Java Programming Exercises

Take the first step in raising your coding skills to the next level, and test your Java knowledge on tricky programming tasks, with the help of the pirate *Captain CiaoCiao*. This is the first of two volumes which provide you with everything you need to excel in your Java journey, including tricks that you should know in detail as a professional, as well as intensive training for clean code and thoughtful design that carries even complex software.

Features:

- About 200 tasks with commented solutions on different levels
- For all paradigms: object-oriented, imperative, and functional
- Clean code, reading foreign code, and object-oriented modeling

With numerous best practices and extensively commented solutions to the tasks, these books provide the perfect workout for professional software development with Java.

Java Programming Exercises
Volume One: Language Fundamentals and Core Concepts

Christian Ullenboom

CRC Press
Taylor & Francis Group
Boca Raton London New York

CRC Press is an imprint of the
Taylor & Francis Group, an **informa** business

A CHAPMAN & HALL BOOK

Designed cover image: Mai Loan Nguyen Duy, Rheinwerk Verlag GmbH

First edition published 2025
by CRC Press
2385 NW Executive Center Drive, Suite 320, Boca Raton FL 33431

and by CRC Press
4 Park Square, Milton Park, Abingdon, Oxon, OX14 4RN

CRC Press is an imprint of Taylor & Francis Group, LLC

ISBN: 978-1-032-59397-5 (hbk)
ISBN: 978-1-032-57984-9 (pbk)
ISBN: 978-1-003-45450-2 (ebk)

DOI: 10.1201/9781003454502

Typeset in Times
by codeMantra

Access the Support Material: https://routledge.com/9781032579849

Contents

About the Author   xv

Introduction   **1**
Previous Knowledge and Target Audience   1
Working with This Book   2
The Suggested Solutions   2
Use of This Book   3
Required Software   3
Used Java Version in the Book   4
    JVM   4
    Development Environment   4
Conventions   4
Helping Captain CiaoCiao and Bonny Brain   5

1 Introduction to the Java Ecosystem   **6**
Bytecode and JVM   6
    Porting Java Programs ★   6
Tools for Java Developers   7
    Get to Know Error Messages of the IDE ★   7
Suggested Solutions   8
    Porting Java Programs ★   8
    Get to Know Error Messages of the IDE ★   8

2 Imperative Programming   **9**
Screen Output   9
    Learn about the SVG Specification   9
    Write an SVG Circle on the Console ★   10
Variables and Data Types   11
    Access Variables and Output Their Assignments ★   12
    Quiz: Value Ranges ★   12
    Quiz: Does This Add Up? ★★★   12
    Generate Random Circles ★   13
    Quiz: Dazed and Confused ★   14
    Process User Input ★   14
Expressions, Operands, and Operators   14
    Quiz: Check In-Between ★   14
    Check If Loot Can Be Shared Fairly ★   15
    Do Two Numbers Share the Same Digit? ★★   15
    Convert Currency Amount to Coins ★★   15
    One Bottle of Rum, Ten Bottles of Rum ★   16
    Quiz: The Zero Effect ★   17

Control Flow   18
    Payday ★   18
    Quiz: Wrong Branching ★   18
    Convert Liters ★★   19
    Create SVG Circles with Random Colors ★   19
    Quiz: To Which Block Does the Else Belong? ★★   20
    Quiz: Recognize Negative Days and Hours ★   20
    Evaluate Input Strings for Approval ★   20
    Rewrite Switch Statement to Switch Expression ★   21
Loops   21
    Create Rotated SVG Rectangles ★   21
    Create SVG-Pearl-Chain ★   22
    Sum Numbers from the Command Line ★   23
    Go through a Mathematical Phenomenon ★   24
    Quiz: How Many Stars? ★   24
    Calculate Products for Faculties ★   25
    Determine If a Number Is Formed by Factorial ★   25
    Find the Smallest and Largest Digit of a Number ★   26
    Quiz: Not Like This from 1 to 100 ★★   27
    A Flag in the Wind through Nested Loops ★   28
    Output Simple Chessboard ★   28
    It's Christmastime: Displaying Trees with Ornaments ★   29
    Draw Fishy Stitching Motifs ★   30
    Trying Instead of Thinking ★★   31
    Get the Number of Digits of a Number ★★   32
Methods   33
    Drawing Hearts ★   33
    Implement Overloaded Line Methods ★   34
    Standing Straight ★   34
    Create a Multiplication Table ★   35
    Cistercian Numerals Script ★★★   36
    Quiz: What Does Ding-Dong Do? (Recursion) ★★   37
    Quiz: Repdigit (Recursion) ★★   37
    Calculate Collatz Sequence (Recursion) ★   38
    Ancient Egyptian Multiplication (Recursion) ★★   38
Suggested Solutions   40
    Write an SVG Circle on the Console ★   40
    Access Variables and Output Their Assignments   41
    Quiz: Value Ranges   42
    Quiz: Does This Add Up?   43
    Generate Random Circles   43
    Quiz: Dazed and Confused   44
    Process User Input   44
    Quiz: Check In-Between   44
    Check If Loot Can Be Shared Fairly   45
    Do Two Numbers Share the Same Digit?   45
    Convert Currency Amount to Coins   46
    One Bottle of Rum, Ten Bottles of Rum   47
    Quiz: The Zero Effect   47
    Payday   47
    Quiz: Wrong Branching   48

Convert Liters   48
Create SVG Circles with Random Colors   49
Quiz: To Which Block Does the Else Belong?   50
Quiz: Recognize Negative Days and Hours   50
Evaluate Input Strings for Approval   51
Rewrite Switch Statement to Switch Expression   52
Create Rotated SVG Rectangles   52
Create SVG-Pearl-Chain   53
Sum Numbers from the Command Line   53
Go through a Mathematical Phenomenon   54
Quiz: How Many Stars?   55
Calculate Products for Faculties   55
Determine If a Number Is Formed by Factorial   57
Find the Smallest and Largest Digit of a Number   58
Quiz: Not Like This from 1 to 100   58
A Flag in the Wind through Nested Loops   59
Output Simple Chessboard   60
It's Christmastime: Displaying Trees with Ornaments   60
Draw Fishy Stitching Motifs   61
Trying Instead of Thinking   62
Get the Number of Digits of a Number   63
Drawing Hearts   65
Implement Overloaded Line Methods   65
Standing Straight   66
Create a Multiplication Table   68
Cistercian Numerals Script   69
Quiz: What Does Ding-Dong Do? (Recursion)   72
Quiz: Repdigit (Recursion)   72
Calculate Collatz Sequence (Recursion)   73
Ancient Egyptian Multiplication (Recursion)   75

3 Classes, Objects, and Packages   **78**
Creating Objects   78
    Draw Polygons ★   78
Working with References   80
    Quiz: The Short Life of Points ★   80
    Build Triangles ★   80
    Quiz: == vs. equals(…) ★   81
    Quiz: Protect against NullPointerException ★   81
Suggested Solutions   82
    Draw Polygons   82
    Quiz: The Short Life of Points   83
    Build Triangles   83
    Quiz: == vs. equals(…)   84
    Quiz: Protect against NullPointerException   84
Note   85

4 Arrays   **86**
Everything Has a Type   86
    Quiz: Array Types ★   86
One-Dimensional Arrays   87

Loop Arrays and Output Wind Speed, Wind Direction ★   87
Detect Continuous Revenue Growth ★   88
Array of Points ★   88
Search Consecutive Strings and Determine If Salty Snook Is Coming ★   89
Reverse an Array ★   89
Find the Nearest Cinema ★★   90
Raid the Candy Store and Share Fairly ★★   90
Enhanced for Loop   91
Numbers Well Shuffled ★★   92
Draw Mountains ★★   93
Two- and Multidimensional Arrays   94
Check Mini-Sudoku for Valid Solution ★★   94
Enlarge Image ★★   95
Variable Argument Lists   96
Create SVG Polygons with a Variable Number of Coordinates ★   96
Check for Approval ★   97
Help, Tetraphobia! Put All Fours Last ★★   97
The Utility Class Arrays   98
Quiz: Copy Arrays ★   98
Quiz: Compare Arrays ★   98
Suggested Solutions   99
Quiz: Array Types   99
Loop Arrays and Output Wind Speed, Wind Direction   99
Reverse an Array   100
Array of Points   101
Search Consecutive Strings and Determine if Salty Snook is Coming   102
Reverse an Array   103
Find the Nearest Cinema   104
Raid the Candy Store and Share Fairly   105
Draw Mountains   106
Check Mini-Sudoku for Valid Solution   107
Enlarge Image   109
Create SVG Polygons with Variable Number of Coordinates   109
Check for Approval   110
Help, Tetraphobia! Put All Fours Last   111
Quiz: Copy Arrays   112
Quiz: Compare Arrays   112

5 **Character and String Processing**   **114**
The String Class and Its Members   114
Quiz: Is String a Built-In Keyword? ★   114
Building HTML Elements with Simple Concatenation ★   114
Check Safe Transmission by Doubling Characters ★   115
Swap Y and Z ★   116
Give Defiant Answers ★   117
Quiz: String Comparisons with == and Equals(...) ★   117
Quiz: Is Equals(...) Symmetric? ★   118
Test Strings for Palindrome Property ★   118
Check if Captain CiaoCiao is in the Middle ★   119
Find the Shortest Name in the Array ★   120
Count String Occurrences ★   120

Determine the Larger Crew Size ★ 121
Build Diamonds ★★ 122
Check for a Good Password ★ 123
Bake Peanut Butter Cookies ★★ 123
Calculate Sum of Digits ★ 124
Decolumnize Texts ★★ 125
Draw a Meadow with Favorite Flowers ★★ 126
Detect Repetitions ★★★ 128
Constrain Line Boundaries and Wrap Lines ★★ 128
Quiz: How Many String Objects? ★ 129
Test If the Fruit Is Wrapped in Chocolate ★★ 129
From Top to Bottom, from Left to Right ★★★ 130
Dynamic Strings with StringBuilder 131
Fill Strings ★ 131
Practicing the Alphabet with a Parrot ★ 132
Quiz: Lightly Attached ★ 133
Convert Number to Textual Unary Encoding ★ 133
Lose Weight by Moving Digits ★ 134
Remove Vowels ★ 135
Don't Shoot the Messenger ★ 136
Compress Repeated Spaces ★★ 137
Insert and Remove Crackles and Pops ★ 137
Split CamelCase Strings ★ 138
Underline Words ★★ 138
Implement Caesar Encryption ★★★ 138
Suggested Solutions 140
Quiz: Is String a Built-In Keyword? 140
Building HTML Elements with Simple Concatenation 140
Check Safe Transmission by Doubling Characters 140
Swap Y and Z 141
Give Defiant Answers 143
Quiz: String Comparisons with == and Equals(…) 143
Quiz: Is Equals(…) Symmetric? 143
Test Strings for Palindrome Property 144
Check if Captain CiaoCiao is in the Middle 146
Find the Shortest Name in the Array 146
Count String Occurrences 147
Determine the Larger Crew Size 148
Build Diamonds 149
Check for a Good Password 151
Bake Peanut Butter Cookies 152
Calculate Sum of Digits 153
Decolumnize Texts 154
Draw a Meadow with Favorite Flowers 156
Detect Repetitions 158
Constrain Line Boundaries and Wrap Lines 159
Quiz: How Many String Objects? 160
Test if the Fruit is Wrapped in Chocolate 160
From Top to Bottom, from Left to Right 161
Fill Strings 162
Practicing the Alphabet with a Parrot 163

Quiz: Lightly Attached   164
Convert Number to Textual Unary Encoding   165
Lose Weight by Moving Digits   166
Remove Vowels   167
Don't Shoot the Messenger   169
Compress Repeated Spaces   170
Insert and Remove Crackles and Pops   171
Split CamelCase Strings   172
Underline Words   173
Implement Caesar Encryption   174

6 Writing Your Own Classes   **176**
Class Declaration and Object Properties   177
Declare Radio with Instance Variables and a Main Program ★ 177
Implementing Methods of a Radio ★   177
Private Parts: Make Instance Variables Private ★   178
Create Setters and Getters ★   178
Static Variables Methods   178
Convert Station Names to Frequencies ★   178
Write Log Output with a Tracer Class ★   179
Quiz: Nothing Stolen ★   180
Simple Enumerations   181
Give Radio an AM–FM Modulation ★   181
Set Valid Start and End Frequency for Modulation ★   181
Constructors   181
Writing Radio Constructors ★   182
Implement Copy Constructor ★   182
Realize Factory Methods ★   182
Associations   183
Connect Monitor Tube with TV ★   183
Quiz: Association, Composition, and Aggregation ★   184
Add Radios with a 1:n Association to the Ship ★★   184
Inheritance   185
Introduce Abstraction into Electrical Devices via Inheritance ★ 185
Quiz: Three, Two, and One ★   185
Quiz: Private and Protected Constructor ★   186
Determine the Number of Switched on Electrical Devices ★   186
Ship Should Hold Any Electronic Device ★   186
Take Working Radios on the Ship ★   187
Solve Equivalence Test with Pattern Variable ★   187
Fire Alarm Does Not Go Off: Overriding Methods ★   188
Calling the Methods of the Superclass ★★   188
Polymorphism and Dynamic Binding   189
Holiday! Switch Off All Devices ★   189
The Big Move ★   190
Quiz: Bumbo Is a Great Drink ★★   191
Quiz: Vodka with Taste ★   192
Quiz: Rum-Paradise ★★   192
Abstract Classes and Abstract Methods   192
Quiz: Consumer Devices as an Abstract Superclass? ★   193
TimerTask as an Example for an Abstract Class ★★   193

Suggested Solutions   194
  Declare Radio with Instance Variables and a Main Program   194
  Implementing Methods of a Radio   195
  Private Parts: Make Instance Variables Private   196
  Create Setters and Getters   197
  Convert Station Names to Frequencies   198
  Write Log Output with a Tracer Class   198
  Quiz: Nothing Stolen   199
  Give Radio an AM–FM Modulation   199
  Set Valid Start and End Frequency for Modulation   200
  Writing Radio Constructors   201
  Implement Copy Constructor   202
  Realize Factory Methods   202
  Connect Monitor Tube with TV   204
  Quiz: Association, Composition, and Aggregation   205
  Add Radios with a 1:n Association to the Ship   205
  Introduce Abstraction into Electrical Devices via Inheritance   206
  Quiz: Three, Two, and One   207
  Quiz: Private and Protected Constructor   208
  Determine Number of Switched on Electrical Devices   208
  Ship Should Hold Any Electronic Device   209
  Take Working Radios on the Ship   209
  Solve Equivalence Test with Pattern Variable   210
  Fire Alarm Does Not Go Off: Overriding Methods   210
  Calling the Methods of the Superclass   211
  Holiday! Switch Off All Devices   212
  The Big Move   212
  Quiz: Bumbo Is a Great Drink   212
  Quiz: Vodka with Taste   213
  Quiz: Rum-Paradise   213
  Quiz: Consumer Devices as an Abstract Superclass?   214
  TimerTask as an Example for an Abstract Class   214
Note   215

7 Records, Interfaces, Enumerations, and Sealed Classes   216
Records   216
  Quiz: Which Statements Are True for Records? ★   216
  Develop Record for Complex Numbers ★   216
  Quiz: Records with Static Variables ★   217
  Record Patterns ★   217
Interfaces   218
  Compare Consumption of Electrical Devices ★   218
  Find Electronic Devices with the Highest Power Consumption ★   219
  Use Comparator Interface for Sorting ★   220
  Static and Default Methods in Interfaces ★★★   220
  Delete Selected Elements with Predicate ★★   220
Enumeration Types (enum)   221
  Enumeration for Candy ★   221
  Deliver Random Candies ★   222
  Tagging Candy with Addictive Value ★★   223
  Interface Implementations via an enum ★★   224

Quiz: Aviso and Brig ★	225
Suggested Solutions	225
Quiz: Which Statements Are True for Records?	225
Quiz: Records with Static Variables	226
Quiz: Records with Static Variables	227
Compare Consumption of Electrical Devices	228
Find Electronic Devices with the Highest Power Consumption	229
Use Comparator Interface for Sorting	230
Static and Default Methods in Interfaces	230
Delete Selected Elements with Predicate	231
Enumeration for Candy	232
Deliver Random Candies	233
Tagging Candy with Addictive Value	233
Interface Implementations via an enum	236
Quiz: Aviso and Brig	237

8 Nested Types — **238**

Declare Nested Types	238
Set AM–FM Modulation to Radio Type ★	238
Write Three Kinds of Watt-Comparator Implementations ★	239
Nested Types Quiz	239
Quiz: Pirate Could Have Waved ★	239
Quiz: Name in a Bottle ★★	240
Quiz: Get Me Another Bottle of Rum ★	240
Suggested Solutions	241
Set AM–FM Modulation to Radio Type	241
Write Three Kinds of Watt-Comparator Implementations	242
Quiz: Pirate Could Have Waved	243
Quiz: Name in a Bottle	243
Quiz: Get Me another Bottle of Rum	243

9 Exception Handling — **244**

Catching Exceptions	244
Get the Longest Line of a File ★	244
Identify Exceptions, Laughing All the Time ★	245
Convert String Array to Int Array and Be Lenient on Nonnumbers ★	245
Quiz: And Finally ★	246
Quiz: A Lonely Try ★	246
Quiz: Well Caught ★	246
Quiz: Too Much of a Good Thing ★	247
Quiz: Try-Catch in Inheritance ★★	247
Throwing Custom Exceptions	247
Quiz: Throw and Throws ★	247
Quiz: The Division Fails ★	248
Writing Your Own Exception Classes	248
Show Impossible Watt with Own Exception ★	248
Quiz: Potatoes or Other Vegetables ★	248
Try-with-Resources	249
Write Current Date to File ★	249
Read Notes and Write Them to a New ABC File ★★	249

Quiz: Excluded ★ 250
Suggested Solutions 251
Get the Longest Line of a File 251
Identify Exceptions, Laughing All the Time 252
Convert String Array to Int Array and Be Lenient on Nonnumbers 254
Quiz: And Finally 255
Quiz: A Lonely Try 255
Quiz: Well Caught 256
Quiz: Too Much of a Good Thing 256
Quiz: Try-Catch in Inheritance 257
Quiz: Throw and Throws 257
Quiz: The Division Fails 257
Show Impossible Watt with Own Exception 258
Quiz: Potatoes or Other Vegetables 260
Write Current Date to File 260
Read Notes and Write Them to a New ABC File 261
Quiz: Excluded 262

10 Lambda Expressions and Functional Programming   **263**
Lambda Expressions 264
Quiz: Recognize Valid Functional Interfaces ★ 264
Quiz: From Interface Implementation to Lambda Expression ★ 264
Write Lambda Expressions for Functional Interfaces ★ 265
Quiz: Write Lambda Expressions Like This? ★ 266
Developing Lambda Expressions ★ 266
Quiz: Contents of the Package java.util.function ★ 266
Quiz: Know Functional Interfaces for Mappings ★ 266
Method and Constructor References 268
Rewriting Lambda Expressions ★★ 268
Selected Functional Interfaces 268
Delete Entries, Remove Comments, Convert to CSV ★ 268
Suggested Solutions 269
Quiz: Recognize Valid Functional Interfaces 269
Quiz: From Interface Implementation to Lambda Expression 270
Write Lambda Expressions for Functional Interfaces 271
Quiz: Write Lambda Expressions Like This? 271
Developing Lambda Expressions 271
Quiz: Contents of the Package java.util.function 271
Quiz: Know Functional Interfaces for Mappings 272
Rewriting Lambda Expressions 273
Delete Entries, Remove Comments, and Convert to CSV 273
Note 274

11 Special Types from the Java Class Library   **275**
Absolute Superclass java.lang.Object 275
Generate `equals(Object)` and `hashCode()` ★ 276
Existing equals(Object) Implementations ★★ 276
Interfaces Comparator and Comparable 277
Quiz: Natural Order Or Not? ★ 277
Handle Superheroes 277

Compare Superheroes ★★   279
Concatenate Hero Comparators ★   280
Using a Key Extractor to Easily Create a Comparator ★★   280
Sort Points by Distance to Center ★   282
Find Stores Nearby ★★   283
Autoboxing   283
Quiz: Handling Null Reference in Unboxing ★   283
Quiz: Unboxing Surprise ★★   284
Suggested Solutions   284
Generate `equals(Object)` and `hashCode()`   284
Existing equals(Object) Implementations   287
Quiz: Natural Order Or Not?   289
Compare Superheroes   289
Concatenate Hero Comparators   290
Using a Key Extractor to Easily Create a Comparator   291
Sort Points by Distance to Center   291
Find Stores Nearby   292
Quiz: Handling Null Reference in Unboxing   293
Quiz: Unboxing Surprise   294
Notes   294

Appendix A: Most Frequent Types and Methods in the Java Universe   **295**
A.1 Packages with the Most Common Types   295
A.2 100 Most Common Types   296
A.3 100 Most Common Methods   299
A.4 100 Most Common Methods Including Parameter List   302

About the Author

Christian Ullenboom started his programming journey at the tender age of ten, typing his first lines of code into a C64. After mastering assembler programming and early BASIC extensions, he found his calling on the island of Java, following his studies in computer science and psychology. Despite indulging in Python, JavaScript, TypeScript, and Kotlin vacations, he remains a savant of all things Java.

For over 20 years, Ullenboom has been a passionate software architect, Java trainer (check out http://www.tutego.com), and IT specialist instructor. His expertise has resulted in a number of online video courses and reference books:

- *Java: The Comprehensive Guide* (ISBN-13: 978-1493222957)
- *Spring Boot 3 and Spring Framework 6* (ISBN-13: 978-1493224753)
- *Java ist auch eine Insel: Java programmieren lernen mit dem umfassenden Standardwerk für Java-Entwickler* (ISBN-13: 978-3836287456)
- *Java SE 9 Standard-Bibliothek: Das Handbuch für Java-Entwickler* (ISBN-13: 978-3836258746)
- *Captain CiaoCiao erobert Java: Das Trainingsbuch für besseres Java* (ISBN-13: 978-3836284271)

Christian Ullenboom has been spreading Java love through his books for years, earning him the coveted title of Java Champion from Sun (now Oracle) way back in 2005. Only a select few—about 300 worldwide—have achieved this status, making him a true Java superstar.

As an instructor, Ullenboom understands that learning by doing is the most effective way to master a skill. So, he has compiled a comprehensive catalog of exercises that accompany his training courses. This book features a selection of those exercises, complete with documented solutions.

His roots are in Sonsbeck, a small town in the Lower Rhine region of Germany.

Introduction

Many beginners in programming often ask themselves, "How can I strengthen my skills as a developer? How can I become a better programmer?" The answer is simple: study, attend webinars, learn, repeat, practice, and discuss your work with others. Many aspects of programming are similar to learning new skills. Just as a book can't teach you how to play a musical instrument, watching the *Fast and the Furious* movie series won't teach you how to drive. The brain develops patterns and structures through repeated practice. Learning a programming language and a natural language have many similarities. Consistent use of the language and the desire and need to express and communicate in it (just as you need to do so to order a burger or a beer) lead to gradual improvement in skills.

Books and webinars on learning a programming language are available, but reading, learning, practicing, and repeating are just one aspect of becoming a successful software developer. To create effective software solutions, you need to creatively combine your knowledge, just as a musician regularly practices finger exercises and maintains their repertoire. The more effective your exercises are, the faster you will become a master. This book aims to help you progress and gain more hands-on experience.

Java 21 declares more than 2,300 classes, about 1,400 interfaces, close to 140 enumerations, around 50 exceptions, and a few annotation types and records are included as well. However, only a fraction of these types are relevant in practice. This book selects the most important types and methods for tasks, making them motivating and following Java conventions. Alternative solutions and approaches are also presented repeatedly. The goal is to make nonfunctional requirements clear because the quality of programs is not just about "doing what it should". Issues such as correct indentation, following naming conventions, proper use of modifiers, best practices, and design patterns are essential. The proposed solutions aim to demonstrate these principles, with the keyword being *Clean Code*.

PREVIOUS KNOWLEDGE AND TARGET AUDIENCE

The book is aimed at Java developers who are either new to Java or are already advanced and wish to learn more about the core language features. The intended audience includes:

- Computer science students.
- IT specialists.
- Java programmers.
- Software developers.
- Job applicants.

The book is centered around tasks and fully documented solutions, with detailed explanations of Java peculiarities, good object-oriented programming practices, best practices, and design patterns. The exercises are best solved with a textbook, as this exercise book is not a traditional textbook. A useful approach is to work through a topic with a preferred textbook before attempting the exercises that correspond to it.

DOI: 10.1201/9781003454502-1

The first set of tasks is designed for programming beginners who are new to Java. As you gain more experience with Java, the tasks become more challenging. Therefore, there are tasks for both beginners and advanced developers.

Additionally, this book does not require the use of tools like profiling tools, as these are beyond the scope of this book.

WORKING WITH THIS BOOK

The task book is organized into different sections. The first section covers the Java language, followed by selected areas of the Java standard library, such as data structures or file processing. Each area is accompanied by programming tasks and "quiz" questions that contain surprises. Each section starts with a small motivation and characterization of the topic, followed by the exercises. Additional tips and hints are provided for particularly challenging assignments, while other exercises offer optional extensions for further exploration.

The majority of exercises are independent of each other, making it easy for readers to dive in anywhere. However, in the chapter on imperative programming, some tasks build on each other to develop a larger program, and the same goes for the chapter on object-oriented programming. The problem definitions make this clear, and more complex programs help to provide context for understanding different language characteristics. Furthermore, a more complex program can motivate readers to continue.

The exercises are rated with one, two, or three stars to indicate their complexity, although this rating is subjective to the author.

1 star ★: Simple exercises, suitable for beginners. They should be easy to solve without much effort. Often only transfer of knowledge is required, for example, by writing down things that are in a textbook differently.

2 stars ★★: The effort is higher here. Different techniques have to be combined. Greater creativity is required.

3 stars ★★★: Assignments with three stars are more complex, require recourse to more prior knowledge, and sometimes require research. Frequently, the tasks can no longer be solved with a single method, but require multiple classes that must work together.

THE SUGGESTED SOLUTIONS

The task book provides at least one suggested solution for each problem. The term "sample solution" is not used to avoid implying that the given solution is the best one and that all other solutions are useless. Readers are encouraged to compare their solutions with the proposed solution and can be satisfied if their solution is more refined. All proposed solutions are commented, making it possible to follow all steps well.

The suggested solutions are compiled at the end of each chapter to reduce the temptation to look into a solution directly after the task, which takes the fun out of solving the task. The suggested solutions can also be found on the website https://github.com/ullenboom/captain-ciaociao. Some solutions contain comments of the type //tag::solution[], which marks the parts of the solutions printed in the book.

USE OF THIS BOOK

To become a software developer, you must master the art of turning problems into code, and that's where practice and role models come in. While there are plenty of exercises available online, they're often disorganized, poorly documented, and outdated. That's where this book shines, by offering a systematic approach to tasks and well-thought-out solutions. Studying these solutions and reading code in general helps the brain develop patterns and solutions that can be applied to future coding challenges. It's like reading the Bible; you need to read to understand and learn. Surprisingly, many software developers write code without bothering to read others' code, which can lead to confusion and misunderstanding. Reading good code elevates our writing skills by building patterns and solutions that our brains unconsciously transfer to our own code. Our brains form neuronal structures independently based on templates, and the quality of the input we receive matters greatly. Therefore, we should only feed our brains with good code, as bad solutions make for bad models. The book covers important topics such as exception handling or error handling, discussing the correct input values, identifying erroneous states, and how to handle them. In software, things can and will go wrong, and we must be prepared to deal with the less-than-perfect world.

It's easy for developers to get stuck in their ways of writing code, which is why it's important to explore new approaches and "expand our vocabulary", so to speak. For Java developers, libraries are their vocabulary, but too many enterprise Java developers write massive, non-object-oriented code. The solution is to continuously improve object-oriented modeling, which is precisely what this book demonstrates. It introduces new methods, creates new data types, and minimizes complexity. Additionally, functional programming is becoming increasingly important in Java development, and all solutions in this book take advantage of modern language features.

While some solutions may appear overly complex, the tasks and proposed solutions in this book can help developers improve their ability to concentrate and follow through with steps. In practice, the ability to concentrate and quickly comprehend code is crucial for developers. Often, developers must join a new team and be able to understand and modify unfamiliar source code, and possibly fix bugs. Those who wish to expand upon existing open-source solutions can also benefit from honing their concentration skills through these exercises.

In addition to its emphasis on the Java programming language, syntax, libraries, and object orientation, this book provides numerous side notes on topics such as algorithms, the historical evolution of programming, comparisons to other programming languages, and data formats. These additional insights and perspectives offer readers a more well-rounded understanding of software development beyond just the technical aspects.

If you're looking for one more reason to add this book to your collection, it doubles as a fantastic sleep aid!

REQUIRED SOFTWARE

While solving a task with just a pen and paper is possible in theory, modern software development requires the proper use of tools. Knowing programming language syntax, object-oriented modeling, and libraries is just the tip of the iceberg. Understanding the JVM (Java Virtual Machine), using tools like Maven and Git for version management, and becoming proficient in an IDE (Integrated Development Environment) are all crucial aspects of professional software development. Some developers can even perform magic in their IDE, generating code and fixing bugs automatically.

USED JAVA VERSION IN THE BOOK

While Java version 8 remains still strong in enterprise settings, it's crucial for learners to become acquainted with the latest language features. Accordingly, whenever feasible, the suggested solutions in this book leverage Java 21. Not only is this version equipped with long-term support (LTS), but runtime environment providers also offer extensive support, ensuring that the release retains its relevance for an extended period.

JVM

If we want to run Java programs, we need a JVM. In the early days, this was easy. The runtime environment first came from Sun Microsystems, later from Oracle, which took over Sun. Today, it is much more confusing. Although a runtime environment can still be obtained from Oracle, the licensing terms have changed, at least for Java 8 up to Java 16. Testing and development are possible with the Oracle JDK, but not in production. In this case, Oracle charges license fees. As a consequence, various institutions compile their own runtime environments from the OpenJDK, the original sources. The best known are *Eclipse Adoptium* (https://adoptium.net/), *Amazon Corretto* (https://aws.amazon.com/de/corretto), *Red Hat OpenJDK* (https://developers.redhat.com/products/openjdk/overview), and others such as those from *Azul Systems* or *Bellsoft*. There is no specific distribution that readers are required to follow.

Development Environment

Java source code is just plain text, so technically a simple text editor is all you need. However, relying solely on Notepad or vi for productivity is like trying to win a race on a tricycle. Modern integrated development environments support us with many tasks: color highlighting of keywords, automatic code completion, intelligent error correction, insertion of code blocks, visualization of states in the debugger, and much more. It is therefore advisable to use a full development environment. Four popular IDEs are: *IntelliJ*, *Eclipse*, *Visual Studio Code*, and *(Apache) NetBeans*. Just like with Java runtime environments, the choice of IDE is left to the reader. Eclipse, NetBeans, and Visual Studio Code are all free and open-source, while IntelliJ Community Edition is also free, but the more advanced IntelliJ Ultimate Edition will cost you some cash.

Halfway through the book, we delve into implementing project dependencies using Maven in a few places.

CONVENTIONS

Code is written in `fix width font`, filenames are *italicized*. To distinguish methods from attributes, methods always have a pair of parentheses, such as in "the variable `max` contains the maximum" or "it returns `max()` the maximum". Since methods can be overloaded, either the parameter list is named, as in `equals(Object)`, or an ellipsis abbreviates it, such as in "various `println(…)` methods". If a group of identifiers is addressed, * is written, like `print*(…)` prints something on the screen.

In the suggested solutions, there are usually only the relevant code snippets, so as not to blow up the book volume. The name of the file is mentioned in the listing caption, like this:

VanillaJava.java

```
class VanillaJava { }
```

Sometimes, we need to flex our terminal muscles and execute programs from the command line (also known as console or shell). Since each command-line program has its own prompt sequence, it is symbolized here in the book with a $. Example:

```
$ java -version
openjdk version "21.0.1" 2023-10-17
OpenJDK Runtime Environment (build 21.0.1+12-29)
OpenJDK 64-Bit Server VM (build 21.0.1+12-29, mixed mode, sharing)
```

If the Windows command line is explicitly meant, the prompt character > is set:

```
> netstat -e
Interface Statistics

                           Received              Sent

Bytes                      218927776          9941980
Unicast packets               162620            64828
Non-unicast packets              276              668
Discards                           0                0
Errors                             0                0
Unknown protocols                  0
```

HELPING CAPTAIN CIAOCIAO AND BONNY BRAIN

Ahoy there! Once upon a time, Captain CiaoCiao and Bonny Brain lent ye a hand with a certain matter we won't speak of. And now, ye owe them a favor. But fear not, for it will be worth yer while to assist them on their latest venture. Join the daring duo and their loyal crew as they sail the seven seas, striking deals with unsavory characters across the globe. Their secret hideout is on the island of Baloo, where the currency of choice is Liretta.

Introduction to the Java Ecosystem

1

Many newcomers get caught in "tutorial hell": they read a lot, watch countless videos. This chapter is here to help you break out of your shell and get comfortable with practical programming. You'll not only learn your way around the development environment, but you'll also be able to flex your skills by running programs from the command line. In the process, we will get to know our development environment better, be able to run programs from the command line, and see more clearly the division of tasks between the Java compiler and the runtime environment.

Prerequisites

- Understand the task of Java compiler, bytecode, and JVM.
- Be able to compile Java programs on the command line.
- Know the difference between `java` and `javac` programs.
- Set up and be able to operate Java development environment.

BYTECODE AND JVM

In the early days of Java, the usual way for compilers was to generate a directly executable machine file. Sun Microsystems wanted something different: a platform-independent programming language—this led to Java. To achieve this, the compiler is no longer allowed to generate machine code, but the Java compiler generates bytecode. This bytecode is not bound to a machine. So that the bytecode can be executed, a runtime environment and a function library must exist, called *Java Runtime Environment* (short *JRE*). Part of the JRE is the *Java Virtual Machine*, short *JVM*, which executes the bytecode.

Porting Java Programs ★

Anyone starting in programming is bound to have come across a classic: the Hello World output. In the mid-1970s, this small example appeared in a C tutorial and has since been ported to various programming languages. Although the program is small, it serves an important purpose: to test whether all the development tools are installed and working correctly.

Task:

Save the following program named *Application.java*. Pay attention to the upper/lower case.

Application.java

```java
public class Application {
  public static void main( String[] args ) {
    System.out.println( "Aye Captain!" );
  }
}
```

DOI: 10.1201/9781003454502-2

We can now compile the program with

```
$ javac Application.java
```

and start it with

```
$ java Application
```

Question:

- Would it be possible to copy the file `Application.class` from a Windows operating system to a Linux operating system and *java* can run the program?
- What software must be installed on the computer?

TOOLS FOR JAVA DEVELOPERS

The choice of development environment often depends on personal taste, and they all handle the core tasks well:

- IntelliJ.
- Eclipse.
- Visual Studio Code.
- (Apache) NetBeans IDE.

This workbook is completely independent of the IDE. All developers should work intensively with the shortcuts, the debugger, and the other tools. The web pages of the developers and YouTube offer plentifully material for it, a small selection:

- Eclipse: https://help.eclipse.org/, https://www.youtube.com/user/EclipseFdn/playlists?view= 50&sort=dd&shelf_id=6
- IntelliJ: https://www.youtube.com/user/intellijideavideo

Get to Know Error Messages of the IDE ★

This task is about getting to know the development environment a little better.

Let's take the following program again:

Application.java

```java
public class Application {
  public static void main( String[] args ) {
    System.out.println( "Aye Captain!" );
  }
}
```

Task:

- Transfer *Application.java* to the IDE.
- Deliberately build errors into the program code, and observe the error messages. Some suggestions:

- Change the file name.
- Change the case, for example, write `Class` instead of `class`.
- The main program is not started until the class has a special method `public static void main(String[] args)`. What happens if the method is not called `main`, for example, but something else, e.g., `Main` or `run`?
- Try to output Greek letters or hearts, can you do that?
- White space is often used, so spaces (usually not a tab) and line breaks appear after each statement. Is the following valid like this?

```
public class Application{public static void main(String[]args){System.
out.println("Aye Captain!");}}.
```

SUGGESTED SOLUTIONS

Porting Java Programs ★

If the *Application.class* file is copied from a Windows operating system to a Linux machine, it will run there as well. To run the file, a runtime environment like Oracle JDK is always required.

Get to Know Error Messages of the IDE ★

You could deliberately include the following errors:

- If the class is `public`, the filename must be the same as the class. So, we could change the filename or class name. The IDE recognizes the error and suggests a renaming.
- Keywords are always lowercase in Java. What happens if you capitalize a keyword like `public` or `class` or capitalize single letters? In that case, there is a compiler error.
- If the start method is not declared as `public static void main(String[] args)`, but differently, the editor cannot guess, but the compiler will translate the program correctly because `public static void run(String[] args)` could, in general, be a method we want. It is a *semantic error* and not a *syntactic error*, which the editor or the compiler cannot notice. But the runtime environment will throw an error that the `main(...)` method is not present when the program is to be started (semantic error).
- A method consists of a sequence of statements—these statements are in a block enclosed in curly braces. The same is true for the class, which consists of a collection of methods that must also be placed in a block altogether. Indentations are not significant in Java. You can provoke an error by omitting the curly braces completely.
- Every open curly bracket requires a closing curly bracket. If you omit a curly bracket, it will cause a compiler error.
- String literals are enclosed with different symbols in different programming languages. Some programming languages use double quotes ("), other programming languages use a single quote ('), and some programming languages use backticks (`). Java can accept the strings only in double quotes; otherwise, there will be compiler errors. Single quotes are used for single characters (data type `char`).
- In Java, white space is used to make the source code clearer, especially to make the blocks visible. You can save some white space. You can try to find out which of the whitespace characters you are allowed to delete and which you are not. The code given in the task is fine.

Imperative Programming

2

At its core, the virtual machine does nothing more but evaluates expressions and executes statements. The exercises in this chapter focus on the different data types, various operators, and conditional execution.

Prerequisites

- Be able to do simple screen output.
- Receive user input.
- Be able to distinguish between data types.
- Be able to declare variables.
- Know assignment and operators.
- Be able to use conditional statements.
- Be able to use loops for repetitions.
- Be able to use nested loops.
- Be able to declare and implement subroutines with methods.
- Know the difference between argument and parameter.
- Be able to use overloaded methods.

Data types used in this chapter:

- `java.lang.System`
- `java.lang.Math`
- `java.lang.ArithmeticException`
- `java.util.Scanner`

SCREEN OUTPUT

In the first chapter, the Java program implemented a simple output. Let's build on that and learn how to write special characters (such as quotes), set line breaks, or achieve simple formatted output.

Learn about the SVG Specification

Graphical representations encourage us to engage in playing, which is why we want our Java programs to draw something. Java SE includes a library that allows you to open a window and draw content, but it's not done with a few lines of code. Therefore, we want to go a different way, using *SVG*. The abbreviation stands for *Scalable Vector Graphics*, a standard for vector graphics. With SVG, we can easily describe two-dimensional graphics in text and write text from our Java programs.

DOI: 10.1201/9781003454502-3

Task:

- Learn about SVG with a small example at https://tutego.de/go/trysvgcircle.
- Change the size of the circle on the web page.

Write an SVG Circle on the Console ★

There are several approaches for screen output in Java. Usually, the method `print(...)`, `println(...)`, or `printf(...)` is used. These methods are located at the `System.out` object. Besides `System.out` there is `System.err`, but this is reserved for error output. Some developers also use the `Console` object for output, we stick with `System.out.print*(...)`.

Captain CiaoCiao needs a filled circle for shooting exercises, which can be printed later. For this purpose, we want to develop a new Java program.

For screen output, we can use:

```
System.out.print( "Text without subsequent line break" );
System.out.println( "Text followed by a newline" );
System.out.printf( "Text followed by line break%n" );
```

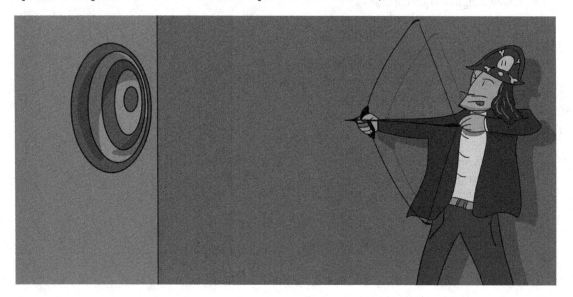

Task:

- Create a new class `SvgCircle1`.
- Create a `main(...)` method so that we can run the program later.
- Use in `main(...)` the known `print*(...)` methods to bring the following text to the console:
  `<svg height='400' width='1000'><circle cx='100' cy='100' r='50' /></svg>`
- Enter the console output to https://tutego.de/go/trysvgcircle, and after clicking Run » you will see a circle. We want to come back to the web page whenever SVG elements are to be displayed in the following.

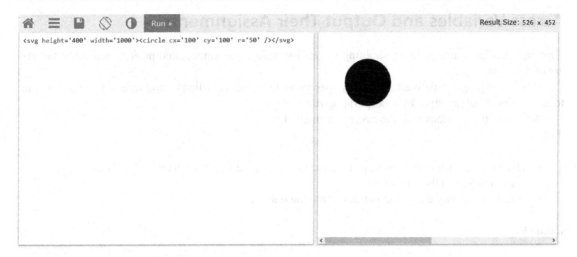

FIGURE 2.1 Display an SVG output.

- Modify the program so that line breaks occur in the output. The output should be:
```
<svg height='400' width='1000'>
  <circle cx='100' cy='100' r='50' />
</svg>
```
- Change the program again so that instead of single quotes, there are now double quotes in the string. The output should be:
```
<svg height="400" width="1000">
 <circle cx="100" cy="100" r="50" />
</svg>
```

VARIABLES AND DATA TYPES

Variables store information, and variables always have a type in Java. The compiler knows at all times what kind of variable is declared, and what type of expression is in front of him.

Java has eight built-in data types: boolean, byte, char, short, int, long, float, and double. You can store numeric values and boolean values into them. The boolean values can be set to true and false. For numeric values, we have three different groups:

- We have numeric values for Unicode characters and use the char data type for them. In addition, we have data types for general integers and floating-point numbers.
- Integers always have signs. We have four different types of them: byte, short, int, and long. The types differ according to their number of bytes, which means that the data types can hold numbers of different sizes.
- For floating-point numbers, we have float and double available; a double has twice as many bits as a float to store.

The size of the data types is fixed in the Java specification and does not depend on the particular architecture or platform.

Access Variables and Output Their Assignments ★

Captain CiaoCiao wants to make shooting targets for novices, advanced, and professionals. The targets are of different sizes.

Our initial program defined a circle by specifying its center coordinates and radius, but we now aim to create a modifiable output by incorporating parameters.

Add from the previous task the `main(…)` method.

Task:

- Declare two `int` variables `x`, `y` and a `double` variable `r` in the `main(…)` method.
- Assign values to the variables.
- Build the assignment of the variables into the output.

Example:

- If, for example, `x=100` and `y=110` and `r=20.5`, then the console output should be:
  ```
  <svg height="100" width="1000">
    <circle cx="100" cy="110" r="20.5" />
  </svg>
  ```
- For manual assignment with `x=10`, `y=10` and `r=2.686`:
  ```
  <svg height="100" width="1000">
    <circle cx="10" cy="10" r="2.686" />
  </svg>
  ```

A black circle on a white background is created.

Quiz: Value Ranges ★

What is the result of this expression `1000000 * 1000000`? Does anything stand out? Why does this result occur?

Quiz: Does This Add Up? ★★★

If you compute `0.1+0.1+0.1+0.1+0.1+0.1+0.1+0.1+0.1 - 1.0`, and output the result with `System.out.println(…)`, is the output surprising?

Generate Random Circles ★

Random numbers play a bigger role in the practice as you might think.

In Java, there is a class `Math` which provides important mathematical methods. Random numbers can be determined like this:

```
double rnd=Math.random();
```

The method `random()` is thus an offering of the `Math` class.
Task:

- Refer to the Javadoc for the range of values in which the result of `random()` is.
- Extend the circle program so that the radius is random, in the range including 10, but keeping it smaller than 20. Let the radius still be a floating-point number.

Example:

- If we run the program twice, the outputs might look like this:
  ```
  <svg height="100" width="1000">
   <circle cx="100" cy="110" r="19.47493300792351" />
  </svg>
  <svg height="100" width="1000">
   <circle cx="100" cy="110" r="10.218243515543868" />
  </svg>
  ```

Alternative variants for forming random numbers in Java are:

```
double rnd1=java.util.concurrent.ThreadLocalRandom.current().nextDouble();
double rnd2=java.util.concurrent.ThreadLocalRandom.current().nextDouble(/* 0
to */max);
double rnd3=java.util.concurrent.ThreadLocalRandom.current().nextDouble(min,
max);
```

```
int rnd4=java.util.concurrent.ThreadLocalRandom.current().nextInt();
int rnd5=java.util.concurrent.ThreadLocalRandom.current().nextInt(/* 0 to */
max);
int rnd6=java.util.concurrent.ThreadLocalRandom.current().nextInt(min, max);
```

Quiz: Dazed and Confused ★

Clean Code is a set of best practices that make code easy to read and understand, as well as maintainable, extensible, and testable. Unfortunately, there are also enough counter-examples.

What is wrong with the following example?

```
double höhe  =12.34;
double breite=23.45;
double tmp=2 * (höhe+breite);
System.out.println( tmp );
tmp=höhe * breite;
System.out.println( tmp );
```

Process User Input ★

So far, we have done screen output, but have not done any input.

Using new java.util.Scanner(System.in).next*(), we can accept input from the command line. Examples:

```
int    number1=new java.util.Scanner( System.in ).nextInt();
double number2=new java.util.Scanner( System.in ).nextDouble();
String line   =new java.util.Scanner( System.in ).nextLine();
```

Captain CiaoCiao wants to be able to determine the position of the SVG circle itself.
Task:

- For the circle, take the assignments for cx and cy as integers from the console, and write the generated SVG fragment back to standard output. The radius remains random.

EXPRESSIONS, OPERANDS, AND OPERATORS

An expression is evaluated and produces a result. Operators can be used to link operands such as literals or variables.

Quiz: Check In-Between ★

To test if a number between is truly greater than min and real less than max, we can write:

```
boolean isBetween=between>min && between<max;
```

Is the following syntax also allowed in Java?

```
boolean isBetween = min < between < max;
```

Check If Loot Can Be Shared Fairly ★

After a raid on the distillery, Captain CiaoCiao and his crew snatch countless bottles. Now the loot must be divided, with Captain CiaoCiao getting half (if the number of bottles is odd, he gets less than half, the captain is that generous). All other robbers should get the same share. But does this add up?
Task:

- Write a program that reads the captured number of bottles from the command line and outputs how much Captain CiaoCiao obtains.
- Output what is left for the crew.
- Ask for the crew size, and see if the loot can be distributed fairly and equally so that each crew member gets the same number of bottles. An answer in the form of true or false is sufficient.

Example:

```
Number of bottles in total?
123000
Bottles for the captain: 61500
Bottles for all crew members: 61500
Number of crew members?
100
Fair share without remainder? true
```

Consider how division and remainder value relate.

Do Two Numbers Share the Same Digit? ★★

Bonny Brain is playing anchor dominoes, which uses tiles with two squares, each containing a value from 0 to 9. She is wondering whether it's possible to place two tiles end-to-end, even if they are rotated, so that the two squares adjacent to each other have the same values.
Task:

1. Write a program that reads in two numbers, where the numbers are to be in the range from 0 to 99 (both limits inclusive).
2. If the numbers are above 100, only the last two digits are to be evaluated; 100 or 200 would then be like 00 (i.e., 0), 1111 would be like 11.
3. Test if the two numbers have a common digit.

Examples:

- 12 and 31 have 1 as a common digit.
- 22 and 33 do not have a common digit.

Note: The common digit is not asked, but simply an output true/false. If the number is a single digit, there is a 0 in front, so 01 and 20 have a common digit, which is 0.

Convert Currency Amount to Coins ★★

In the currency Liretta, there are Liretta coins with denominations of 2 Liretta, 1 Liretta, 50 Lirettacent, 20 Lirettacent, 10 Lirettacent, 5 Lirettacent, 2 Lirettacent, and 1 Lirettacent. 100 lirettacent is equal to 1 liretta.

Task:

1. Create a new class `CoinMachine`.
2. The program should first ask for a floating-point number for an amount of money.
3. Print out how the entered amount can be paid out in Literatta coins. Not all permutations are requested, but only the smallest number of coins.

Example with input `12.91` (English locale):

```
Please enter the amount of money:
12.91
6 x 2 Liretta
0 x 1 Liretta
1 x 50 Lirettacent
2 x 20 Lirettacent
0 x 10 Lirettacent
0 x 5 Lirettacent
0 x 2 Lirettacent
1 x 1 Lirettacent
```

The formatting of the output is not relevant.

The `Scanner` is localized, so it uses the decimal separator of the respective language when entering descendant digits.

One Bottle of Rum, Ten Bottles of Rum ★

Bonny Brain is a hunter of incorrect language, and she always makes sure that labels are grammatically correct. Many languages have specific rules for the plural. Every so often it's "1 bottle" or "99 bottles", but also "0 bottles". Simplifications such as "1 bottle(s)" are typically found in user interfaces.

Task:

- Create a variable noOfBottles and assign a value to it greater than or equal to 0.
- Program a grammatically correct output depending on whether there are 0, 1, or many bottles.

Example:

- "0 bottles of rum".
- "1 bottle of rum".
- "99 bottles of rum".

The condition operator (?-:-operator) makes the code compact.

Quiz: The Zero Effect ★

Does the following class translate? If so, and you run the program, what is the result?

```java
class Application {
 public static void main( String[] args ) {
    int zero=0;
    int ten=10;
    double anotherTen=10;
    System.out.println( anotherTen / zero );
    System.out.println( ten / zero );
  }
}
```

CONTROL FLOW

Conditional statements such as `if-else` statements are crucial imperative concepts. For the upcoming exercises involving user input validation and processing, we rely on the capability to selectively execute sections of code based on conditions.

Payday ★

Tort Ellini purchased an antique pocket watch from Bonny Brain for 1,000 Liretta and is now responsible for paying for it.

Task:

1. Write a program that reads in the amount of money on the command line using `new java.util.Scanner(System.in).nextDouble()`.
2. Bonny Brain is always in a good mood, so she is happy with 10% less. She is also pleased when Tort offers 20% more. However, if Tort voluntarily pays more than 20%, Bonny Brain has the impression that something is wrong and the pocket watch probably has a valuable hidden function or holds a secret. Consider how to set up the program so that few code changes are needed when the limits shift on a whim.
3. When Tort has the appropriate amount together, the screen displays `"Good boy!"`; if the amount is too low or an attempt is made to bribe, it displays `"You son of a bi***!"`.

Quiz: Wrong Branching ★

The following piece of code wants to swap the contents of the variables x and y if x is greater than y. Is this correct?

```
int x=2; y=1;
if ( x>y )
```

```
    int swap=x;
    x=y;
    y=x;
// x should be 1 and y 2
```

Convert Liters ★★

A program should convert liquid quantities into a form that is easy for Captain CiaoCiao to read.
Task:

- From the command line, read in a floating-point number, the order of magnitude is liters.
- Convert the number according to the following pattern:
    - 1.0 and greater: output in liters, such as `approx. 4 l` for the input 4.
    - 0.1 and greater: output in centiliters, about `approx. 20 cl` when entering 0.2.
    - 0.001 and larger: output in milliliters, about `approx. 9 ml` when entering 0.009.
- The result will always be an integer, and rounding is acceptable.

Example:

- Conversion to mL:
  ```
  Enter quantity in liters:
  0.0124134
  approx. 12 ml
  ```
- Conversion in cL:
  ```
  Enter quantity in liters:
  0.9876
  about 98 cl
  ```
- Message if the value is too small:
  ```
  Enter quantity in liters:
  0.00003435
  Value too small to display
  ```
- Input is already in liters:
  ```
  Enter quantity in liters:
  98848548485.445
  approx. 98848548485 l
  ```

Create SVG Circles with Random Colors ★

In a previous assignment, Captain CiaoCiao called for a black circle on a white background. But there should be more colors in the mix!
Task:

- Create a new class with a `main(...)` method.
- Output on the command line randomly, and with equal probability, `red`, `green`, and `blue`.
- In SVG, for circles, you can specify the color with the `fill` attribute, like this: `<circle cx="20" cy="20" r="5" fill="blue " />`. Give the circle a random color.

Example:

- With three program starts, there could be the following screen outputs:
  ```
  <circle cx="20" cy="20" r="5" fill="green" />
  ```

```
<circle cx="20" cy="20" r="5" fill="blue" />
<circle cx="20" cy="20" r="5" fill="blue" />
```

Quiz: To Which Block Does the Else Belong? ★★

Indentations are among the most important principles of clean code. If the indentations are wrong, a reader may misunderstand the program.

What output does the following program produce?

```
if ( true ) {
if ( false )
if ( 3!=4 )
;
else
System.out.println( "ship's kobold" );
else
System.out.println( "Pumuckl" );
}
```

Find the result without translating the program.

Hint: First indent the program correctly.

Quiz: Recognize Negative Days and Hours ★

For tests if one of two values is negative, Giggi Giggles always uses expressions like hours < 0 || minutes < 0. Now something strange appears in a program:

```
System.out.println( "Enter number of hours" );
int hours=new java.util.Scanner( System.in ).nextInt();
System.out.println( "Enter number of minutes" );
int minutes=new java.util.Scanner( System.in ).nextInt();
if ( (hours | minutes)<0 ) // Magic. Do not touch.
  System.out.println( "Either the minutes or hours have been negative." );
else
  System.out.println( "Minutes in total: "+(60 * hours+minutes) );
```

Instead of the familiar operator || there is only one slash |. Is this an error? Or why could the result of hours < 0 || minutes < 0 and (hours | minutes) < 0 be the same?

Evaluate Input Strings for Approval ★

Bonny Brain expects approval for new projects, and the approval can vary.
Task:

- Ask for a string from the command line. We assume that the input is always lowercase.
- If the input string is "ay", "aye", "ay, ay", "ja", or "joo", the message "Keep it up!" should be printed on the screen, all other input strings result in "Don't you dare!".
- Solve this exercise using the switch statement or switch expression.

Rewrite Switch Statement to Switch Expression ★

Java 14 has introduced an extended syntax for the switch statement, allowing for more concise writing of existing code.
Task:

- Given is the following code with the classic switch statement:

```
int month=new java.util.Scanner( System.in ).nextInt();
int year=new java.util.Scanner( System.in ).nextInt();
boolean isLeapYear= ((year % 4 == 0) && (year % 100 != 0))
                    || (year % 400 == 0);

int days;
switch ( month ) {
  case 2:
    days=isLeapYear ? 29 : 28;
    break;
  case 4:
  case 6:
  case 9:
  case 11:
    days=30;
    break;
  default:
    days=31;
}
```

- Shorten the program with the switch expression.

LOOPS

Besides if statements, repetitions are the second important imperative property. Java provides different language constructs for loops:

- while loop.
- do-while loop.
- for loop.
- extended for loop.

Create Rotated SVG Rectangles ★

After a raid, Captain CiaoCiao often comes back stressed. To relax, he colors geometric, recurring patterns. Bonny Brain is supposed to prepare sheets for him, but she dislikes doing it; a program is supposed to take care of it.

The following vector graphic in SVG rotates a rectangle around the center point (100, 100), by 60 degrees:

```
<svg height="200" width="200">
 <rect x="50" y="50" width="100" height="100" stroke="black" fill="none"
       transform="rotate(60 100 100)" />
</svg>
```

Task:

- Write a program that rotates 36 SVG rectangles 10 degrees on top of each other and outputs them to the screen.

Example:

- The output starts with:
  ```
  <svg height="200" width="200">
   <rect x="50" y="50" width="100" height="100" stroke="black"
         fill="none" transform="rotate(0 100 100)" />
   <rect x="50" y="50" width="100" height="100" stroke="black"
         fill="none" transform="rotate(10 100 100)" />
   <rect x="50" y="50" width="100" height="100" stroke="black"
         fill="none" transform="rotate(20 100 100)" />
   ...
  </svg>
  ```

Create SVG-Pearl-Chain ★

Captain CiaoCiao wants to give a pearl necklace to his beloved Bonny Brain. This is made of three different gemstones: Sapphire (blue), Emerald (green), Spessartite Garnet (orange). He would like to have a design proposal in which the colors are randomly arranged.

The following is for an SVG document with three circles:

```
<svg height="100" width="1000">
 <circle cx="20" cy="20" r="5" fill="blue" />
 <circle cx="30" cy="20" r="5" fill="green" />
 <circle cx="40" cy="20" r="5" fill="orange" />
</svg>
```

Task:

- Create an SVG output on the command line with 50 circles side by side.

Sum Numbers from the Command Line ★

Captain CiaoCiao needs a program to enter a number of captured Loretta from his individual raids. This should be entered from the command line to add them up.

Task:

- Create a new class `SummingCalculator`.
- Use the `Scanner` to input numbers until 0 is entered. Negative numbers are allowed since Captain CiaoCiao is occasionally been robbed. Ignore any potential overflows resulting from numbers that are too large.
- After 0 is entered, the sum should be printed.

Example:

```
12
3
-1
0
Sum: 14
```

Go through a Mathematical Phenomenon ★

In mathematics, an iteration is a repeated calculation starting with a starting value until a certain condition is met. In calculations, iterations are an important procedure to improve the solution at each additional step after an initial approximation.
Task:

- Declare a `double` variable `t` between 0 (inclusive) and 10 (exclusive) with the following line:
  `double t =Math.random() * 10;`
- Multiply `t` by 2 if `t < 1`. However, if `t >= 1`, subtract `1`.
- Put this calculation into a `while` loop that should end when `t` is less than or equal to 0.

Example:

- The output might evolve like this:
  ```
  9.835060881347246
  8.835060881347246
  7.835060881347246
  6.835060881347246
  ...
  0.75
  1.5
  0.5
  1.0
  ```

Quiz: How Many Stars? ★

How many asterisks would appear on the console for loop A and B?
  A:

```
for ( int stars=0; stars <= 7; stars=stars+2 )
  System.out.println( "***" );
```

B:

```
for ( int stars=10; stars<0; stars++ )
  System.out.println( "**" );
```

Remember: `stars++` is an abbreviation for `stars=stars+1`.

Calculate Products for Faculties ★

For the new fleet, Rigel VII, Bonny Brain must select the lead officers; the choices are Paul Peldrion, Kate Muggle, Robinson Langdon, and Lienn Langdon. However, Bonny Brain is unsure which person should take which role; there are: commander, first officer, second officer, and third officer.

There are many possibilities of which person takes which role. How many possible arrangements of different elements there are in a row is told by the so-called *permutation*. A permutation without repetition is calculated by the *factorial*. With four persons, there are $1 \times 2 \times 3 \times 4 = 24$ possible arrangements.

The factorial of a natural number (positive integer) is the product of all positive integers up to that number. It is defined as follows:

$$n! = 1 \times 2 \times 3 \times \ldots \times (n-1) \times n$$

It holds that $0! = 1$.
Task:

- Write a Java program that reads a nonnegative integer from the command line and displays the calculation.

Example:

- Input: 9 → Output: `9!=1 * 2 * 3 * 4 * 5 * 6 * 7 * 8 * 9=362880`.
- Input: 3 → Output: `3!=1 * 2 * 3=6`.
- Input: 0 → Output: `0!=1`.
- Input: 1 → Output: `1!=1`.
- Input: -1 → Output: `Number must not be negative`.

Use the data type `long` internally.

Question: From which number will there be "problems"? How do the issues show up, and how can we detect them? Can `Math.multiplyExact(long x, long y)` help us?

Determine If a Number Is Formed by Factorial ★

Jar Jar Dumbs has been instructed by Bonny Brain to write down all possible arrangements for a given number of people. Before looking at the list, she counts the number to determine if all permutations have been listed.

We saw how to calculate the factorial for a natural number in the previous assignment. But how can we find out if a number is a factorial? We know that 9!=362880, but what about 212880 or 28?
Task:

- Write a program that reads a natural number from the command line, and outputs whether the number is a factorial.

Example:

- Number is factorial:
  ```
  Enter a number:
  362880
  362880=9!
  ```
- Number is not a factorial:
  ```
  Enter a number:
  1000
  1000 is not a factorial
  ```

Test if the number is divisible by 2, 3, 4, 5 …

Find the Smallest and Largest Digit of a Number ★

Bonny Brain knows, of course, that decimal numbers consist of digits from 0 to 9. Since the boat ride is long and boring, she came up with a game: she gives the crew an integer, and the fastest person to name its largest and smallest digits wins one Liretta.

Task:

- Given any whole number (positive or negative), stored in a `long`.
- Using a program, help find the smallest and largest digits of the stored number.

Examples:

- 12345 → 1, 5
- 987654 → 4, 9
- 11111 → 1, 1
- 0 → 0, 0
- -23456788888234567L → 2, 8

Quiz: Not Like This from 1 to 100 ★★

The compiler does the work for us of checking programs syntactically. Now let's play compiler!

The following program is supposed to add the numbers from 1 and up to 100 and output the result. Unfortunately, there are some errors in the program.

```java
class Sümme {
  private static int getSum() {
    int j == 0;
    for ( /* int */i=0, i <= 100, j++);
      j += i
    ;
  }
  public static void Main( String aarg ) {
    system.out.println( getsum() );
  }
}
```

Assign the errors to the following types:

1. Syntactic errors.
2. Semantic errors.
3. Style guide violations.

A Flag in the Wind through Nested Loops ★

The sailors were in for a surprise when they realized that their flag had gone for a swim in the rough sea! Captain CiaoCiao, being the witty captain that he is, demanded that his crew whip up a new one ASAP. Let's just hope it doesn't decide to take another dip anytime soon!

Task:

- Create the following output that looks like a small flag:

```
1
2 2
3 3 3
4 4 4 4
5 5 5 5 5
```

Optional: The output should appear as a tree, in the sense that all lines are centered.

Output Simple Chessboard ★

Captain CiaoCiao is a fan of German Checkers, which is a variant of the game of checkers. He frequently takes part in competitions and has noticed that the board size can vary. Sporadically, it is 8×8 squares, and sometimes 10×10 squares; he has also experienced 12×12 and 14×14.

For Captain CiaoCiao to prepare for all possible board sizes, a program should output a chessboard on the screen.

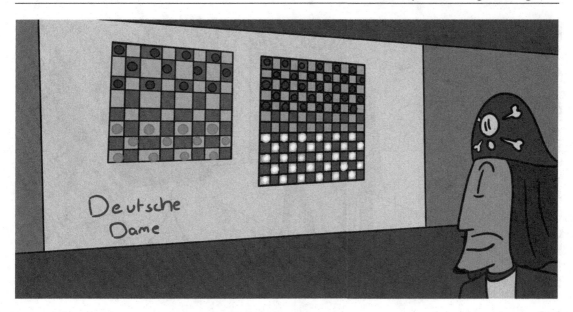

Task:

- Obtain from the command line the height and width of the game board.
- Draw the board according to its given dimensions by the symbols # and _ .

Example:

```
Checkerboard width: 10
Checkerboard height: 5
_#_#_#_#_#
#_#_#_#_#_
_#_#_#_#_#
#_#_#_#_#_
_#_#_#_#_#
```

It's Christmastime: Displaying Trees with Ornaments ★

Christmas is coming soon, and Bonny Brain wants to print Christmas cards. For this, trees of different sizes are needed.

Task:

- Using loops, write a triangular tree top with a maximum width on the screen.
- In each line, the string becomes wider by two characters until it becomes >= width.
- Centering is achieved by preceding spaces.
- The leaves of the tree consist of the multiplication character *.
- Randomly sprinkle o characters representing Christmas balls into the tree.

Example:

- Tree of width 7 (equal to a tree of width 8):
  ```
     *
    *o*
   ***o*
  *o*****
  ```

Draw Fishy Stitching Motifs ★

Bonny Brain loves the sea and wants a scarf with a fish pattern. The sewing machine can stitch ><
and > motifs using the symbols ><> and <><.

The following forms a pattern with a repetition of 1, so that first a fish swims to the right and then a
fish swims to the left.

><> <><

Task:

- Write a program that, according to the assignment of a variable `repetitions`, first places the fish ><> `repetitions` times one after the other and then places the fish <>< `repetitions` times one after the other. The line should itself be `repetitions` times below the other.

Examples:

- If `repetitions` is equal to 2, the output shall be:
  ```
  ><> ><> <>< <><
  ><> ><> <>< <><
  ```
- If `repetitions` = 3 the program shall result in the following output:
  ```
  ><> ><> ><> <>< <>< <><
  ><> ><> ><> <>< <>< <><
  ><> ><> ><> <>< <>< <><
  ```

Trying Instead of Thinking ★★

Today's computers are so fast to try different things at the same time. Password cracking programs work on this principle.

Captain CiaoCiao flips through the "Pirates Daily" and finds a brainteaser:

$$
\begin{array}{cccc}
  & X & O & L \\
+ & L & X & X \\
\hline
= & T & L & T \\
\end{array}
$$

He has to find a digit for each of the letters L, O, T, and X to make the calculation correct. The prize for the puzzle is an old compass, which Captain CiaoCiao desperately wants to win. But unfortunately, he lacks the desire to think.

Task:

- Develop a program that finds a solution by trying all possibilities.
- Print out all the solutions and indicate which solutions have X, O, L, and T all different from each other.

Get the Number of Digits of a Number ★★

Bonny Brain wants to right-justify numbers. To accomplish this, spaces are placed in front of the numbers. For example, if you want the width to be 10 characters and the number is 123 (three digits), then seven spaces must be placed before the number to make the width 10.

The first step to determine the number of spaces is to determine the number of digits in a number.
Task:

- Given is a positive integer n of type int. Output the number of digits of the number. Do not use (""+n).length(), that would be too simple …

Examples for n and the expected output:

- `1234 → 4`
- `3 → 1`
- `0 → 1`
- `Integer.MAX _ VALUE → 10`

METHODS

Methods are important because this way we can centralize common code and also give objects an API to access for clients.

Drawing Hearts ★

Since Captain CiaoCiao loves his crew, there can't be enough hearts.

Task:

1. Create a new class `LinePrinter`. Put a static method `line()` into the class, which writes a line of ten hearts. Java can store and output the Unicode character "♥" in strings.
2. Create a new class `LinePrinterDemo` that has a `main(..)` method and calls `line()`.

Implement Overloaded Line Methods ★

Next, let's look at methods that can be passed something. Furthermore, a method name can be used multiple times: we talk about *overloaded methods*.
Task:

- A method `line(int len)` will print a line of length `len` with a minus sign (`"-"`) on the console. For example, `line(3)` will print `---` onto the screen.
- The method `line(int len, char c)` shall be callable with custom fill characters. So `line(2, 'x')` outputs the line `xx` on the screen. Can the first method use the second?
- Add another overloaded method `line(String prefix, int len, char c, String suffix)` that sets a start string before the line and an end string after the line. For example, `line("╠", 3, '=', "╣")` returns `╠===╣`. The line inside is three characters long, not the entire string.

Remember: you don't have to implement all three methods completely with a loop. If you're smart, you'll forward from one method to the other.
    Add the overloaded methods to the class `LinePrinter`.

Standing Straight ★

Back in the day, the nincompoops would hoist the mast at the wrong angle. A pirate can be a bit crooked, but the mast better be straight as an arrow!

    If you take a triangle, it can come in a variety of shapes. There are acute-angled triangles, obtuse-angled triangles, equilateral triangles, and right-angled triangles, among others. As a reminder, triangles are right-angled if $c^2 = a^2 + b^2$.

Task:

- Create a new class `RightTriangle` and write a new method; use the following code as a template:

```
class RightTriangle {
  public static boolean isRightTriangle( double a, double b, double c )
  {
      // Your implementation goes here
  }
}
```
- The method should take three sides of a triangle and return `true` if it is a right triangle, `false` otherwise.
- Remember: each of parameters a, b, and c can stand for the cathetus or hypotenuse.

Example:

- `isRightTriangle(3, 4, 5)` → `true`
- `isRightTriangle(5, 4, 3)` → `true`
- `isRightTriangle(5, 12, 13)` → `true`
- `isRightTriangle(1, 2, 3)` → `false`
- `isRightTriangle(1, 1, Math.sqrt(2))` → `false`

The last example shows well that computational inaccuracy is a problem. `Math.sqrt(2)` * `Math.sqrt(2)` is (in the output) 2.00000000000004 and not exactly 2.

Create a Multiplication Table ★

Bonny Brain is spicing things up over at the *Magical Company*. She's now selling two new products: a flamethrower for 500 Liretta and a fire extinguisher for a measly 100 Liretta.

To be able to read quickly what the price is in case of a larger purchase, a table should be created in HTML:

QUANTITY	FLAMETHROWER	FIRE EXTINGUISHER
1	500	100
2	1,000	200
3	1,500	300
...	...	...

In HTML, a table is represented as follows:

```
<html>
<table>
<tr><th>Quantity</th><th>Flamethrower</th></tr>
<tr><td>1</td><td>500</td></tr>
<tr><td>2</td><td>1000</td></tr>
</table>
</html>
```

Task:

- On the screen, create the HTML table shown with the number 1–10.
- Consider where own methods would be useful.

You can copy the generated HTML at https://jsfiddle.net/ and "run" it to see the result.

Cistercian Numerals Script ★★★

A *numeral system* is a system that consists of symbols used to represent numbers. There are different types of numeral systems that have been used in different cultures and time periods. Examples are the *Roman numeral system* (MCMLXXIII would be 1973) and the *Arabic numeral system* with the well-known numerals 0, 1, 2, 3, 4, 5, 6, 7, 8, and 9, which is used in most parts of the world today.

The Cistercian Order is known for the *Cistercian numeral system*, in which the numbers from 1 to 9,999 can be expressed in a single glyph. The construction plan is as follows:

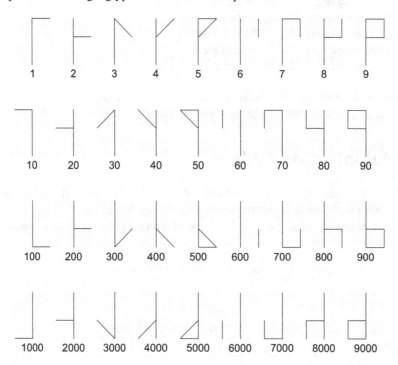

FIGURE 2.2   Cistercian numbers.

A few examples:

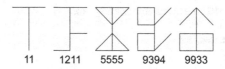

FIGURE 2.3   Examples of Cistercian numerals.

Task:

- Write a program that generates SVG on the command line for any four-digit number according to the presented pattern.

Example:

- For 9394 the following SVG could be generated:

  https://jsfiddle.net/Lt0djpz3/

```
<svg height="1400" width="1400">
<g style="stroke:grey;stroke-linecap:round;stroke-width:2">
<line x1="100" y1="85" x2="100" y2="115" />
<line x1="100" y1="95" x2="110" y2="85" />
<line x1="100" y1="85" x2="90" y2="85" />
<line x1="100" y1="95" x2="90" y2="95" />
<line x1="90" y1="85" x2="90" y2="95" />
<line x1="100" y1="115" x2="110" y2="105" />
<line x1="100" y1="115" x2="90" y2="115" />
<line x1="100" y1="105" x2="90" y2="105" />
<line x1="90" y1="115" x2="90" y2="105" />
</g>
</svg>
```

- https://commons.wikimedia.org/wiki/File:Cistercian1-9999.png shows all possible characters.

Note the horizontal and vertical mirroring.

Quiz: What Does Ding-Dong Do? (Recursion) ★★

The following method appears in a long lost program:

```
static long ding( long dong ) {
  return dong == 0 ? 0
                   : (dong % 10+ding( dong / 10 ));
}
```

What does the method do? How could it be better named?

Quiz: Repdigit (Recursion) ★★

A *repdigit* (from *repeated digits*) has only identical digits.
    The following Java method recursively determines whether a number is a repdigit:

```
static boolean isRepdigit( long n ) {
```

```
  if ( (n % 100) / 10 != n % 10 )
    return n<10;
  return isRepdigit( n / 10 );
}
```

Task:

- How does the method work?
- The boolean expression inside the if statement
  if ((n % 100) / 10 != n % 10).
- Can be rewritten to
  if (n % 100 % 11 != 0).
- Why?

Calculate Collatz Sequence (Recursion) ★

Lothar Collatz defined a sequence of numbers in 1937 that is now known as the *Collatz sequence*. It is defined as a mapping that follows a number n as follows:

- $n \rightarrow n/2$, if n is even,
- $n \rightarrow 3n+1$, if n is odd.
- The sequence is finished when 1 is reached.

If we start, say, with $n=7$, the algorithm runs through the following numbers:

- $7 \rightarrow 22 \rightarrow 11 \rightarrow 34 \rightarrow 17 \rightarrow 52 \rightarrow 26 \rightarrow 13 \rightarrow 40 \rightarrow 20 \rightarrow 10 \rightarrow 5 \rightarrow 16 \rightarrow 8 \rightarrow 4 \rightarrow 2 \rightarrow 1$

Every sequence ends with 4, 2, 1, but the reason is still an unsolved one in mathematics.
Task:

- Create a class Collatz with a method void collatz(long n).
- Create a main(...) method, and compute the Collatz sequence with a starting value of 27.
- Write a new method long collatzMax(long n), which returns the largest intermediate value reached.
- How can we program collatz(...) recursively so that the method returns the maximum assumed value as result? Attention, the signature must be changed! (Why?)

Ancient Egyptian Multiplication (Recursion) ★★

Computers rely heavily on arithmetic operations, which form an essential part of their tasks. Basic operations such as addition and subtraction are straightforward, and even multiplication and division by two can be easily achieved by shifting bits left and right.

In earlier processors, multiplication was not natively implemented, so software-based solutions were needed. To ensure fast performance, these solutions were limited to using only basic operations such as addition, subtraction, division by two, and multiplication by two. Interestingly, a calculation method for multiplication using these limited operations was already known to the Ancient Egyptians over 5,000 years ago.

The concept is the following: $a \times b$ is equivalent to $1/1 \times a \times b$, which is equivalent to $2/2 \times a \times b$, which is equivalent to $(a/2) \times (2 \times b)$. Let's test that:

$$4 \times 3 = (4/2) \times (3 \times 2) = 2 \times 6 = 12$$

From 4×3 we have come to 2×6. And that would be by the same rule $(2/2) \times (6 \times 2) = 1 \times 12 = 12$. You see: when the multiplier is 1, the multiplicand has the result. (A product results from the multiplication of factors. The first factor is called a **multiplier**, and the second is **multiplicand**).

A second example:

MULTIPLIER	MULTIPLICAND
8	7
4	14
2	28
1	56

The multiplier has reached 1 and the multiplicand contains the result with 56.

An algorithm would be quickly formulated: a loop runs as long as the multiplier is >0. In the body of the loop, divide the multiplier by 2 and multiply the multiplicand by 2. However, there is a problem ...

The multiplier is not always an even number. If the product of 11×6 is to be calculated, 5.5×12 will, of course, give the same result, but we don't want to work with floating-point numbers. If we calculate 11×6 as known, the result of the integer division will be $(11/2) \times (6 \times 2) = 5 \times 12 = 60$. The correct result is 66. We are missing 6. The multiplicand is also 6. Is this a coincidence?

Odd and even numbers are always different by one. If a is an odd number, $a-1$ is an even number. If we want to calculate $a \times b$, it is like $(a-1+1) \times b$, and expanding the product leads to $(a-1) \times b + b$. For example, $11 \times 6 = (11-1+1) \times 6 = (10+1) \times 6 = 10 \times 6 + 6 = 66$. That's right. You could continue like this and calculate 10×6 as well.

Let's come back to the algorithm that divides the multiplier by two until one is reached. If a multiplier is odd, the multiplier is reduced by one so that it is even again for the next division step and a "correction value" is noted. Since there can be multiple corrections, they are all summed.

PRODUCT	MULTIPLIER ODD?	REWRITE IF MULTIPLIER IS ODD	CORRECTION VALUE
22×3	No		
11×6	Yes	$(10+1) \times 6 = 10 \times 6 + \mathbf{6}$	6
5×12	Yes	$(4+1) \times 12 = 4 \times 12 + \mathbf{12}$	12
2×24	No		
1×48	Yes	$(0+1) \times 48 = 0 + \mathbf{48}$	48

The sum of $6+12+48$ is 66, and that is 22×3. Written in a nested way:

$$22 \times 3 = 11 \times 6 = (10 \times 6) + 6 = ((4 \times 12) + 12) + 6 = ((48) + 12) + 6 = 66.$$

Multiplying any integer would only require adding values, multiplying by 2, and dividing by 2. And, it must be possible to test whether a number is even or odd.

Task:

- Implement the algorithm in Java code, with and without recursion.
- If addition costs as much as multiplication and division, how can the number of iterations be optimized?

SUGGESTED SOLUTIONS

Write an SVG Circle on the Console ★

com/tutego/exercise/lang/SvgCircle1.java

```java
package com.tutego.exercise.lang;
public class SvgCircle1 {
  public static void main( String[] args ) {
    System.out.println(
      "<svg height='400' width='1000'><circle cx='100' cy='100' r='50' /></
svg>"
    );
  }
}
```

In the first step, we build a new class because program code outside of classes is not allowed in Java. Next, we put the special main method into the class. The JVM calls main(...) by itself when the program starts, so we put in here exactly the part we want to be executed at the beginning.

To better group the solutions thematically, they are placed in Java packages; this is what the first declaration, `package com.tutego.exercise.lang` stands for. Packages are introduced in chapter *Classes, Objects, and Packages*, the own solutions do not need to use packages for this time.

To print the circle, we can create a file *circle.html*, open it in the editor and copy the SVG part into it, then open the file with the web browser and print the page.

com/tutego/exercise/lang/SvgCircle2.java

```
System.out.println( «<svg height='400' width='1000'>» );
System.out.println( « <circle cx='100' cy='100' r='50' />» );
System.out.println( «</svg>» );

System.out.println(
  «<svg height='400' width='1000'>\n <circle cx='100' cy='100' r='50' />\n</
svg>»
);
```

The difference between print(…) and println(…) is that the latter method automatically writes a newline. So if the task is to write several lines one below the other, we can write each line with the println(…) method.

There is another way, and that is to put a newline inside the string. A string inside double quotes cannot span multiple lines. A line break inside a string is therefore wrong. The solution is a so-called *escape sequence*; for a line break, this is \n. If we use the method println(…), we do not have to put \n at the end, unless we want to have two line breaks at the end.

Large strings can be split into multiple substrings using the plus operator so that they are more readable. This way, we can convert each of them into one line of Java code.

com/tutego/exercise/lang/SvgCircle3.java

```
System.out.println(   "<svg height=\"400\" width=\"1000\">\n"
            +" <circle cx=\"100\" cy=\"100\" r=\"50\" />\n"
            +"</svg>" );
```

The last part of the exercise is also solved with an escape sequence. Besides \n the escape sequence \" puts a double quote in a string.

As of Java 15, there are *text blocks* for multiline texts. This allows another solution:

com/tutego/exercise/lang/SvgCircle4.java

```
System.out.println( """
            <svg height="400" width="1000">
            <circle cx="100" cy="100" r="50" />
            </svg>""" );
```

Access Variables and Output Their Assignments

Below, you find three alternative solutions that differ in how the SVG element is output to the screen.

com/tutego/exercise/lang/SvgCircleWithVariables1.java

```
int x=100;
int y=110;
double r=20.5;

System.out.println( "<svg height=\"100\" width=\"1000\">" );
System.out.print( " <circle cx=\"" );
```

```
System.out.print( x );
System.out.print( "\" cy=\"" );
System.out.print( y );
System.out.print( "\" r=\"" );
System.out.print( r );
System.out.println( "\" />" );
System.out.println( "</svg>" );
```

The first solution simply splits the constant and variable parts into different System.out.println(…) and System.out.print(…) calls.

com/tutego/exercise/lang/SvgCircleWithVariables2.java

```
int x=100, y=110;
double r=20.5;

System.out.println(
    "<svg height=\"100\" width=\"1000\">\n"
 +" <circle cx=\""+x+"\" cy=\""+y+"\" r=\""+r+"\" />\n"
 +"</svg>"
);
```

The second solution uses the ability to concatenate strings with the + operator. When concatenating, Java is flexible enough that anything that is not a string is converted to a string and then appended.

com/tutego/exercise/lang/SvgCircleWithVariables3.java

```
int x=100, y=110;
double r=20.5;

System.out.printf(    "<svg height=\"100\" width=\"1000\">\n"
                 +" <circle cx=\"%d\" cy=\"%d\" r=\"%s\" />\n"
                 +"</svg>\n%n",
                  x, y, r );
```

Furthermore, the third solution results in the same string, and we only use a format string and the method printf(…). There are three placeholders in the format string. That is twice %d for the integer, and we format the floating-point number using %s. This format specifier is so generic that it can be used for all data types. We then get the English representation where the decimal places are separated by a period, which is the correct notation for floating-point numbers with decimal places for the SVG specification. %n results in a platform-specific end-of-line character and is an alternative to \n.

Quiz: Value Ranges

The product of $1{,}000{,}000 \times 1{,}000{,}000$ is $1E+12$, and that exceeds the value range of the int data type, which only goes as high as 2,147,483,647. $1E+12$ needs 40 bits, and int offers only a width of 32 bits, so the upper 8 bits are truncated. The situation is different with long, which is 64 bits long and allows a range of values up to 9,223,372,036,854,775,807 (no, you don't have to remember the ranges digit by digit).

The following gives the correct output because the integers are multiplied as long:

```
long number=1_000_000;
System.out.println( number * number );
```

Large numbers can be made more readable in Java by using an underscore.

Alternatives:

```
System.out.println( 1_000_000 * 1_000_000L );
System.out.println( 1_000_000L * 1_000_000 );
System.out.println( 1_000_000L * 1_000_000L );
System.out.println( (long) 1_000_000 * 1_000_000 );
System.out.println( 1_000_000 * (long) 1_000_000 );
```

Quiz: Does This Add Up?

The result is not exactly 0.0. The reason is that double cannot represent the number 0.1 precisely. 0.1 is a difficult number which, simply put, cannot be represented as a sum of fractions of the type $1/2^n$. 0.1 has in the IEEE-754 format the bit pattern 0|01111011|1001 _ 1001 _ 1001 _ 1001 _ 101, symbolically | separates the sign bit from the exponent and from the mantissa, and the underscore makes the period visible. This bit pattern corresponds back to 0.1000000001490116119384765625, an error of about 1.49×10^{-9}. If 0.1000000001490116119384765625 is now added ten times, 1.0 cannot come out.

There are several solutions to the problem:

1. Instead of double, use the class BigDecimal.
2. Accept the inaccuracy and round in the output, which can be done with printf(…).
3. A monetary amount can be stored internally in cents; instead of storing 0.1 Liretta, for example, a program can store 10 Lirettacent and display that later in the output as 0.1.

Generate Random Circles

com/tutego/exercise/lang/SvgCircleWithRandomRadius.java

```
int x=100, y=110;
double r=Math.random() * 10+10;

System.out.printf(
  "<svg height=\"100\" width=\"1000\">\n "
+ "<circle cx=\"%d\" cy=\"%d\" r=\"%s\" />\n</svg>\n%n",
  x, y, r );

System.out.printf(
  Locale.ENGLISH,
  "<svg height=\"100\" width=\"1000\">\n "
+ "<circle cx=\"%d\" cy=\"%d\" r=\"%.2f\" />\n</svg>\n%n",
  x, y, r );
```

The method Math.random() produces a floating-point number from 0 to a true less than 1. If we multiply the result by 10, we get a floating-point number between 0 and less than 10. If we add 10 to this, the random number will be between 10 and less than 20.

Since the floating-point number is random, it also has many decimal places. The format specifier %s also lists all the decimal places. It might look like this:

```
<svg height="100" width="1000">
 <circle cx="100" cy="110" r="17.807835163311744" />
</svg>
```

There is another solution, and the listing shows an alternative. We no longer use the `%s` format specifier, but `%f`. This is precisely the format specifier intended for floating-point numbers. However, it has one property that now gets in the way: the output is localized, i.e., in a local language. If we use our program on a different localized operating system, the separator for the decimal places might not be `.`, but `,`. This is wrong for SVG. The solution is to pass the language as the first argument of the `printf(...)` method. We can also specify the number of decimal places. To complete this, we make the format specifier a bit more precise. Instead of just `%f` it will be `%.2f` for two decimal places. You can see from the output that rounding is also done here.

```
<svg height="100" width="1000">
 <circle cx="100" cy="110" r="17.81" />
</svg>
```

Quiz: Dazed and Confused

There are three problems:

1. Variables should be in English, and not contain for example, German umlauts.
2. `tmp` is not a good name, it is about perimeter or area, so the variable should be called `area` or `diameter`.
3. The function's variable should remain consistent throughout the program's execution. Consequently, it's preferable to use two local variables:

```
double diameter = 2 * (height + width);
System.out.println( diameter );
double area = height * width;
System.out.println( area );
```

Process User Input

com/tutego/exercise/lang/SvgCircleWithConsoleCoordinates.java

```
int x=new java.util.Scanner( System.in ).nextInt();
int y=new java.util.Scanner( System.in ).nextInt();

double r=Math.random() * 10+10;

System.out.printf(
    Locale.ENGLISH,
    "<svg height=\"100\" width=\"1000\">\n "
  +"<circle cx=\"%d\" cy=\"%d\" r=\"%.2f\" />\n</svg>\n%n",
    x, y, r );
```

As stated in the exercise, `new java.util.Scanner(System.in).nextInt()` can be used to read in an integer. We do this twice. The rest of the program remains the same as the previous one.

Quiz: Check In-Between

While Python is capable of performing range checks of the form `min<between<max`, the same cannot be done in Java due to type incompatibility. In Java, the expression `min<between` results in a `boolean`

value, and a comparison between a `boolean` and a `double` is not valid. For this reason, attempting to perform such a comparison in Java will result in a compilation error such as `operator '<' cannot be applied to 'boolean', 'double'`.

Check If Loot Can Be Shared Fairly

com/tutego/exercise/lang/FairShare.java

```java
System.out.println( "Number of bottles in total?" );
int bottles =new java.util.Scanner( System.in ).nextInt();

int captainsBottles =bottles / 2;
int crewsBottles =bottles - captainsBottles;

System.out.println( "Bottles for the captain: " +captainsBottles );
System.out.println( "Bottles for all crew members: " +crewsBottles );

System.out.println( "Number of crew members?" );
int crewMembers =new java.util.Scanner( System.in ).nextInt();
System.out.println( "Fair share without remainder? " + (crewsBottles %
crewMembers == 0) );
```

In the first step, we read in an integer via the `Scanner` and initialize our variable `bottles` for the loot. Since the captain gets half of the bottles, we divide the input by 2. In the next step, we calculate what the crew members get, and don't choose the solution that we divide by 2 again because with odd numbers, we get the problem that the two halves don't add up anymore. (If you want to try this out, give the result of 5 / 2 + 5 / 2.) To make sure this doesn't happen, we subtract the captain's share from `bottles` to obtain what the crew gets.

Finally, we have to find out if the number of leftover bottles can be divided fairly by the number of crew members. To achieve this, the program first asks for the number of crew members. The remainder operator will tell us if the division pans out or if there is a remainder. If the division goes up, the remainder will be 0. In that case, the loot can be divided fairly.

Do Two Numbers Share the Same Digit?

com/tutego/exercise/lang/HasCommonDigits.java

```java
System.out.println( "Enter two numbers between 0 and 99:" );
int number1=new java.util.Scanner( System.in ).nextInt() % 100;
int number2=new java.util.Scanner( System.in ).nextInt() % 100;

int number1digit1 = number1 / 10;
int number1digit2 = number1 % 10;
int number2digit1 = number2 / 10;
int number2digit2 = number2 % 10;

boolean hasCommonDigits= number1digit1 == number2digit1
                      || number1digit1 == number2digit2
                      || number1digit2 == number2digit1
                      || number1digit2 == number2digit2;
System.out.println( hasCommonDigits );
```

First, we read in two numbers, and the % 100 expression ensures that the numbers do not go over 100, but are correctly—truncated to the range from 0 to 99 as required by the specification—.

To understand the solution, let's go back to the example from the problem definition. We have the numbers 12 and 31. How do we proceed? Ultimately, we have to test whether 1 occurs in 31 or 2 occurs in 31. In other words, we have to test whether 1 equals 3, or 1 equals 1 or 2 equals 3 or 2 equals 1. In our case, 1 equals 1, so the result is true.

To translate the entire procedure into a Java program, we need to extract the first and second digits. For this, we need a bit of mathematics. If we divide an integer by 10, it cuts off the last digit. If we divide 12 by 10, we are left with 1. The operations on integers lead to a result that is again an integer. On the other hand, we use the remainder operator % to obtain the very last digit. Thus, 12 % 10 is equal to 2.

This way, we create four variables and test if we can find digits of the first number in the second number.

Convert Currency Amount to Coins

com/tutego/exercise/lang/CoinMachine.java

```java
System.out.println( "Please the enter the amount of money:" );
double input=new java.util.Scanner( System.in ).nextDouble();
int cents=(int) (input * 100);

System.out.println( cents / 200+" x 2 Liretta" );
cents %= 200;

System.out.println( cents / 100+" x 1 Liretta" );
cents %= 100;

System.out.println( cents / 50+" x 50 Lirettacent" );
cents %= 50;

System.out.println( cents / 20+" x 20 Lirettacent" );
cents %= 20;

System.out.println( cents / 10+" x 10 Lirettacent" );
cents %= 10;

System.out.println( cents / 5+" x 5 Lirettacent" );
cents %= 5;

System.out.println( cents / 2+" x 2 Lirettacent" );
cents %= 2;

System.out.println( cents+" x 1 Lirettacent" );
```

The task's solution can be implemented using the division and remainder operators. After the command prompt and reading the floating-point number, we perform the first trick: we convert the amount to cents. This way it is easier to calculate.

The next steps always occur in pairs. First, we calculate the number of coins, then we calculate how many coins remain. Let's take the example of 12.91 Liretta; that's 1,291 Lirettacent. The total number of cents divided by 200 gives us a positive integer and is precisely the result of how many 2-Liretta pieces are in total. Now we need to move on to the remainder, and this is where the remainder operator is helpful. If we take cents % 200, we get a smaller number, and we can continue next with the 1-Liretta piece, which is 100 cents. The game continues like this until we get to one cent. Then there is nothing left.

One Bottle of Rum, Ten Bottles of Rum

com/tutego/exercise/lang/NumberOfBottles.java

```
int noOfBottles=1;   // or 0, 1, 99, ...

System.out.println(  noOfBottles+" "
                   +(noOfBottles !=1 ? "bottles" : "bottle")+" of rum" );

System.out.printf( "%d bottle%s of rum%n",
                   noOfBottles, noOfBottles !=1 ? "s" : "" );
```

Depending on the variable noOfBottles we choose the ending. Two ideas are realized here:

1. The first suggestion uses string concatenation and builds bottle or bottles there depending on noOfBottles. The methods print(…) and println(…) allow only one argument, so a string must be concatenated before.
2. The second suggestion uses printf(…), which consists of two parts: the formatting string and several formatting arguments. Here we take the ending as a single string, which is either "s" or empty. In the formatting string, %s accesses this ending.

Quiz: The Zero Effect

The program compiles but throws an exception at runtime. The output is:

```
Infinity
Exception in thread "main" java.lang.ArithmeticException:
/ by zero
...
```

The first println(10.0/0) works because you can divide two floating-point numbers by 0, and the result is Infinity, i.e., positive infinity. Although zero is an integer, since the dividend is a floating-point number, the divisor is also converted to a double.

For integers, a division by 0 is a cause for an ArithmeticException. The different behavior is perhaps strange, but easy to explain: integers have no special bit pattern that can map to infinity. Floating-point numbers, on the other hand, have a special bit pattern for three special values: NaN (Not a Number) and plus as well as minus infinity—these are quite "normal numbers."

Payday

com/tutego/exercise/lang/PayDay.java

```
double tortsPayment=new java.util.Scanner( System.in ).nextDouble();

double minPayment=1000;
minPayment -= minPayment * 0.1;
double maxPayment=1000;
maxPayment += maxPayment * 0.2;

// Solution 1
if ( tortsPayment >= minPayment && tortsPayment <= maxPayment )
  System.out.println( "Good boy!" );
```

```
else
  System.out.println( "You son of a bi***!" );

// Solution 2
if ( tortsPayment<minPayment || tortsPayment>maxPayment )
  System.out.println( "You son of a bi***!" );
else
  System.out.println( "Good boy!" );
```

After asking for Tort's payment, we next calculate the amount Tort must not go below and the amount Tort must not go above. 10% of 1,000 is 100, so Tort must not go below 900 Liretta. For the maximum, it is the other way around, 20% of 1,000 is 200, so Tort must not go above 1,200 Liretta. What is given here as fixed numbers are calculated dynamically in the program. The advantage is that we can change the bound later and the percentage is calculated dynamically.

Now there are two alternative solutions. The first solution tests whether Tort's payment is within the bounds. In the second solution, we work with negation and test if Torts payment is not in the range. You can easily see that the if statement is inverted, and also the blocks in the if-else branch are inverted. In practice, it will always be the case that for case distinctions with if-else both variants work and one chooses which one thinks is better understandable. The first solution should be better because it should be more understandable to test if payment is in a range instead of asking if payment is not in a range.

Quiz: Wrong Branching

Two errors are in the program code: first, the block is indented, but the curly braces are missing; visual indentation does not change semantics in Java. If we were to indent the program correctly without the braces, the first error becomes obvious:

```
if ( x >y )
  int swap =x;
x =y;
y =x;
```

As a side note, this causes a compiler error because a variable declaration is not allowed at this point.
We use curly braces for the if block to fix the first error.
There is also a logical error. The program code is wrong because both variables get the same value. This is because x is replaced by y. Therefore, a temporary variable swap is necessary. Correct is:

```
if ( x >y ) {
  int swap =x;
  x =y;
  y =swap;
}
```

Convert Liters

com/tutego/exercise/lang/HumanReadableLiter.java

```
System.out.println( "Enter quantity in liters:" );
double value=new java.util.Scanner( System.in ).nextDouble();

if ( value >=1 )
  System.out.printf( "approx. %d l", (long) value );
```

```
else if ( value >= 0.1 )       // 1 l = 100 cl
   System.out.printf( "approx. %d cl", (long) (value * 100) );
else if ( value >= 0.001 )     // 1 l = 1000 ml
   System.out.printf( "approx. %d ml", (long) (value * 1000) );
else
   System.err.println( "Value too small to display" );
```

The program starts with a screen output and then asks for a floating-point number. We have to remember that the `Scanner` reads floating-point numbers in a localized way.

The actual logic is then like this: we start with the largest unit of measure (liter), and if the number is greater than or equal to the one we are looking for, the program formulates the output. If the value is smaller, the `else` block checks the next smaller unit. Therefore, there are also three `if` statements. Without the `else` block, the program will not work either because we must only run into a single block.

Within a block, we multiply the input by a conversion factor, either 1, which we omit, by 100, or by 1,000. Furthermore, the floating-point number will be converted to an integer. The result will be printed on the screen.

During the conversion, it makes sense to use `long` as a data type because this allows the given numbers to be much larger than with an int. Before the type conversion will initiate, the program could test if the floating-point number is larger than `long.MAX _ VALUE`. If the `double` number is larger than `long.MAX _ VALUE`, the result after the type conversion will always be 9223372036854775807. Example:

```
System.out.println( (long)385823752375823563765. ); // 9223372036854775807
System.out.println( (long)365827359283847475 6474. ); // 9223372036854775807
```

We could consider introducing constants for 100 and 1000:

```
final int CENTILITERS_PER_LITER = 100;
final int MILLILITERS_PER_LITER = 1000;
```

However, we would have to ask ourselves whether this makes the program more readable.

Create SVG Circles with Random Colors

com/tutego/exercise/lang/RandomColor.java

```
String color;
double random = Math.random();

if ( random < 1. / 3 )
   color = "red";
else if ( random < 2. / 3 )
   color = "green";
else
   color = "blue";
System.out.println( color );
System.out.printf( "<circle cx=\"20\" cy=\"20\" r=\"5\" fill=\"%s\"/>",
                   color );
```

`Math.random()` returns us a floating-point number between 0 and less than 1. Each number is equally probable, which is also true for the value ranges. Numbers between 0 and less than 0.5 are equally probable as numbers between 0.5 and less than 1.0.

We use this to select the three random colors. Random numbers between 0 and smaller 1/3 are assigned to the color red, numbers between 1/3 and smaller 2/3 are assigned to the color green. Otherwise, the color is blue. Of course, it could have been the other way around.

Quiz: To Which Block Does the Else Belong?

It is easy to see from the example that the lack of indentation causes us difficulty in understanding. This should be a reminder to always indent source code correctly so as not to get in the way of the reader. Let's, therefore, catch up with the indentation:

```
if ( true ) {
 if ( false )
   if ( 3!=4 )
     ;
   else
     System.out.println( "ship's kobold" );
 else
   System.out.println( "Pumuckl" );
}
```

Practically, there is little reason to write truth values directly as literals in the condition statements. However, you should not be afraid of this notation either because it shows what is happening at the core. Each condition statement expects a truth value, and based on it, the block is either executed or not.

Let's simplify the program. The first statement is an `if(true)`, and consequently this block is always executed.

```
if ( false )
  if ( 3!=4 )
    ;
  else
    System.out.println( "ship's kobold" );
else
  System.out.println( "Pumuckl" );
```

The next condition statement checks with `if(false)`, and that means that the block is not executed. This also means that the embedded condition statement including the inner `else` is not executed either. Consequently, the output `pumuckl` remains.

Quiz: Recognize Negative Days and Hours

To answer the question, we need to recall two Java features. The first is the binary operator `|`, which performs an OR operation. As a reminder, two integers can be mentally processed as a bit pattern and if one of the bits is set, then the bit in the result is also 1. An example for a byte:

```
  01010110
| 10100010
  --------
  11110110
```

Secondly, integers are written in two's complement. Let's take a look at some numbers written according to this format as an example:

TABLE 2.1   Numbers in two's complement

POSITIVE DECIMAL NUMBER	BINARY REPRESENTATION	NEGATIVE DECIMAL NUMBER	BINARY REPRESENTATION
0	00000000	−128	10000000
1	00000001	−127	10000001
2	00000010	−126	10000010
3	00000011	−125	10000011
126	01111110	−2	11111110
127	01111111	−1	11111111

For negative numbers, the first bit (from the left) is always set, thus is 1.

Combining both pieces of information yields the following: if two arbitrary numbers are OR-linked and one of the two numbers is negative, then after the OR-linking, the most significant bit will always be set. Only if both numbers are positive, the most significant bit will be 0. If the most significant bit is set, then the number is negative, that is, less than zero. Therefore, (hours | minutes) < 0 is a valid alternative notation.

Evaluate Input Strings for Approval

The switch statement is flexible in Java and can be used as a statement and as an expression. In the notation, you find labels with colon and also the newer arrow notation. Three proposed solutions are shown.

com/tutego/exercise/lang/DoYouAgree.java

```java
String input=new java.util.Scanner( System.in ).nextLine();

switch ( input ) {
  case "ay":
  case "aye":
  case "ay, ay":
  case "ja":
  case "joo":
    System.out.println( "Keep it up!" );
    break;

  default:
    System.out.println( "Don't you dare!" );
}
```

After Scanner has read the line with nextLine(), switch compare it with different constants—since the input may contain white space, we cannot use the Scanner method next() because otherwise, the return will contain only a string up to the first white space.

Quite intentionally, the first proposed solution takes advantage of switch's ability to map multiple case blocks to the same program code. Furthermore, crucial is the break after the console output so that the program does not accidentally run from one case block into the other when this is not intended. If the yes block does not catch, it goes into the default block. The default block is executed whenever none of the case blocks have been caught.

The second proposed solution uses the modern arrow notation, where a break is no longer necessary and where case blocks can be combined:

com/tutego/exercise/lang/DoYouAgree.java

```
switch ( input ) {
  case "ay", "aye", "ay, ay", "ja", "joo" -> System.out.println( "Keep it up!"
);
  default -> System.out.println( "Don't you dare!" );
}
```

The console output is a code duplication that can be removed; to solution three:

com/tutego/exercise/lang/DoYouAgree.java

```
System.out.println(
    switch ( input ) {
      case "ay", "aye", "ay, ay", "ja", "joo" -> "Keep it up!";
      default -> "Don't you dare!";
    }
);
```

Here, `switch` is used as an expression and returns a string that goes to the screen.

Rewrite Switch Statement to Switch Expression

com/tutego/exercise/lang/LengthOfMonth.java

```
days=switch ( month ) {
  case 2 -> isLeapYear ? 29 : 28;
  case 4, 6, 9, 11 -> 30;
  default -> 31;
};
```

The lines of code shown in the task are common to Java programs with `switch` statements. However, if each `case` block of a `switch` statement always assigns a variable, then a `switch` expression can supply exactly this value and thus the variable can be written.

When using `switch` expressions, there must always be a result. This works perfectly in the example because if the `case` blocks do not return 29, 28, or 30 days, then the `default` branch returns 31.

Create Rotated SVG Rectangles

com/tutego/exercise/lang/SvgRotatingRect.java

```
System.out.println( "<svg height=\"200\" width=\"200\">" );

int angle=10;
for ( int rotation=0; rotation<360; rotation += angle )
  System.out.printf( """
                    <rect x="50" y="50" width="100" height="100" \
                    stroke="black" fill="none" \
                    transform="rotate(%d 100 100)" />%n""", rotation );

System.out.println( "</svg>" );
```

The solution consists of three parts. The first part writes the header of the SVG container. A variable `angle` stands for the desired rotation angle, which can be changed without problems. 0 should not be the value, of course.

In the second part, a loop consistently advances the `rotation` variable by `angle` increments. The variable `rotation` starts at 0 degrees and ends when the angle is equal or above 360 degrees. The loop condition does not test for the number of iterations, but whether one "goes around it once and comes back again" in the circle. In the body of the loop, an SVG rectangle is built and output with the value of `rotation`. A text block is helpful. Otherwise, the strings would have to mask out many double quotes. The backslash at the end makes the line continue.

Create SVG-Pearl-Chain

com/tutego/exercise/lang/BonnysPearls.java

```java
System.out.println( "<svg height=\"100\" width=\"1000\">" );
for ( int i=0; i<50; i++) {
  double random=Math.random();
  String color=random<1./3 ? "blue" :
                  random<2./3 ? "green" : "orange";
  System.out.printf( "<circle cx=\"%d\" cy=\"20\" r=\"5\" fill=\"%s\"/>%n",
                  20+(i * 10), color );
}
System.out.println( "</svg>" );
```

The assignment mentions 50 circles, so there is also a loop in the center that is executed 50 times. In the body of the loop, we form a random number `random` for the random color. The random number is between 0 and less than 1, and we divide it into three ranges, as we did in a previous solution: There are values between 0 and <1/3, between 1/3 and <2/3, and between 2/3 and <1. Instead of an `if` statement, the solution uses nested condition operators. We could, of course, compute `int random=(int)(Math.random() * 3.0)` to get random integer values 0, 1, or 2.

To allow the loop counter `i` to determine the circle center `cx`, we multiply `i` by 10 and add 20 so that in each step the circle moves 10 units to the right. The y-axis and the radius remain the same; only the x-axis and the color are parameterized in the formatting string. Another solution would be to introduce a new variable `cx`, which is incremented by 10 in each loop pass. However, since `cx` can be calculated directly from `i`, this second variable is not necessary.

Sum Numbers from the Command Line

Let's look at two solutions below.

com/tutego/exercise/lang/SummingCalculator.java

```java
final int END_OF_INPUT=0;
int sum   =0;
int input=0;

do {
  input=new java.util.Scanner( System.in ).nextInt();
  sum += input;
} while ( input != END_OF_INPUT );

System.out.printf( "Sum: %d%n", sum );
```

Whenever a program needs to do something first and then asks if it will continue, a do-while loop is appropriate. This is what the first program does. Since the algorithm must sum, we declare a variable sum and initialize it with 0. Another variable input stores the user input. Because the input ends with 0 and 0 is a magic value, we declare a constant END _ OF _ INPUT. A value that causes the loop to end is also called a *sentinel*.

Unfortunately, the variable must be declared outside the loop body, but that is because it must be accessed in the while part. Inside the loop, we ask for the input and add it to the sum. Since 0 is the neutral element in the addition, we don't need to check at this point if the input is already terminated by 0. Instead, we move the check to the while part. Here, we check if the variable input is not equal to END_OF_INPUT, i.e., 0, and in that case, it goes back to the body for input. If the input was equal to END_OF_INPUT, the loop terminates, and we output the sum to the console.

Not ideal in this program is that the variable input takes a larger scope than necessary. This is something one would like to avoid in programming: local variables should not be valid far beyond their use to the end. You want variables that are only used in the loop to be valid there. One solution would be, of course, to artificially create a block with { }, but there is another variant. Whether the following notation is better can be doubted because the complexity is also higher.

com/tutego/exercise/lang/SummingCalculator.java

```java
final int END_OF_INPUT=0;
int sum=0;

for ( int input;
       (input=new java.util.Scanner(System.in).nextInt()) != END_OF_INPUT; )

  sum += input;
System.out.printf( "Sum: %d%n", sum );
```

In the second solution, there is also a variable for the sum. However, we declare the input variable input inside the for loop. The for loop allows three different segments: In the first one, we can declare variables, which are then only valid within the loop; in the second segment, there is the condition; and in the third part, there is the continuation expression, which may also be empty. The condition in the for loop is somewhat complex in this solution because it combines two steps: first, the variable input is assigned, and after the variable has been written to, a check is made whether the input was 0 or not. If the input was not 0, the loop continues into the body, where the input is added to the variable sum. If the user enters 0, 0 is also not summed as in the first solution, but the loop terminates and the console output follows.

Go through a Mathematical Phenomenon

com/tutego/exercise/lang/AlwaysEnding.java

```java
double t=Math.random() * 10;

while ( t>0 ) {
  System.out.println( t );

  //System.out.printf("%64s%n",Long.toBinaryString(Double.
  doubleToLongBits(t)));
  if ( t<1 )
    t *= 2;
  else // t >= 1
    t--;
}
```

After initializing the variable t with a random value between 0 and less than 10, the loop condition t > 0 decides whether the loop body is executed or not. This sounds different from the task: "Loop until t is less than or equal to 0". However, it is the same because the problem statement refers to when the loop should end. After all, we always need to specify when the loop should continue, not when it should terminate, in the loop conditions. Therefore, we must negate the condition, and from *not* t <= 0 follows t > 0.

The condition statements are as in the assignment. We have two alternatives: once t < 1 can be, once t >= 1. We should be careful to execute the condition statement as a real alternative and not omit the else block. This is because there is a dependency: if t < 1, t is multiplied by 2, which can cause t >= 1, so it runs into the next condition statement. In our program, it doesn't matter because on the next loop pass we'll end up in that condition statement anyway, but such dependencies between values are something we as developers need to keep in mind. It may well be that developers want to go to the code and include a counter for how many times the loop has been run, and then suddenly this loop counter would no longer be correct. This is because the if-else variant results in more runs on average than if there were two if blocks in a row.

It is interesting why the program ends at all. This is due to two characteristics that "reduce" the set bits:

1. Subtraction makes the number smaller, and the number "loses" bits.
2. Multiplication doubles the number, but it is less accurate afterward, and thus "loses" bits. The number possibly becomes larger than 1 by the multiplication, but then in the next step, the number becomes smaller again.

If you want to see the bit pattern of the numbers, you can display the bits by using:

```
System.out.printf( "%64s%n",
    Long.toBinaryString( Double.doubleToLongBits( t ) ) );
```

Quiz: How Many Stars?

A:
There are 12 asterisks in the first for loop.
B:
There is no pass in the second for loop because 10 < 0 is false, so the loop never passes and the loop body never enters.

Calculate Products for Faculties

com/tutego/exercise/lang/Factorial.java

```
System.out.println( "Enter a number:" );
int n=new java.util.Scanner( System.in ).nextInt();
if ( n<0 )
  System.err.println( "Number must not be negative" );
else if ( n<2 )
  System.out.printf( "%d!=1%n", n );
else {
  System.out.printf( "%d!=1", n );
  long factorial=1;

  for ( int multiplier=2; multiplier <=n; multiplier++) {
```

```
        System.out.printf( " * %d", multiplier );
        factorial *= multiplier;
    }

    System.out.println( "="+factorial );
}
```

After entering an integer, we test in the first condition whether the number is negative. If it is, we output a message and terminate the program because the following alternatives are in `else` branches.

The next condition checks whether the input was 0 or 1. Then, we print a screen message because the factorial of 0 is valid, and 0! and 1! are both 1.

If the program enters the second `else` branch, then the number entered is greater than or equal to 2. We, therefore, start with a screen output showing the beginning of the sequence. In the following iterations, pairs of a multiplication sign and a number are always written.

The number from the input is of type `int`, but we have to declare the result with the data type `long` because the multiplication quickly leads to huge numbers. Our variable `factorial` is initialized with 2 because this is the next multiplier after 1—we do not have to multiply with 1, the neutral element. The loop will keep the multiplier running until we reach the input. In the body of the loop, we output the pair of the multiplication sign, and the multiplier to the console; multiply the multiplier by the previous factorial, and update the factorial to the next value.

At the end of the loop, we put an equal sign, output the result, and the program is finished.

Factors quickly become massive, and the range of values of an `int` value is quickly exhausted. Even a `long` eventually comes to an end.

TABLE 2.2 Magnitude

FACTORIAL/CONSTANT	VALUE
1!	1
2!	2
3!	6
12!	479.001.600
Integer.MAX_VALUE	2.147.483.647
13!	6.227.020.800
20!	2.432.902.008.176.640.000
Long.MAX_VALUE	9,223,372,036,854,775,807
21!	51.090.942.171.709.440.000

While the factorial of 20 is still representable, we are close to the edge of the largest representable `long` number. Calculating 21! with the program yields the astonishing result -4249290049419214848; the number is suddenly negative because the sign is stored in the uppermost bit and multiplication leads to a bit pattern in which the uppermost bit is set.

There are three strategies to deal with larger numbers:

1. We can use the previous code if we know that the value ranges are so limited that we never run out of the value range.
2. If we know that huge numbers occur, `long` will not help us. Java provides a data type `BigInteger` that can represent integers of any size. Thus, the numbers are limited only by the size of the memory space.
3. Java does not alert us to an overflow, so if we exceed the range of values, Java just keeps calculating. There is a useful method in the `Math` class that the exercise is talking about: the method `Math.multiplyExact(long x, long y)` helps us to detect overflows because it throws

an exception when the numbers cannot be multiplied anymore because they become too large for a `long`.

Determine If a Number Is Formed by Factorial

com/tutego/exercise/lang/IsFactorial.java

```
System.out.println( "Enter a number:" );
long n=new Scanner( System.in ).nextLong();

if ( n<1 )
  System.err.println( "Factorials are always >=1" );
else {
  long number =n;
  long divisor=2;

  while ( number % divisor ==0 ) {
    number /=divisor;
    divisor++;
  }

  if ( number ==1 )
    System.out.printf( "%d=%d!%n", n, divisor - 1 );
  else
    System.out.printf( "%d is not a factorial%n", n );
}
```

From the command line, we ask for a number, and since factorials can get huge, we will query it as `long`. If the factorial is less than 1, i.e., 0 or negative, we print a message on the command line and terminate the program because the rest of the code is executed only if n is greater than or equal to 1.

The algorithm is as described in the tip. We start by dividing the factorial by 2, then by 3, 4, and so on. Let us take 6 as an example. The variables `number` and `divisor` also occur in the program:

TABLE 2.3 Iterations for backward calculation of recursion

STEP	NUMBER	DIVISOR	QUOTIENT	REMAINDER
1	6	2	6 / 2 = 3	6 % 2 = 0
2	3	3	3 / 3 = 1	3 % 3 = 0
3	1	4	irrelevant	1 % 4 ≠ 0

In the third step, the remainder is not 0, and the loop ends.

The variable `number` is initialized with the factorial, i.e., the largest value. We divide this variable `number` repeatedly by the divisor. We do this as long as we have no remainder after an integer division. Whether a number can be divided by a divisor without a remainder is answered by the remainder operator `%`. If `number % divisor` is equal to 0, the division came out without remainder.

At the end, the loop will stop because there is always a case where the number cannot be divided by the divisor. The variables `number` and `divisor` run toward each other. `number` gets smaller and smaller with each division, and `divisor` gets larger and larger due to the increment. In the last step, there will be a remainder != 0. When `number` has arrived at 1, we know that we could divide so many times until we arrive at the beginning of the factorial chain and the user input is a factorial; this is what we output on the screen. If the number is not 1, then it is not factorial.

Find the Smallest and Largest Digit of a Number

com/tutego/exercise/lang/SmallestLargestDigit.java

```java
final long n=30;

long largest =0;
long smallest=n ==0 ? 0 : 9;
for ( long value=Math.abs( n ); value != 0; value /= 10 ) {
  long lastDigit=value % 10;
  largest =Math.max( lastDigit, largest );
  smallest=Math.min( lastDigit, smallest );
}

System.out.println( smallest+","+largest );
```

Given a number n, which can be positive or negative. By repeating the operations of division and calculating the remainder, we extract digit by digit and update two local variables: largest should later contain the largest digit value and smallest the smallest digit value. We initialize the variable largest with 0, and it can become larger in the following, if the number for testing is not equal to 0. For the smallest digit in the variable smallest, we can only start with 9 and perhaps find a smaller number if n is not 0. The condition operator checks exactly this case because if n is 0, then the smallest and also the largest digit value is also 0. The following loop is also not run through.

Positive and negative numbers are to be treated the same, so the Math method abs(...) turns negative numbers into positive numbers.

It is true that Math.abs(Integer.MIN _ VALUE) equals Integer.MIN _ VALUE, so the result remains negative. The program does not check this special case.

Since we do not want to change the assignment of n, it is final, we introduce a new variable value with the absolute value in the for loop. If this value is not 0, then the body of the method is executed where the remainder operator extracts the last digit, and then the variable largest and smallest are adjusted, if necessary. After the loop is run, value is divided by 10. If the result is then not equal to 0, it goes back into the loop body. If the result is 0, then there are no more digits to look at, the loop is aborted, and the smallest and largest values are output to the screen.

Quiz: Not Like This from 1 to 100

```java
class Sümme { //'ü' - violation of style guide, should be English
  private static int getSum() { // prefix get unfavorable - tends to violate
style guide
    int j == 0; // == instead of=- syntactic error
    for ( /* int */i=0, i <= 100, j++);
      // int must be declared - syntactic error
      // twice , instead of ; - syntactic error
      // 100 ->100 - syntactic error
      // j instead of i - semantic error
      // ';' at the end of the line is wrong - semantic error
      j += i
    ; // ; place at the preceding line - style guide
    // return j missing - semantic error
  }
```

```
public static void Main( String aarg ) {
    // cannot be started with this particular method - semantic error
    // array specification must be included - semantic error if program
should be executed
      system.out.println( getsum() ); // 'S' instead of 's' - 2 * syntactic
error
  }
}
```

A Flag in the Wind through Nested Loops

com/tutego/exercise/lang/NestedLoopsForTrees.java

```
final int MAX=5;

// Normal output
for ( int i=1; i <=MAX; i++ ) {
  for ( int j=1; j <=i; j++ )
    System.out.print( i );

  System.out.println();
}

System.out.println();

// Centered output
for ( int i=1; i <=MAX; i++ ) {
  for ( int indent=0; indent<(MAX - i); indent++ )
    System.out.print( " " );

  for ( int j=1; j <=i; j++ )
    System.out.print( i+" " );

  System.out.println();
}
```

The main method contains the logic that produces a left-aligned output, and then the centered output. Beforehand, we declare a final variable MAX that determines the number of lines. If we want to modify the number of lines to be output, we simply change this variable and do not have to make changes in various places in the source code, such as changing 5 to 9.

The outer loop runs a loop counter i from 1 to 5. In this case, it takes over the job of executing program code for five lines. The inner loop with the loop counter j writes a single line. The loop counter j is written in the line. The end of the loop counter j is in itself bound to the loop counter i of the outer loop. If the outer loop counter i becomes larger, the line is also getting longer. In the body of the loop, we have to work with print(...) instead of println(...) because we want to output the numbers one after the other, but only set a newline at the end of the line. Therefore, the line break is not in the inner loop, but in the body of the outer loop, after everything in the line has been written next to each other.

For centered output of any kind, the line starts with white space at the beginning. We first have to calculate how much white space is needed, and in the next step, we also have to write this white space. In our case, the width depends on the line. Each new line leads to a different indentation. But the special thing in our example is that the dependency is reversed: the more lines there are, the less indented it is, and in the first line the indentation is maximum.

If we want to produce or output a string with a certain length in Java, we have different ways: special methods can be used, but in this case, we would like to focus on a fairly straightforward method of manually putting spaces in a row to achieve indentation. Before we write the actual line, we prepend a custom `for` loop that produces spaces. This loop uses a counter `indent`. The variable `indent` is bound to `i`, but inversely: if `i` gets larger, the indentation gets smaller, so `indent` only goes up to `MAX - i`.

It is left to the reader as an exercise to display this tree reasonably centered as well for numbers larger than 10.

Output Simple Chessboard

com/tutego/exercise/lang/Checkerboard.java

```
System.out.print( "Checkerboard width: " );
int width=new java.util.Scanner( System.in ).nextInt();

System.out.print( "Checkerboard height: " );
int height=new java.util.Scanner( System.in ).nextInt();

for ( int y=0; y<height; y++ ) {
  for ( int x=0; x<width; x++ )
    System.out.print( (x+y) % 2 ==1 ? '#' : '_' );
  System.out.println();
}
```

First, we read the width and height of the checkerboard. Since the checkerboard in our task does not have to be square, two inputs are needed.

Whenever it comes to drawing rectangles or any form of tables, they are usually nested loops. Therefore, we have an outer loop that goes over all the rows and an inner loop that goes over all the columns. We name the variables x and y, alternatively `row` and `col` would also have been appropriate.

The exciting part is inside the loop when we have to decide whether to write a # or an underscore. A little logic is needed here. The characters depend on their position. If x and y change, it has a direct effect on the character. The question now is: how can we make the character to be written dependent on x and y? Let's test what happens when x and y are added:

0	1	2	3
1	2	3	4
2	3	4	5
3	4	5	6

The even numbers are set in bold, and from this, we can see the solution: we add the numbers and test with the remainder operator whether the result is even or odd.

We do not have to handle incorrect values specially. If negative numbers or 0 are entered, there is no loop pass.

It's Christmastime: Displaying Trees with Ornaments

Before we get into the solution of the problem, let's see the relationships between the number of spaces for indentation and the width of the tree.

TABLE 2.4 Indentation (symbolized by underscore) and tree width

LINES	INDENTATION	ASTERISK/WIDTH
*	3	1
***	2	3
*****	1	5
******	0	7

It is easy to see that the indentation decrements in ones, while the asterisks increase in twos. In the same way, we can formulate our program that uses two variables in a loop, for indentation, and width, and then decrements and increments the variables accordingly.

com/tutego/exercise/lang/XmasTree.java

```java
int width=7;

for ( int stars=1, indentation=(width - 1) / 2;
      stars <= width;
      stars += 2, indentation-- ) {

  for ( int i=0; i<indentation; i++ )
    System.out.print( ' ' );

  for ( int col=0; col<stars; col++ )
    System.out.print( Math.random()<0.9 ? '*' : 'o' );

  System.out.println();
}
```

The variable width stores the width of the tree, which we initialize with 7 in our example. The loop declares the variables stars and indentation, where indentation is calculated from half the width. We subtract 1 from width so that if the width is odd, we don't mistakenly put an extra space in front. In the body of the main loop, there are two more loops that create the line. In the first step, we have to write the indentation; in the second step, we have to output the asterisks of the tree. There is a 90% probability that an asterisk will be output, and a 10% probability that a small o will be output. At the end of the line, we set a new line, and then the loop continues.

Draw Fishy Stitching Motifs

com/tutego/exercise/lang/FishPattern.java

```java
int repetitions=3;

final String RIGHT_FISH="><>";
final String LEFT_FISH ="<><";
final String SPACER    =" ";
for ( int row=0; row<repetitions; row++ ) {
  for ( int col=0; col<repetitions; col++ )
    System.out.print( RIGHT_FISH+SPACER );
  for ( int col=0; col<repetitions; col++ )
    System.out.print( LEFT_FISH+SPACER );
  System.out.println();
}
```

For the right and left swimming fish, we declare two constants and additionally a constant for the distance between the fish. This spacing is also set at the end of the line, but since the white space is not visible, this is not a problem.

The next loop generates several lines. The number of lines is determined by the value of `repetitions`. Within each line, we use two more loops. The first loop prints `repetitions` of right swimming fish, and the second loop prints `repetitions` of left swimming fish. At the end of the line, a new line is set, and then we can continue with the main loop.

What is striking about the proposed solution is that the two inner `for` loops are identical, except for the body. We can solve this kind of code duplication as follows:

com/tutego/exercise/lang/FishPattern.java

```
for ( int row=0; row<repetitions; row++ )
  for ( int col=0; col<repetitions * 2; col++ ) {
    System.out.print( col<repetitions ? RIGHT_FISH : LEFT_FISH );
    System.out.print( col != repetitions * 2 - 1 ? SPACER : "\n" );
  }
```

Instead of running two single loops to `repetitions`, one loop can also run to 2 * `repetitions`; then only the body has to decide whether the right or left fish is printed. But this information is provided by the loop counter itself: if it is below half, the fish swims to the right, in the second half it swims to the left. And also a second time the condition operator is used. A test checks if the loop counter col is for the last element: If no, white space is output, otherwise a line break. The first variant will probably be easier to understand when reading.

Trying Instead of Thinking

com/tutego/exercise/lang/XOLLXXTLT.java

```
for ( int l=0; l<10; l++ ) {
  for ( int o=0; o<10; o++ ) {
    for ( int x=0; x<10; x++ ) {
      for ( int t=0; t<10; t++ ) {
        int xol=100 * x+10 * o+l;
        int lxx=100 * l+10 * x+x;
        int tlt=100 * t+10 * l+t;

        if ( xol+lxx == tlt ) {
          if ( (l != o) && (l != x) && (l != t) &&
               (o != x) && (o != t) && (x != t) )
            System.out.print( "All variables are different: " );

          System.out.printf( „l=%d, o=%d, x=%d, t=%d%n", l, o, x, t );
        }
      } // end for t
    } // end for x
  } // end for o
} // end for l
```

The twist in the solution is to produce all possible assignments of the four variables. We do this with four nested loops. Each of these loops produces all values from 0 to 9. With four loops, there are $10 \times 10 \times 10 = 10,000$ in total repetitions, which is manageable in terms of execution performance. If we had more variables and larger ranges of values, then the runtime would increase rapidly. Our solution would then probably no longer be feasible.

Once we have generated all possible values by the loops, we calculate xol, 1xx, and tlt by multiplying by 10 and 100 to move the variables to the right place. This is a property of the positional notation. The number 234 is nothing but $2 \times 100 + 3 \times 10 + 4$, and so xol is nothing but x * 100 + o * 10 + 1.

Next, we test if xol + 1xx is equal to tlt. There are numerous solutions here; however, if we want to have only the solutions in which all four variables have different assignments, we must test that. This is done by the inner if statement. If all the values are different, we output them to the screen.

More of these nice tasks are provided by *Alphametic Puzzles* (https://www.gtoal.com/wordgames/alphametic/examples).

Get the Number of Digits of a Number

For the exercise, we want to review different ways of solving the problem. Variants 1 and 2 use loops, and therefore the task is also positioned in this section.

The first approach is the following: we divide a number by 10 until the result is 0. Let us take the following three statements as an example:

```
System.out.println( 123 / 10 );   // 12
System.out.println(  12 / 10 );   // 1
System.out.println(   1 / 10 );   // 0
```

By dividing by 10, the number gets smaller and smaller until the result is 0 at some point. We just have to loop the divisions, increment a counter, and the number of digits is determined. The termination criteria are when the result of the division is 0.

com/tutego/exercise/lang/NumberOfDigits.java

```
int digits=1;
for ( int number=n / 10; number != 0; number /= 10 )
  digits++;
System.out.println( digits );
```

The number of digits is at least 1, which is why the variable digits default to 1.

Divisions are relatively expensive for the computer, so we can also work with the reverse way, multiplying a number by 10 until it is above the given number. This is what the second solution does:

com/tutego/exercise/lang/NumberOfDigits.java

```
int digits=1;
for ( long powersOfTen=10; powersOfTen <= n; powersOfTen *= 10 )
  digits++;
System.out.println( digits );
```

One detail is the data type long because if we multiply a giant integer by 10, it will cause an overflow and the comparison would not be correct.

The other proposed solutions do not use loops, but a slightly different approach.

Suggested solution 3 uses the idea of binary search. However, we do not search for any element, but the number of digits.

com/tutego/exercise/lang/NumberOfDigits.java

```
if ( n >= 10_000 ) {
  if ( n >= 10_000_000 ) {
    if ( n >= 100_000_000 ) {
```

```
    if ( n >= 1_000_000_000 )
      System.out.println( 10 );
    else
      System.out.println( 9 );
  }
  else
    System.out.println( 8 );
}
else if ( n >= 10_0000 ) {
  if ( n >= 1_000_000 )
    System.out.println( 7 );
  else
    System.out.println( 6 );
}
else
  System.out.println( 5 );
}
else if ( n >= 100 ) {
  if ( n >= 1000 )
    System.out.println( 4 );
  else
    System.out.println( 3 );
}
else if ( n >= 10 )
  System.out.println( 2 );
else
  System.out.println( 1 );
```

Numbers of type int can be at most ten digits long. So first we query whether the number has more or less than five digits, i.e., is greater or less than 10 _ 000. If the number is smaller, then we take half of five digits, rounded three digits, and ask if the value is greater or smaller than 100. If the value is greater than 10 _ 000, then we calculate the arithmetic mean between five digits and ten digits, rounded eight digits, so 10 _ 000 _ 000. We hard-code all possibilities for one digit, two digits, three digits, up to ten digits.

This procedure has advantages and disadvantages. The advantage is that the number of maximum comparisons is clear in advance; a binary search has a logarithmic runtime. A disadvantage could be that the algorithm does not favor ranges of numbers. If we know that smaller numbers are more likely to occur, then we could do something different with the algorithm.

This is what proposed solution 4 does. It works with several nested condition operators and prefers small numbers. The larger the numbers are, the more comparisons need to be made.

com/tutego/exercise/lang/NumberOfDigits.java

```
int digits=n<10 ? 1 :
           n<100 ? 2 :
           n<1000 ? 3 :
           n<10000 ? 4 :
           n<100_000 ? 5 :
           n<1_000_000 ? 6 :
           n<10_000_000 ? 7 :
           n<100_000_000 ? 8 :
           n<1_000_000_000 ? 9 :
           10;
System.out.println( digits );
```

The last proposed solution does not use loops or condition statements at all, but uses the logarithm. To repeat:
$$b^x = a \Leftrightarrow x = \log_b(a) \text{ for all } a, b > 0 \text{ and } b \neq 1.$$

If we choose $b=10$, we get:

$10^x=a \Leftrightarrow x=\log_{10}(a)$ for all $a>0$.

If we put on the right for a again 10^x, one recognizes nicely:

$\log_{10}(10^x)=x$

For a number like 10^x, x is the number of digits we are looking for. We do not have powers of ten, but we can bring the floating-point number to an `int`.

TABLE 2.5 Logarithm for different numbers, relation with the number of digits

LOG_{10}	RESULT (DOUBLE)	RESULT (INT)
1	0	0
9	0.954242509439	0
10	1	1
19	1.27875360095	1
99	1.9956351946	1
100	2	2

So, we have to calculate the logarithm, adjust the result to `int` and increase it by 1.

com/tutego/exercise/lang/NumberOfDigits.java

```
int digits=n == 0 ? 1 : (int) Math.log10( n )+1;
  System.out.println( digits );
}
```

For numbers between 0 and 1, the result of a logarithm is negative. Approaching 0 from the right, the function value goes to minus infinity. Therefore, we consider 0 as a special case and return the 1 digit.

Drawing Hearts

com/tutego/exercise/lang/LinePrinter.java

```
public static void line() {
  System.out.print( "♥♥♥♥♥♥♥♥♥♥" );
}
```

The implementation can be done without much trouble. The only important thing is that the method is static so that we can call it from another class without necessarily having to build an object of the class.

com/tutego/exercise/lang/LinePrinterDemo.java

```
LinePrinter.line();
```

Since the `line()` method comes from `LinePrinter` and is not present in `LinePrinterDemo`, to access the static method, we need to put the `LinePrinter` class name in front of the method name.

Implement Overloaded Line Methods

com/tutego/exercise/lang/LinePrinter.java

```
public static void line( int len, char c ) {
  while ( len-->0 )
```

```
        System.out.print( c );
}

public static void line( int len ) {
   line( len, '-' );
}

public static void line( String prefix, int len, char c, String suffix ) {
   System.out.print( prefix );
   line( len, c );
   System.out.print( suffix );
}
```

We need to implement three methods. The first method we want to implement is the most important one: the method line(int len, char c), which prints a character c a certain number of len on the screen. This is the typical case for a loop. The solution uses a while loop that counts down the number until it becomes 0. Solutions of this type have a disadvantage in practice because after the while loop the parameter is destroyed, which means that if after the while loop the variable len had to be accessed again for some reason, we would have a problem. However, since our method is very compact, this is fine for us; we don't need len again.

For the second method, which outputs a minus by default, it is convenient that we can refer to the previously implemented method, which sets in any character a certain number. We can call this method and thus move the "responsibility" for the output away from us.

The last method also delegates, but writes a prefix beforehand on the screen and a suffix after the character in the line.

A call to the methods looks like this:

com/tutego/exercise/lang/LinePrinterDemo.java

```
int len=new java.util.Scanner( System.in ).nextInt();
LinePrinter.line( len );
System.out.println();

LinePrinter.line( 4, '*' );
System.out.println();

LinePrinter.line( „{„, 4, '*', „}" );
System.out.println();
```

Standing Straight

If triangles are right-angled, they satisfy the equation $c^2 = a^2 + b^2$. But this only works if a and b are smaller than c. Let's discuss two possible solutions.

com/tutego/exercise/lang/RightTriangle.java

```
public static boolean isRightTriangle( double a, double b, double c ) {
   return      a * a == b * b + c * c
          || b * b == a * a + c * c
          || c * c == b * b + a * a;
}
```

If it is unclear in which order the variables come into the method, all possibilities can be tested, i.e., first assume that a is the hypotenuse, then whether b is the hypotenuse, or c.

The multiplications are sometimes done several times. A good compiler will optimize this, but if you want to do it yourself, you could, of course, write:

```
double aˣa=a * a;
double bˣb=b * b;
double cˣc=c * c;
return aˣa == bˣb+cˣc || bˣb == aˣa+cˣc || cˣc == bˣb+aˣa;
```

The symbol ˣ is the Unicode character U+02E3 and is intended to be symbolic of the multiplication sign.

Another approach is to sort the variables a, b, and c in such a way that in the end, c contains the largest number.

com/tutego/exercise/lang/RightTriangle.java

```java
public static boolean isRightTriangle( double a, double b, double c ) {
  // Step 1: propagate the largest value into c

  // If a>c then swap
  if ( a>c ) {
    double swap=a;
    a=c;
    c=swap;
  }

  // If b>c then swap
  if ( b>c ) {
    double swap=b;
    b=c;
    c=swap;
  }

  // Step 2: The test
  return a * a+b * b == c * c;
}
```

To make sure that c contains the largest number, we first test whether a is larger than c. If so, we swap the contents of a and c. We do the same with b and c: if b is greater than c, we swap b and c. The order of a and b is not critical, only that the largest number is in c at the end. We realize the actual swap operation by an intermediate variable.

The actual test is simple, with a * a+b * b == c * c. However, there remains a problem with computational precision because an exact == test is difficult with floating-point numbers. Tests with accepted inaccuracies are an option. One possibility would be to use an additional parameter double tolerance for this, as a tolerance that within the range the values are considered equal. A method could look like this:

```java
public static boolean almostEqual( double a, double b, double tolerance ) {
  return Math.abs( a - b )<tolerance;
}
```

Create a Multiplication Table

com/tutego/exercise/lang/MultiplicationTable.java

```java
private static void startTable() { System.out.println( "<table>" ); }

private static void endTable() { System.out.println( "</table>" ); }

private static void startRow() { System.out.print( "<tr>" ); }

private static void endRow() { System.out.println( "</tr>" ); }

private static void headerCell( String value ) {
  System.out.print( "<th>"+value+"</th>" );
}

private static void dataCell( String value ) {
  System.out.print( "<td>"+value+"</td>" );
}

private static void dataCell( int value ) {
  dataCell( Integer.toString( value ) );
}

public static void main( String[] args ) {
  final int BASE_PRICE_FLAMETHROWER     =500;
  final int BASE_PRICE_FIRE_EXTINGUISHER=100;

  startTable();

  startRow();
  headerCell( "Quantity" );
  headerCell( "Flamethrower" );
  headerCell( "Fire extinguisher" );
  endRow();

  for ( int i=1; i <=10; i++) {
    startRow();
    dataCell( i );
    dataCell( BASE_PRICE_FLAMETHROWER * i );
    dataCell( BASE_PRICE_FIRE_EXTINGUISHER * i );
    endRow();
  }

  endTable();
}
```

HTML is a markup language that is part of the technology, but all technological aspects should be separated from the "business logic". In our case, we write several methods, each of which outputs the HTML tags on the command line. The actual main program then doesn't see what's happening in the background. Two methods take care of the start and end of a table; two more methods take care of the start and end of a table row. The two dataCell(...) methods are an exception because they frame the data in HTML tags. dataCell(...) is overloaded with two parameters, so we can call the method flexible with an integer as well as with a string. Of course, we don't need to implement both methods completely; it's enough that the one method with the integer converts it to a string and then delegates it to the other method. For the table header, we have a separate method headerCell(String).

`main(...)` starts the table and starts the first row. Then three table cells are written for the columns for the header, and the row is completed. This is followed by a loop that generates rows from 1 to 10. We have to start each table row in HTML, and then the loop counter can be written directly into the first column. The second column is given by 500 (price of a flamethrower) times the loop counter; the last column is given by 100 (price of a fire extinguisher) times the loop counter for the row. Finally, we end the row, and at the end of the loop, we end the table. Since the prices might change, the program introduces constants.

Cistercian Numerals Script

We are in the section about methods, so the primary task is to define appropriate subroutines that will draw the given symbol as a result. The foundation is always a line. Therefore, let's start with our own method that outputs an SVG line string:

com/tutego/exercise/lang/CistercianDigits.java

```java
static void printSvgLine( int x, int y, int dx1, int dy1, int dx2, int dy2 )
{
  System.out.printf( "<line x1=\"%d\" y1=\"%d\" x2=\"%d\" y2=\"%d\" />\n",
                     x+dx1, y+dy1, x+dx2, y+dy2 );
}
```

There are several ways to define a line. One way is to use the start and end coordinates, another is by using the start coordinates and then relatively defining the end point. The method described here is a bit more general. First, a reference point is passed. The start point of the line is given by the reference point plus the displacement in the x and y axes, and the end point is also given by the reference point plus a displacement.

Let's recall the construction plan of the numbers:

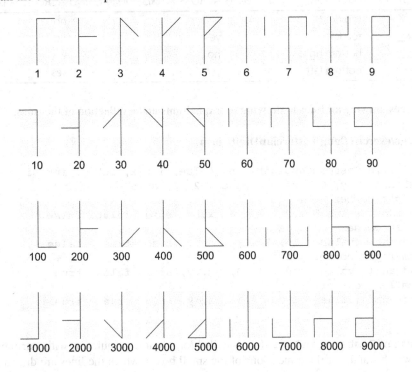

FIGURE 2.4   Cistercian numbers.

Basically, there is a vertical line in the middle; this does not pose a problem when drawing. How to proceed with the number representation? A simple approach would be to extract the ones, tens, hundreds, thousands and then draw all the lines for the digits 1 through 9 in a large case distinction. For example, if the number is 11, then there is a line at the top right and a line at the top left.

If you look closely at the glyph, you can see four quadrants. (In the figures, one quadrant is shown as a box slightly grayed out.) Each of the four quadrants represents a digit. The key insight, however, is that depending on the digit, the lines in the quadrant are mirrored horizontally (on the x-axis) or vertically (on the y-axis). This is indicated by the four small mirror symbols.

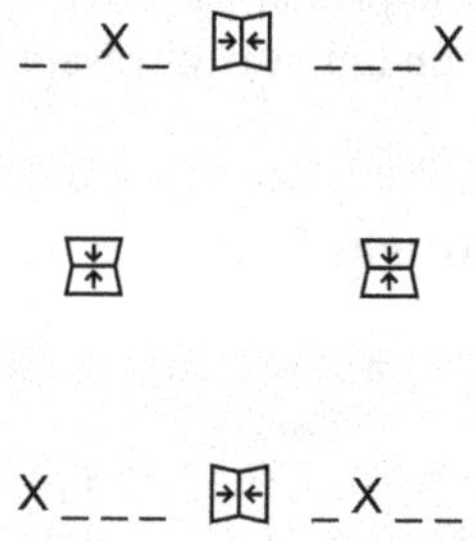

FIGURE 2.5   Mirrors areas.

The rules for mirroring on the axes are as follows:

TABLE 2.6   Four quadrants with mirrored lines

POSITION	LOCATION	MIRRORING ACROSS X-AXIS	MIRRORING ACROSS Y-AXIS
___X	top right	no	no
__X_	top left	yes	no
_X__	bottom right	no	yes
X___	bottom left	yes	yes

This reduces drawing all lines to drawing four quadrants and a reflection of the lines.

com/tutego/exercise/lang/CistercianDigits.java

```java
static void printCistercianDigit( int value, int x, int y, int size ) {
  printSvgLine( x, y, 0, -size - size / 2, 0, size+size / 2 );
  // top right corner     (___X)
  printQuadrant( value % 10,              x, y, size, false, false );
  // top left corner      (__X_)
  printQuadrant( (value / 10) % 10,   x, y, size, true,  false );
  // bottom right corner (_X__)
  printQuadrant( (value / 100) % 10,  x, y, size, false, true );
  // bottom left corner  (X___)
  printQuadrant( (value / 1000) % 10, x, y, size, true,  true );
}
```

The method `printCistercianDigit(...)` is called for a four-digit number, with starting coordinates and a `size`, which stands for the dimensions of the small box in which the lines are drawn. The middle line is placed, and the four quadrants are handled by a separate method. The x/y-coordinate of the center, as well as the size, does not change, only the two passed truth values, which stand for the reflection.

A single quadrant suffices to depict nine distinct scenarios, rather than sketching individual quadrants for each case. While it is possible to include only the necessary lines for each scenario, there exists a fascinating correlation that could be utilized. Any number greater than six possesses a line on its right side. For instance, 7 is a composite of 6 and 1, 8 is a combination of 6 and 2, and 9 is a blend of 7 and 2. Similarly, 5 is a union of 1 and 4. This association is linked to a binary pattern that, when merged, produces a higher value.

The proposed solution does not use this property, but something simpler: each digit from 1 to 9 has lines at certain places. A case statement can place the corresponding line for each digit. This is how printQuadrant(...) is implemented:

com/tutego/exercise/lang/CistercianDigits.java

```java
static void printQuadrant( int value, int x, int y, int size,
                           boolean mirroredX, boolean mirroredY ) {
  int dx=mirroredX ? -size : size;
  int dy=mirroredY ? -size : size;
  y -= 0.5 * dy;

  switch ( value ) {
    case 1, 5, 7, 9 -> printSvgLine( x, y, 0, -dy, dx, -dy );
  }
  switch ( value ) {
    case 2, 8, 9 -> printSvgLine( x, y, 0, 0, dx, 0 );
  }
  switch ( value ) {
    case 3 -> printSvgLine( x, y, 0, -dy, dx, 0 );
    case 4, 5 -> printSvgLine( x, y, 0, 0, dx, -dy );
    case 6, 7, 8, 9 -> printSvgLine( x, y, dx, -dy, dx, 0 );
  }
}
```

The method has two tasks. On the one hand, the information of the horizontal or vertical mirroring has to be translated into a coordinate and on the other hand, the corresponding line has to be shown for each digit. From the information, whether the representation is to be mirrored horizontally or vertically, variables dx and dy are assigned in such a way that the line is drawn from the starting point either to the right or to the left and/or up or down. Furthermore, the variable y is modified; although the quadrants top left and top right are directly next to each other, as well as the quadrants bottom left and bottom right, the top and bottom quadrants shall have a small distance. Therefore, the y-coordinate is additionally shifted by half of dy.

All nine digits are expressed by a total of five different lines. Different digits have different lines; therefore, a translation of the different digits into the corresponding lines follows in the method at the end.

The main program just has to define the size of the box, the start coordinates, start the SVG container, and then can set the symbol. At the end, the SVG element must be closed again:

com/tutego/exercise/lang/CistercianDigits.java

```java
public static void main( String[] args ) {
  final int SIZE=10;
  final int startX=20;
  final int startY=20;
  System.out.println( """
    <svg height="1400" width="1400">
    <g style="stroke:grey;stroke-linecap:round;stroke-width:2">""" );
  printCistercianDigit( 9394, 100, 100, SIZE );
```

```
//     int value=1;
//     for ( int _i=0; _i <= 34; _i++ ) {
//       for ( int i_=0; i_ <= 34; i_++ ) {
//         printCistercianDigit( value, startX+(i_ * 40), startY+(_i * 40),
SIZE );
//         value++;
//       }
//     }

  System.out.println( "</g>\n</svg>" );
}
```

The nested loops from the commented out block draw a large grid with different numbers.

Quiz: What Does Ding-Dong Do? (Recursion)

The parameter and the return of the method indicate that we are working with an integer-to-integer mapping. Before we look for a more suitable name, let's rename dong to value and the method to f:

```
static long f( long value ) {
  return value ==0 ? 0
                   : (value % 10+f( value / 10 ));
}
```

Recursive calls generally consist of two parts: a stopping condition and a new recursive call. The invocation is terminated when the parameter reaches 0, and the outcome is 0. During the recursive call, we can observe division by 10, indicating that the number is gradually decreasing. Specifically, the last digit is removed, and the function is recursively called with the remaining digits. The primary summand, along with the remainder of 10, extracts the rightmost digit. Let's apply this procedure to the value 192:

```
⊟ f(192)
  >f(19)
    >f(1)
      >f(0)
      <0
    <1+0=1
  <9+1=10
⊟ 2+10=12
```

Written out: $2+(9+(1+0))=12$.

  The method sums digit by digit with a zero at the end. This gives the *cross sum*, so the English method name digitSum(...) would be appropriate.

Quiz: Repdigit (Recursion)

As previously discussed, recursive functions consist of two components: the recursive call and the termination condition. Both of these aspects can be readily observed in the following method:

```
static boolean isRepdigit( long n ) {
  if ( (n % 100) / 10 !=n % 10 )
    return n<10;
  return isRepdigit( n / 10 );
}
```

- The recursive call divides the passed number by 10, which truncates the trailing digit and makes the number smaller and smaller.
- The repeated calls subsequently make the number so small that the recursive call must be terminated. This is taken care of by the case distinction.

The expression (n % 100) / 10 returns the second digit of a number (from the right), while n % 10 leads to the first digit (from the right). If the two digits are equal, the if statement does not enter the body and the number is divided by 10 and the recursion continues. If the last two digits are not equal, it does not automatically mean that the number is not a repdigit number, because if only one digit remains, that is, the number is less than 10, that is fine. Only when we have two digits that are not equal, it can no longer be a repdigit.

Let's negate the condition for a moment. The expression (n % 100) / 10 == n % 10 tests whether the last two digits of a number are equal. This is also done by the expression n % 100 % 11 == 0. The following table makes this visually clear:

TABLE 2.7   Characteristics of numbers with two equal digits

LAST TWO DIGITS	% 11	% 11 == 0
00	0	true
11	0	true
22	0	true
33	0	true
44	0	true
55	0	true
66	0	true
77	0	true
88	0	true
99	0	true
12	1	false
89	1	false

The table shows all numbers less than 100 where the two digits are equal. They fulfill a simple mathematical law: the numbers are divisible by 11. For exactly this test the remainder operator comes into play, which checks whether the number is divisible by 11 or not. If the number is divisible by 11, there is no remainder, the result is 0. If the number is *not* divisible by 11, then % 11 == 0 gives false.

Since the if statement is not to check whether the digits are equal, but not equal, the condition is negated.

Calculate Collatz Sequence (Recursion)

com/tutego/exercise/lang/Collatz.java

```java
static void collatz( long n ) {
  while ( n>1 ) {
    System.out.print( n+" -> " );
    if ( n % 2 == 0 )
      n /= 2;
    else
      n = 3 * n+1;
  }
```

```
    System.out.println( 1 );
}

static long collatzMax( long n ) {
  long max=n;
  while ( n>1 ) {
    if ( n % 2 == 0 )
      n /= 2;
    else {
      n = 3 * n+1;
      if ( n>max )
        max=n;
    }
  }
  return max;
}

static long collatz( long n, long max ) {
  if ( n <= 1 ) {
    return max;

  if ( n % 2 == 0 )
    return collatz( n / 2, Math.max( n, max ) );
  return collatz( 3 * n+1, Math.max( n, max ) );
}

public static void main( String[] args ) {
  collatz( 27 );
  System.out.println( collatzMax( 27 ) );
  System.out.println( collatz( 27, 0 ) );
  collatz( 20 );
  System.out.println( collatzMax( 20 ) );
  System.out.println( collatz( 20, 0 ) );
}
```

We write the method collatz(long) and assume an integer n. We need to repeat if n is greater than 1, and abort if n=1. To find out whether the number is even or odd, we resort to the remainder operator. If the number is even, we divide it by 2; otherwise, we multiply the number by 3 and add 1. n /= 2 is a shortcut for n=n / 2. We cannot abbreviate n=3 * n+1 by n *= 3+1, not only because the readability should be worse, but because n *= 3+1 becomes n=n * (3+1).

If we want to determine the maximum, the algorithm is almost identical to the previous one. The only difference is in the declaration of the variable max. At the start, max is initialized with the argument from the passing and possibly updated during the loop. Since dividing by 2 results in a smaller value, we do not need to adjust max. But during the loop, if the number is increased by multiplying by 3, we update the variable max if necessary.

In the recursive implementation, the parameter list is adjusted to transfer the maximum from one recursion step to the next. The method operates as follows: If the current number n is greater than 1, the recursion continues, as further steps in the Collatz sequence need to be performed. Once n equals 1, the last maximum is returned, as the sequence is completed. If n is greater than 1, it is checked whether the number is even or odd. Depending on this result, the next value of the Collatz sequence is calculated and stored in a new intermediate variable next for readability. This intermediate variable, along with the updated maximum, is recursively called to determine the maximum of the entire Collatz sequence. The mathematical utility method Math.max(...) is used to determine and return the maximum between two numbers.

Ancient Egyptian Multiplication (Recursion)

Let's first start with a direct implementation of the algorithm in the imperative form:

com/tutego/exercise/lang/PeasantMultiplication.java

```java
private static boolean isOdd( int value ) {
  return value % 2 != 0;
}

static int multiply( int a, int b ) {
  int sum=0;

  while ( a>0 ) {
    if ( isOdd( a ) )
      sum=sum+b;

    a=a / 2;
    b=b * 2;
  }

  return sum;
}
```

A helper method isOdd(...) enhances the readability when checking if a number is odd. Odd numbers cannot be divided by two.

The code is almost a direct mapping of the calculation steps. The first parameter a is divided by 2, and the second parameter b is multiplied by 2. The loop continues until a becomes 1 (i.e., as long as a is greater than 0). The sum adds the correction value b only if it is odd. Although it might seem that the case distinction is unnecessary if a is always even, in the last step, a is always 1, so odd, so b is counted at least once toward the sum.

To optimize the code, it is necessary to reduce the number of runs, which is directly dependent on a because it is divided by 2 that many times. Therefore, the smaller the value of a, the fewer iterations are required. The value of b is not relevant. However, since multiplication is commutative, and a * b=b * a, we can swap values of a and b if b is less than a:

com/tutego/exercise/lang/PeasantMultiplication.java

```java
static int multiply( int a, int b ) {
  if ( a>b ) {
    int swap=b;
    b=a;
    a=swap;
  }

  int sum=0;
  // ...
  return sum;
}
```

If you want to optimize the code further (toward nonreadability and perhaps for speed), you can look at the following:

com/tutego/exercise/lang/PeasantMultiplication.java

```
static int obfuscatedMultiply( int a, int b ) {
  int sum=0;
  for ( ; a>0; a /=2, b *=2 )
    sum += -(a & 1) & b;       //  sum += (a & 1) * b;

  return sum;
}
```

Any while loop can be rewritten to a for loop, and that is the first change. The initialization part remains empty, the condition remains the same and in the continuation expression a is halved and b is doubled as known. But why is the if missing?

Let's start with an intermediate step, and first consider why the if statement was needed in the first place: it controls whether b should be added or not.

```
if ( value % 2 !=0 )
  sum=sum+b;
```

The test value % 2 != 0 can be rewritten if the last bit is set; then the number is odd and not divisible by 2:

```
if ( a & 1 ==1 )
  sum=sum+b;
```

Written another way:

```
if (a & 1 ==1 )
  sum=sum+b;
else
  sum=sum+0;
```

Rewrite that:

```
sum=sum+((a & 1 ==1) ? b : 0 );
```

a & 1 can only be 0 or 1, and therefore is equivalent to:

```
sum=sum+(a & 1) *b;
```

The multiplications can be replaced precisely because (a & 1) can only take the value 0 or 1: (a & 1) * b is equivalent to -(a & 1) & b. Why this is so, shown by the two cases:

   a **odd**

- (a & 1) is 1.
- (a & 1) *b=1 *b=b
- -(a & 1) & b=-1 & b=0b11111111 _ 1111111111 _ 1111111111 & b=b

a **even**

- (a & 1) is 0.
- (a & 1) *b=0 *b=b
- -(a & 1) & b=-0 & b=0 & b=0

The key concept here is that when all bits of a number are flipped to 1, an AND operation will retain the second operand, whereas an AND operation with 0 will result in the extinction of the second operand.

Finally, the recursive variant:

com/tutego/exercise/lang/PeasantMultiplication.java

```java
public static int recursiveMultiply( int a, int b ) {
  if ( a == 1 )
    return b;

  if ( isOdd( a ) )
    return recursiveMultiply( a / 2, b * 2 )+b;
  else
    return recursiveMultiply( a / 2, b * 2 );
}
```

On each recursive call, a is halved and b is doubled. For odd numbers, the correction value comes on the result. When a arrives at 1, b contains the result.

In the proposed solution, we could, of course, also have swapped a and b and also used the bit tricks.

Classes, Objects, and Packages

3

In the previous chapters, we used classes as containers for static methods. We did not intentionally build new objects with new. In this chapter, the following exercises deal with creating new objects, object references, and the special null reference.

Prerequisites

- Know the difference between object type and reference type.
- Be able to use new.
- Know the purpose and basic operation of the automatic garbage collector.
- Be able to pass objects to methods and return them.
- Be able to build packages.
- Be able to import types.
- Be able to separate equivalence and identity.
- Understand the problem with null reference.

Data types used in this chapter:

- `java.awt.Polygon`
- `java.awt.Point`

CREATING OBJECTS

For the following examples, we use the classes `Point` and `Polygon` from the package `java.awt`. The `java.awt` package contains various classes, many for graphical interfaces. However, the point and polygon are not graphical, and we will not program graphical interfaces. The Java types for points and polygons, however, are nice simple data types that have publicly accessible instance variables as well as well-understood object methods, so they are quite suitable for our first exercises. We will not use any other data types from the `java.awt` package in the exercise book.

Draw Polygons ★

A polygon is a closed set of lines. The Java library provides a class `java.awt.Polygon` for polygons, which we can "feed" with points.

Captain CiaoCiao goes by ship to the vicinity of the Bermuda Triangle and looks for the water spirit Undine. But the Bermuda Triangle is dangerous and full of killer squids. The sailors must avoid the area at all costs. What would be good now is a map …

DOI: 10.1201/9781003454502-4

Task:

1. Create a new class `BermudaTriangle` with a `main(...)` method.
2. Declare three constants in the method:

```
final int DIMENSION=50;
final String RAINBOW="\uD83C\uDF08";
final String FOG="\uD83C\uDF2B";
final String OCTOPUS="\uD83D\uDC19";
```

3. Create a `java.awt.Polygon` object.
4. A polygon consists of points that are added using a method. What is the name of this method?
5. Create a triangle for the mysterious Bermuda Triangle. Keep the coordinates in the range from 0 to 50.
6. If the ship's position is a point, how can you find out if a chosen point is inside the triangle?
7. Create two nested loops for $0 <= x < 50$ and $0 <= y < 50$, creating a rectangular grid. In the body, test:
   - If the x-y coordinate hits the edge of the virtual screen, write a rainbow character (`RAINBOW`).
   - If the x-y coordinate is a point inside the polygon, output an octopus (`OCTOPUS`), otherwise a fog character (`FOG`).

Starting with Java 9, there is the module system. By default, only the types from `java.base` module are included, and this does not contain GUI (graphical user interface) types. AWT (Abstract Window Toolkit) types are part of the desktop module `java.desktop`. If you use modules (a file `module-info.java` exists in the main directory of the application), you have to include the `java.desktop` module:

```
module com.tutego.bermuda {
  requires java.desktop;
}
```

WORKING WITH REFERENCES

After creating an object with new, we get back a reference to the instance. This reference can be passed to other methods, and methods can also return references.

Quiz: The Short Life of Points ★

Given the following program code, where `Point` is from `java.awt`:

```java
Point p, q, r;
p=new Point();
q=p;
Point s=new Point();
p=new Point();
s=new Point();
// How many objects are left?
```

Question:

- How many reference variables are declared?
- How many objects are created?
- How many objects are referenced at the end of lines at the comment? What can the automatic garbage collection remove?

Build Triangles ★

Captain CiaoCiao is sure that the dangerous places in the Bermuda Triangle can be random—he must be prepared for anything.

Task:

- Create a new static method in the existing `BermudaTriangle` class:
```
static Polygon resetWithRandomTriangle( Polygon polygon ) {
    // return initialized triangle
}
```
   This method should first clear the passed `java.awt.Polygon`, which could still contain points, then fill it with a random triangle and return it at the end.
- Write another static method that returns a *new* random triangle:
```
static Polygon createRandomTriangle() {
    // return random triangle
}
```

Quiz: == vs. equals(...) ★

How will the compiler or runtime environment react?

```
public class EqualsOperatorOrMethod {

 public static void main( String[] args ) {

   int number1=1234;
   int number2=1234;

   if ( number1 == number2 )
     System.out.print( "==" );

   if ( number1.equals( number2 ) )
     System.out.print( "equals" );
 }
}
```

Will the screen print ==, or `equals`, or will neither of the condition statements catch so there is no output, or is there even a compiler error?

Quiz: Protect against NullPointerException ★

If a reference variable might be assigned a `null` value, we should check for `null` to avoid encountering a `NullPointerException`.

We are looking for a condition statement that should check if

1. A `String` variable named `string` is neither `null`.
2. Nor empty.

In other words, test whether a `string` instance exists and the `string` has at least one character. Which of the condition statements tests that correctly?

1. if (!string.isEmpty() && string !=null).
2. if (string !=null & !string.isEmpty()).
3. if (string !=null && !string.isEmpty()).
4. if (!(string ==null || string.isEmpty())).

```
5. if ( !(string ==null | string.isEmpty()) ).
6. if ( Objects.requireNonNull( string ) && !string.isEmpty() ).
7. if ( Objects.requireNonNull( string ) !=null ).
```

There are two properties of Java to consider for a solution:

1. The evaluation takes place from left to right.
2. The logical operators && and || are short-circuit operators: If the result is determined, the other expressions do not have to be evaluated.[1]

SUGGESTED SOLUTIONS

Draw Polygons

com/tutego/exercise/oop/BermudaTriangle.java

```java
java.awt.Polygon bermuda=new java.awt.Polygon();

// Dimensions of the Bermuda triangle
bermuda.addPoint( 10, 40 );
bermuda.addPoint( 20, 5 );
bermuda.addPoint( 40, 20 );

// Inside the Bermuda triangle?
System.out.println( bermuda.contains( 25, 25 ) );  // true

final int DIMENSION=50;
final String RAINBOW="\uD83C\uDF08";
final String FOG    ="\uD83C\uDF2B";
final String OCTOPUS="\uD83D\uDC19";

// For every coordinate pair test if inside triangle
for ( int y=0; y<DIMENSION; y++ ) {
  for ( int x=0; x<DIMENSION; x++ ) {
    // test for border
    if ( x ==0 || y ==0 || x ==DIMENSION - 1 || y ==DIMENSION - 1 )
      System.out.print( RAINBOW );
    else
      System.out.print( bermuda.contains( x, y ) ? OCTOPUS : FOG );
  }
  System.out.println();
}
```

Following the same pattern as a java.awt.Point is built, we build a java.awt.Polygon. We store the reference to the newly built object in a variable bermuda. We add three points to the polygon at the end. That the method is called addPoint(...) can be found in the Java documentation, or via the auto-completion appears after the point (.) following bermuda. The method is now passed x and y coordinates; it was not in the assignment that the values must be random, so we enter three static pairs.

That the method for testing is called contains(...) can again be read from the Java documentation or just guessed in the autocompletion of the IDE (integrated development environment). It is always a good idea to translate what you want from the object into English, and then search for these verbs in the method list or Javadoc. Methods are always verbs, `contains` is a good example. You can see this well with the `Point`, it also has methods like `move` or `translate`.

The last step is the two nested loops. We know this already. We go with the outer loop over all rows and then with the inner loop over the row itself (x-axis). If the point is on the edge, the rainbow should be printed. Otherwise, the point is inside the frame. The condition operator makes the query simple. With `contains(...)` we then test whether points are in the polygon or not. If the points are in the polygon, we draw an octopus, otherwise the rainbow. For the Unicode symbols, there are speaking constants.

Quiz: The Short Life of Points

In total, four reference variables are declared (p, q, r, s) and four objects are built. If we want to know how many objects are created, we just have to count the number of occurrences of `new`.

Not every reference variable is initialized. The variable r remains uninitialized; we would not be allowed to access it because r is not even pre-initialized with the `null` reference.

Of the four constructed objects, three remain at the end because the first initialization of the point s is overwritten by the last line. This means that the point built at `Point s=new Point();` is no longer referenced and can be cleared away by the garbage collector. Moreover, the variable p is reinitialized, nevertheless the first generated `Point` remains in memory because the variable q also points to the object and thus saved it.

Build Triangles

com/tutego/exercise/oop/BermudaTriangle2.java

```
private static final int DIMENSION=50;

static Polygon resetWithRandomTriangle( Polygon poly ) {
  poly.reset();

  Random random=ThreadLocalRandom.current();
  poly.addPoint( random.nextInt( DIMENSION ), random.nextInt( DIMENSION ) );
  poly.addPoint( random.nextInt( DIMENSION ), random.nextInt( DIMENSION ) );
  poly.addPoint( random.nextInt( DIMENSION ), random.nextInt( DIMENSION ) );

  return poly;
}

static Polygon createRandomTriangle() {
  return resetWithRandomTriangle( new Polygon() );
}
```

Let's start with the method `resetWithRandomTriangle(Polygon poly)`, which takes a polygon and returns the reference to exactly that polygon as well. Since the passed polygon might in principle already have elements, we want to remove all elements. Here a look at the documentation is necessary, which leads us to the method `reset()`. Then we create three random points as usual and add them to the polygon. Finally, we return the polygon.

One can ask why a method that expects a polygon also returns this polygon. `resetWithRandomTriangle(...)` could well return `void` because no new polygon object is built inside. However, methods that have returned are fundamentally better than methods that return nothing. Because if we get something back, it is an expression, and expressions are handy.

The use is well seen in the second method `createRandomTriangle()` because it can refer to the previous method `resetWithRandomTriangle(…)` and pass a new polygon there. Since `resetWith-RandomTriangle(…)` also returns this passed polygon directly, we can end the method with a one-liner. If `resetWithRandomTriangle(…)` returned nothing, we would have to introduce an intermediate variable, which we first assign with the new polygon and finally return via `return`. We can save this intermediate variable if `resetWithRandomTriangle(…)` returns the argument at the same time.

Quiz: == vs. equals(…)

Primitive data types are not reference types; consequently, no single method can be called on the primitive data types. It is not allowed in Java to put a dot after the primitive element and then call a method. The situation is different if the primitive data types are automatically converted into the so-called wrapper objects by the compiler, but that is another story. Consequently, there is a compiler error.

Quiz: Protect against NullPointerException

About the individual conditions:

```
if ( !string.isEmpty() && string != null )
```

The expression first checks whether `string` is empty and then whether `string` is null. Since the evaluation is done from left to right and length is checked here first, this notation leads to a `NullPointerException` if `string == null` and avoids none.

```
if ( string != null & !string.isEmpty() )
```

`&&` and `||` are short-circuit operators, and they have a counterpart `&` and `|` that do not operate on the short-circuit principle, i.e., execute all parts. So, this also yields a `NullPointerException` if `string` is `null`, because of the method call.

```
if ( string != null && !string.isEmpty() )
```

This check is correct. The order is correct; first, it tests if `string` is not equal to `null`. If the result is `false`, the right part is not evaluated at all. This avoids a `NullPointerException`.

```
if ( !(string == null || string.isEmpty()) )
```

Logical expressions can be negated twice, leading to the same result. In this case, the individual logical expressions are reversed, an AND becomes an OR, and an OR becomes an AND. In addition, the whole expression is negated—the keyword is *boolean algebra*. Thus, this `if` statement is also correct. It depends on the context whether this simplifies the readability or not; in this special case, probably not.

```
if ( (string == null | string.isEmpty()) )
```

The `|` operator leads to the evaluation of both sides: a `NullPointerException` occurs if `string` is `null`.

```
if ( Objects.requireNonNull( string ) && !string.isEmpty() )
```

There is a compiler error with this notation because `Objects.requireNonNull(...)` returns a reference, but logical operations are only allowed with `boolean`.

```
if ( Objects.requireNonNull( string ) != null )
```

There is no test whether the string also contains characters; this is not a feature of `requireNonNull(...)`. Besides, using it would be counterproductive because if the string was `null`, we would get an exception, which is precisely what we want to avoid. You only use `requireNonNull(...)` if you would like to throw an exception deliberately to report faulty parameters.

NOTE

---

1   https://docs.oracle.com/javase/specs/jls/se21/html/jls-15.html#jls-15.23 and
    https://docs.oracle.com/javase/specs/jls/se21/html/jls-15.html#jls-15.24

Arrays

4

Arrays are important data structures that also appear indirectly in Java, for example, in the enhanced `for` loop or variable argument lists. This chapter includes exercises on creating arrays, traversing arrays, and questions about algorithms, such as how to search for elements in an array.

Prerequisites

- Be capable of creating, accessing, and filling arrays.
- Traverse arrays using an enhanced `for` loop.
- Be able to use both one-dimensional and multidimensional arrays.
- Be capable of constructing variable argument lists.
- Understand the utility methods of the `Arrays` class.

Data types used in this chapter:

- `java.util.Arrays`
- `java.lang.System`

EVERYTHING HAS A TYPE

Before we look at accessing elements, let's take a closer look at types. It is critical to understand the distinction between object type and reference type.

Quiz: Array Types ★

Arrays are covariant in Java, which means, for example, that `String[]` is a subtype of `Object[]`. This sounds a bit academic, it probably is, so the following task is intended to sharpen your understanding of array covariance.

Consider whether all statements compile or work at runtime:

```
/* 1 */ String[] strings1=new String[ 100 ];
/* 2 */ Object[] a1=(String[]) strings1;
/* 3 */ Object[] a2=strings1;
/* 4 */ Object[] strings2=new String[]{ "1", "2", "3" };
/* 5 */ String[] a3=(String[]) strings2;
/* 6 */ String[] strings3={ "1", "2", "3" };
/* 7 */ Object[] a4=strings3;
/* 8 */ Object[] strings4={ "1", "2", "3" };
/* 9 */ String[] a5=(String[]) strings4;
```

DOI: 10.1201/9781003454502-5

```
/*A */int[] ints1=new int[ 100 ];
/*B */Object[] a6=(int[]) ints1;
/*C */Object[] ints2=new int[ 100 ];
/*D */int[] a7=(int[]) ints2;
```

ONE-DIMENSIONAL ARRAYS

An array is a collection of homogeneous elements. One-dimensional arrays contain the elements directly and no other sub-arrays.

Loop Arrays and Output Wind Speed, Wind Direction ★

Captain CiaoCiao is sailing across the sea, the wind is blowing from all sides. He must always keep the wind speed and direction in mind.

Task:

1. Declare two arrays `int[] windSpeed` and `int[] windDirection`.
2. Fill both arrays each with three integer random numbers (in principle the number should be arbitrary), where the wind speed can range between 0 and (less than) 200 km/h and the wind direction can range between 0 and (less than) 360°.
3. Run a loop over the array and output all pairs comma separated.

Example:

- For example, if the array `windSpeed` contains the values {82, 70, 12} and the array `windDirection` contains the values {12, 266, 92}, the output to the screen should be:

```
Wind speed 82 km/h and wind direction 12°, Wind speed 70 km/h and wind
direction 266°, Wind speed 12 km/h and wind direction 92°
```

Keep in mind that the segments are separated by commas and that there is no comma at the end.

Detect Continuous Revenue Growth ★

At the end of a month, Captain CiaoCiao receives a report of the sales he and his crew have generated. The profit on any given day is recorded on the monthly list. It follows this format:

```
//                Day    1,    2,    3,    4,    5 ... up to a maximum of 31
int[] dailyGains ={ 1000, 2000, 500, 9000, 9010 };
```

Captain CiaoCiao is happy with the numbers, and he wants to pay a reward when gains have increased over 5%. From 1000 to 2000 is a whopping 100% jump, from 500 to 9000 is as well, but not from 2000 to 500, nor from 9000 to 9010.

Task:

- Write a method int count5PercentJumps(int[]) that returns the number of sales jumps. A sales jump is given if the sales were 5% higher than the previous day.
- The passed array must not be null, or an exception will be thrown.

Array of Points ★

What is the expected output?

```
Point[] points={ null, null, null, null };
Point p=new Point();
p.setLocation( 1, 2 );
points[ 0 ]=p;
p.setLocation( 3, 4 );
```

```
points[ 1 ]=p;
Point q=points[ 1 ];
q.setLocation( 5, 6 );
points[ 2 ]=points[ 3 ]=q;
System.out.println( Arrays.toString( points ) );
```

Search Consecutive Strings and Determine If Salty Snook Is Coming ★

Captain CiaoCiao watches the flags of passing ships because he is waiting for Salty Snook. He looks at each flag and knows that Salty Snook never comes alone, but moves in a convoy of four ships. He doesn't know the flags themselves, only that they all have the same inscription.

Task:

- Write a new method isProbablyApproaching(String[] signs) that returns true if there are four of the same abbreviation in the array consecutively in a row. Remember that strings are compared using equals(...).
- The array passed must not be null, and no element in the array must be null.

Example:

```
String[] signs1={"F", "DO", "MOS", "MOS", "MOS", "MOS", "WES" };
System.out.println( isProbablyApproaching( signs1 ) );    // true

String[] signs2={"F", "DO", "MOS", "MOS", "WES", "MOS", "MOS" };
System.out.println( isProbablyApproaching( signs2 ) );   // false
```

Reverse an Array ★

Charlie Creevey does the finances for Captain CiaoCiao. However, rather than sorting the income in the ascending order, he sorted it in the descending order. As a result, the list must be flipped.

To *flip* an array means to swap the first element with the last element, the second with the second to last, and so on.
Task:

- Write a new static method `reverse(...)` that flips a given array:

```
public static void reverse( double[] numbers ) {
  // TODO
}
```

- The operation should be *in place*, that is, it should change the array passed. We do not want to create a new array inside the method `reverse(...)`.
- An exception will be thrown if `null` is passed.

Example:

- { } → { }
- { 1 } → { 1 }
- { 1, 2 } → { 2, 1 }
- { 1, 2, 3 } → { 3, 2, 1 }

The representation in the curly braces is purely symbolic.

Find the Nearest Cinema ★★

The class `java.awt.Point` represents points with x/y coordinates. This data type is excellent for positions.
    The new movie »Under the flag of the buccaneers« is playing in the cinema, and Captain CiaoCiao must see it. But where is the nearest movie theater?
Task:

- Given a set of `Point` objects in an array `points` for the cinema positions.
  `Point[] points={ new Point(10, 20), new Point(12, 2), new Point(44, 4) };`
- Write a method `double minDistance(Point[] points, int size)` that returns the distance of the point that has the smallest distance to the zero point. With `size` we can specify how many array elements should be considered, allowing the array to be larger in theory.
- A passed `null` is not allowed, also the points themselves must not be `null`; an exception must be raised.
- What should we change if the return type is `Point`, implying that the point itself should be returned with the shortest distance?

Examine the Javadoc for `java.awt.Point` to see if the point can calculate distances to other coordinates.

Raid the Candy Store and Share Fairly ★★

Captain CiaoCiao and his children Junior and Jackie are robbing a candy store. The candy is displayed on a long shelf, and each item is labeled with its weight. The information is available as an array:

```
int[] values={ 10, 20, 30, 40, 50 };
```

Junior and Jackie are on opposite ends of the shelf, on the left and right, and because Captain CiaoCiao loves both kids equally, they should end up taking home the same amount. Captain CiaoCiao points to candy on the shelf, so all the products to the left of it go to Junior, and all the products to the right of the position (including the one shown) go to Jackie.

Captain CiaoCiao knows what's on the shelf, but he doesn't know where the same total will appear to the left and right.

Deviations of 10% are acceptable for children. We want to use the following formula for the relative difference for the difference:

```java
private static int relativeDifference( int a, int b ) {
  if ( a == b ) return 0;
  int absoluteDifference=Math.abs( a - b );
  return (int) (100. * absoluteDifference / Math.max( a, b ));
}
```

Task:

- Write a method int findSplitPoint(int[]) that finds the index in the array where left and right can be fairly split. Any solution will do, not all solutions are necessary.
- A method must return -1 if there is no fair split.

Examples:

- $10+20+30+40 \approx 40+50$ because $100 \approx 90$, and the index for the return is 4.
- 10 20 30 40 100 results in −1 because there is no valid partitioning.

ENHANCED FOR LOOP

If arrays are to be run from the first element, an enhanced for loop with an invisible loop counter can be used for this purpose. This saves code.

In the following tasks, in some places it is possible to use an extended for loop.

Numbers Well Shuffled ★★

In the dice cup of Bonny Brain there are five game dice with the numbers 1 to 6. With a hearty shake and a mighty toss, the dice be spillin' onto the table like treasure from a loot chest, revealing their fateful numbers for all to see.

Task:

- Write a method `int[] shuffleDice()` that returns an `int` array with five random numbers that are between 1 and 6.
- Write a method `isHomogeneous(int[] values)` that tests if all values in the array are equal. (The word *homogeneous* means *uniform/similar/equal*). In principle, the array may be of any size.
- Write a method `int[] occurrences(int[] values)`, which returns a new array of size 6, which indicates which number occurs how often.
- Write a method `isFullHouse(int[] values)` that checks if three dice have the same value and two other dice have a different same value. For example, {1, 1, 1, 2, 2} is such a case.
- Write a method void `printDiceValues(int[] points)` that writes the dice numbers to the screen as follows:
  - The numbers are sorted in ascending order.
  - The numbers are grouped together.
  - Instead of the eyes as simple numbers on the screen, use the Unicode symbols ⚀ (Unicode character U+2680), ⚁ (U+2681), ⚂ (U+2682), ⚃ (U+2683), ⚄ (U+2684), ⚅ (U+2685).

We can assume that the methods are always called with correct values, so the array is never `null`, the number of elements is always correct, and the values are always in the valid ranges.

Examples:

- `isHomogeneous(new int[]{ 1, 1, 1, 1 })` returns `true`.
- `isHomogeneous( new int[]{ 1, 1, 1, 2, 2 } )` returns `false`.
- `occurrences( new int[]{ 1, 1, 2, 3, 4 })` returns an array with the values {2, 1, 1, 1, 0, 0}.
- `isFullHouse(new int[]{ 1, 1, 1, 2, 2 })` returns `true`.
- `isFullHouse(new int[]{ 1, 1, 1, 1 })` returns `false`.
- `printDiceValues(new int[]{2, 4, 2, 4, 6})` returns 2 × ⚁, 2 × ⚃, ⚅.

Draw Mountains ★★

Preparing for the upcoming treasure hunt, Bonny Brain and her crew must traverse mountains and hills. Before the journey, she is provided with information about the altitude and wishes to gain a preview of the terrain's topography.

Task:

- Write a program with a method `printMountain(int[] altitudes)` that converts an array of altitude meters into an ASCII representation.
- The altitude has to be represented by a multiplication sign * at exactly this altitude from a base-line. The heights can be arbitrary, but not negative.

Example:

- The array { 0, 1, 1, 2, 2, 3, 3, 3, 4, 5, 4, 3, 2, 2, 1, 0 } shall be represented as:

```
5               *
4              * *
3        ***      *
2     **            **
1   **                *
0 *                     *
```
     The first column is for clarification and does not need to be implemented.

Optional extension:

- Instead of *, use the symbols /, \, -, and ^ to indicate whether we are ascending, descending, on a plateau, or at the top.

```
5               ^
4             / \
3        --/     \
2     -/           -\
1   -/               \
0 /                     \
```

TWO- AND MULTIDIMENSIONAL ARRAYS

An array in Java can contain references to other arrays, and this is how you define multidimensional arrays in Java. In Java, there are no true two-dimensional arrays; two-dimensional arrays are nothing more than arrays that reference sub-arrays and the sub-arrays could be of different lengths.

Check Mini-Sudoku for Valid Solution ★★

Since mugging is quite exhausting, Bonny Brain needs a balance and engages in Sudoku. A Sudoku game consists of 81 squares in a 9×9 grid. The grid can be divided into nine blocks, each block is a two-dimensional array of size 3×3. In each of these blocks, each number from 1 to 9 must occurs exactly once—none may be missing.

Task:

- Write a program that tests a two-dimensional array of nine elements to see if all numbers from 1 to 9 occur.
- Missing elements are to be reported.

Example:

- The following array is a valid Sudoku assignment:
  ```
  int[][] array={
      { 1, 2, 3 },
      { 4, 5, 6 },
      { 7, 8, 9 }
  };
  ```
- The following array is not a valid Sudoku assignment:
  ```
  int[][] array={ { 1, 2, 3 }, { 4, 5, 6 }, { 7, 8, 8 } };
  ```
  The error could be reported something like: Missing 9.

Enlarge Image ★★

Captain CiaoCiao is looking for the treasure of one-eyed Billy. The treasure map is small, and his eyes are getting worse. Help him enlarge the map and find the treasure.

Images are often stored in memory as triples of red-green-blue values, where the individual values can range from 0 to 255. Since there are no colors in grayscale images, only one value is needed instead of three.

Task:

- Given a two-dimensional integer array with values from 0 to 255, the array mentally represents a grayscale image.
- Write a method int[][] magnify(int[][] array, int factor) that returns a new array and scales the image by the given factor. So, an image of size 2×3 and factor 2 becomes an image of size 4×6. Image pixels are simply doubled, no interpolation of values is desired.

Example:

- Assume the following array:
  ```
  { {1, 2, 3},
    {4, 5, 6} }
  ```
  Then, after doubling, it follows:
  ```
  { {1, 1, 2, 2, 3, 3},
    {1, 1, 2, 2, 3, 3},
    {4, 4, 5, 5, 6, 6},
    {4, 4, 5, 5, 6, 6} }
  ```

VARIABLE ARGUMENT LISTS

Java allows methods to which you can pass any number of arguments. They are called *vararg methods*. A vararg parameter may only be at the end of a parameter list and is an array. When called with variable arguments, the compiler automatically creates a new anonymous array and passes it to the method.

Create SVG Polygons with a Variable Number of Coordinates ★

Bonny Brain wants to draw a map for her next place of work, and it should always look good printed and on any resolution because every detail matters. The best technology for this is SVG.

In SVG there are different primitives, for example, for lines, circles, or rectangles. There is also an XML element for polylines. Example:

```
<polygon points="200,10 250,190 160,210" />
```

Task:

- Declare a Java method `printSvgPolygon(...)` to which we can pass any number of coordinate pairs. What errors could occur when passing them?
- The method should print a matching SVG output to the screen for the passed pairs.

Example:

- In `printSvgPolygon( 200, 10, 250, 190, 160, 210 )`, 200,10 is a coordinate pair, 250,190 is as well, as is 160, 210. The screen output should be: `<polygon points="200,10 250,190 160,210" />`.

Optional: study the example at https://tutego.de/go/trysvgpolygon.. Copy the self-generated SVG into the web interface.

Check for Approval ★

Captain CiaoCiao gets feedback from his crew members about an order. All members can vote yes or no. Task:

- We are looking for a vararg method `allTrue(…)` that can accept any number of `boolean` values, but must be called at least with one argument.
- If all arguments are `true`, the return is also `true`; if one of the `boolean` values is `false`, the method shall return `false`.
- Since a vararg is internally an array, `null` may be passed—this must lead to an exception.

Example:

- `allTrue(true, true, true)` returns `true`.
- `allTrue(true)` returns `true`.
- `allTrue(true, false)` returns `false`.
- `allTrue(true, null)` throws an exception.
- `allTrue()` cannot be compiled and must give a compiler error.

Help, Tetraphobia! Put All Fours Last ★★

Bonny Brain meets befriended pirates in Hong Kong and finds that many suffer from tetraphobia and have a superstitious fear of the number 4. The accountant must now put all numbers with a 4 to the back.

Task:

- Write a method `fourLast(int... numbers)` that places all numbers containing a 4 after the numbers that do not have a 4. The order of the numbers without 4 must not change, the numbers with a 4 can be anywhere at the end.
- `fourLast(...)` should return the passed array.
- The argument `null` must lead to an exception.

Example:

- `int[] numbers={1, 44, 2, 4, 43}; fourLast(numbers);` modifies the array `numbers` so that 1 and 2 are before 44, 4, and 43 in the array. The 2 must not come before the 1 later.
- `fourLast( 4, 4, 44, 1234 )` returns the array automatically generated by the compiler with the entries, for example, in the order 4, 4, 44, 1234.

THE UTILITY CLASS ARRAYS

In Java, array objects have limited built-in functionalities. Many useful methods for arrays are found in external classes, such as `java.util.Arrays`. For instance, a method to copy arrays resides in the `System` class.

Quiz: Copy Arrays ★

What do these nonsensical variable names stand for, and what is the effect of the following lines?

```
int[] hooey={1, 2, 3, 4 };
int[] shuck=new int[ hooey.length - 1 ];
int bushwa=2;
int kelter=0;
int piddle=0;
System.arraycopy( hooey, kelter, shuck, piddle, bushwa );
System.arraycopy( hooey, bushwa+1, shuck, bushwa, hooey.length - bushwa - 1 );
System.out.println( Arrays.toString( shuck ) );
```

Quiz: Compare Arrays ★

What are the outputs?

```
Object[] array1={ "Anne Bonny", "Fortune", "Sir Francis Drake", new int[]{ 1,
2, 3 } };
Object[] array2={ "Anne Bonny", "Fortune", "Sir Francis Drake", new int[]{ 1,
2, 3 } };
System.out.println( array1 == array2 );
System.out.println( array1.equals( array2 ) );
System.out.println( arrays.equals( array1, array2 ) );
System.out.println( Arrays.deepEquals( array1, array2 ) );
```

SUGGESTED SOLUTIONS

Quiz: Array Types

The variable declarations and assignments from `strings1` to `strings4` and `int1` and `int2` are less interesting; we know the syntax: an array is pre-initialized with either a fixed size or elements.

It's worth noting the following type conversions, which can be performed explicitly or implicitly. We must distinguish between type conversions that are fine for the compiler and type conversions that cause trouble only at runtime. This is an important distinction, which also becomes clear in the terms *object type* and *reference type*. For the compiler there are reference variables and a reference type, the compiler does not know what is going on at runtime. The runtime environment, on the other hand, basically does not know under which variable type a variable was declared, but it does know what kind of object it has in front of it: We, therefore, speak of the object type.

The first statement is the most honest one. For the compiler, it is a string array and for the runtime environment as well.

The type conversions in the second line are irrelevant because `String[]` is a subtype of `Object[]`. This is very significant because exactly this is covariant: **A *String* array is a subtype of an *Object* array, also a *Point[]* is a special *Object[]*.** This is also evident in the third line, where the explicit type conversion is missing because it is implicit.

In the fourth statement, runtime environment and compiler know different things. For the runtime environment, there is still a `String` array in memory, but the compiler knows the `String` array only as an `Object` array. This notation is valid in principle, and again an implicit type conversion takes place.

In the fifth statement, we upgrade the `Object` array to a `String` array. This works at compile time and also at runtime.

In the sixth statement, we again directly build a `String` array and declare it as a `String` array. This is the usual notation. In the seventh statement, we find an implicit type conversion from the `String` array to the `Object` array. This statement is fine.

The eighth and ninth statements are tricky: the compiler does not build a `String` array but an `Object` array and puts `String` references into this `Object` array. As a result, there is no `String` array, only an `Object` array that references strings. In the ninth line, the compiler trusts our decision to cast the `Object` array to a `String` array. The compiler accepts this, and there is no compiler error. However, a problem occurs at runtime. Since the runtime environment knows, of course, that the variable `strings4` holds only an `Object` array and not a better `String` array, the exception `java.lang.ClassCastException: class [Ljava.lang.Object; cannot be cast to class [Ljava.lang.String;` follows.

The last four examples are easier for the compiler to identify as false. While the declaration of `ints1` is still correct, B and C, and D will lead to a compiler error. An `int` array cannot be converted to an `Object` array, either explicitly as in line B or implicitly as in line C. There is no type matching here, just as `Object o=1` is also wrong. Since we already cannot compile line C, line D also leads to a compiler error: there is no type matching from an `Object` array to an `int` array.

Loop Arrays and Output Wind Speed, Wind Direction

com/tutego/exercise/array/Windy.java

```
final int MAX_WIND_SPEED=200;
final int MAX_DEGREE    =360;

final int LENGTH=5;
```

```
int[] windSpeed      =new int[ LENGTH ];
int[] windDirection=new int[ LENGTH ];

for ( int i=0; i<LENGTH; i++) {
  windSpeed[ i ]     =(int) (Math.random() * MAX_WIND_SPEED);
  windDirection[ i ]=(int) (Math.random() * MAX_DEGREE);
}

for ( int i=0; i<LENGTH; i++) {
  System.out.printf( "Wind speed %d km/h and wind direction %d°",
                    windSpeed[ i ], windDirection[ i ] );
  if ( i !=LENGTH - 1 )
    System.out.print( ", " );
}
```

The solution consists of four steps. First, we want to define three constants: for the maximum wind speed and wind force and for the number of elements. We initialize LENGTH with 5 so that we don't have to write the literal 5 as a magic number in the code again later when building the arrays windSpeed and windDirection; we can simply change the variable later if we want larger arrays.

In the second step, we run with a loop variable from 0 to the last element of the array. The array has five elements, so we may run from 0 to 4. In the body of the loop, we create two random numbers and initialize the array elements. Calculating an integer random number from 0 to 200 looks like this: Using Math.random() we get a random number as a floating-point number between 0 and less than 1. Multiplying by 200 gives a random number between 0 and less than 200. If (int) converts the expression to an integer, all decimal places are truncated, so the result is an integer between 0 and 199. Usually, for range specifications, the start is inclusive, and the end is exclusive.

The two arrays are now initialized, and we can output the pairs. We loop through the array; we access the arrays windSpeed and windDirection at the same position i. The output is supported by printf(...) and the format specifier %d for decimal numbers. But we do not put a comma in the format string because there must not be a comma at the end of the string. That there is a comma only at the end can be solved in different ways. The approach here queries the loop counter whether it stands for the last element. If i is not equal to the last element, then a separator is set, otherwise not.

Reverse an Array

com/tutego/exercise/array/BigProfits.java

```
private static int count5PercentJumps( int[] dailyGains ) {

  if ( dailyGains.length<2 )
    return 0;

  final double MIN_PERCENTAGE_INCREASE=5;

  int count=0;

  // Index variable i starting at 1, second element
  for ( int i=1; i<dailyGains.length; i++) {
    double yesterdayGain=dailyGains[ i - 1 ];
    double todayGain     =dailyGains[ i ];

    double percent=todayGain / yesterdayGain * 100 - 100;
```

```
     if ( percent >= MIN_PERCENTAGE_INCREASE )
       count++;
   }

   return count;
}
```

The count5PercentJumps(...) method is passed an array containing, in the best case, a set of integers. It may happen that null is passed, which should not be a valid input for the program. If we fall back to length, there will be a NullPointerException in case of null—this is intended.

If the array object exists but contains no element or only one, we consider that an error and return 0.

Whenever we continue, we know that there are at least two elements in the array. We run a for loop over the array, starting with index i at 1 and asking for two elements at a time: the current element at position i and the element at the position before that, at position i - 1. These elements stand for todayGain and yesterdayGain. In principle, we could have started at 0 and run to< dailyGains.length - 1.

Once we have read the amount for today and yesterday, we need to calculate the relative percentage increase. We do this with a simple formula. However, we make sure that the division is not done on integers, but on floating-point numbers. After all, if two integers are divided, the result is again an integer. If we take the numbers out of the array beforehand and convert them to a double, we will have a more accurate ratio later by dividing two floating-point numbers. This way we avoid problems with rounding because if we want to change the constant at some point, e.g., to a much smaller value, small jumps might not be detected correctly. Special case: days when no sales were generated work because the increase on the following day is Double.Infinity and "Infinity" is greater than MIN_PERCENTAGE_INCREASE.

After calculating the relative increment, we check to see if we get above our constant of 5% and increment the variable count, where we remember all the increments. At the end of the loop, we return count to report how many total increases we found.

Array of Points

The output is:

```
[java.awt.Point[x=5,y=6], java.awt.Point[x=5,y=6], java.awt.Point[x=5,y=6],
java.awt.Point[x=5,y=6]]
```

Let's go through the program line by line:

```
/* 1 */ Point[] points={ null, null, null, null };
/* 2 */ Point p=new Point();
/* 3 */ p.setLocation( 1, 2 );
/* 4 */ points[ 0 ]=p;
/* 5 */ p.setLocation( 3, 4 );
/* 6 */ points[ 1 ]=p;
/* 7 */ Point q=points[ 1 ];
/* 8 */ q.setLocation( 5, 6 );
/* 9 */ points[ 2 ]=points[ 3 ]=q;
/* 10*/ System.out.println( Arrays.toString( points ) );
```

1. The first line creates an array with four elements, all of which are null. The same effect would have been achieved by creating the array with new Point[4].
2. A new Point object is created.
3. The setter is used to set the coordinates to (1, 2).
4. Then, the first element in the array (index 0) is set to this point.

5. The same point is changed and set to the coordinates (3, 4). If one were to access points[0], they would be able to see this change.

6. Then, the point p is also set to the second position in the array (index 1).

7. The reference to this second position is obtained again and stored in the variable q. Thus, q and p both point to the same Point object.

8. Throughout the program, we are only dealing with a single Point object, which ends up with coordinates of (5, 6) in the end.

9. This Point reference is then set at positions 3 and 4 in the array (indices 2 and 3).

10. Ultimately, all elements in the array point to the same Point object, so the output will be the toString() representation of the Point object with coordinates (5, 6) four times.

Search Consecutive Strings and Determine if Salty Snook is Coming

com/tutego/exercise/array/SaltySnook.java

```
public static boolean isProbablyApproaching( String[] signs ) {

  final int MIN_OCCURRENCES=4;
  if ( signs.length<MIN_OCCURRENCES )
    return false;

  for ( int i=0, count=1; i<signs.length - 1; i++) {
    String currentSign=Objects.requireNonNull( signs[ i ] );
    String nextSign   =Objects.requireNonNull( signs[ i+1 ] );
    if ( currentSign.equals( nextSign ) ) {
      count++;
      if ( count == MIN_OCCURRENCES )
        return true;
    }
    else // ! currentSign.equals( nextSign )
      count=1;
  }
  return false;
}
```

We note the number of ships we want in a constant MIN_OCCURRENCES so we can easily change the number later.

First, we check if the array has at least MIN_OCCURRENCES in many elements. If not, the method returns false to the caller. A NullPointerException is thrown when accessing the length attribute with a parameter null, indicating an incorrect parameter.

If we do not get out of the method, there are at least four elements in the array. When comparing subsequent elements in the array, there are usually two approaches:

- Generate an index from 0 to the second last element, and then access two elements via the index and index + 1.
- Generate an index from 1 to the last element and then access two elements via index − 1 and index.

This solution uses the first variant.

The for loop declares two local variables: i for the index, and in the variable count we note the number of successively equivalent strings; since a string occurs at least once, the variable is initialized with 1.

We start in the loop at index 0 and store the element in an intermediate variable currentSign. At position 1, we have the second element to start with, and this assignment is also saved in a talking variable nextSign. Objects.requireNonNull(...) will throw an exception at this point if one of the array elements is null.

Strings have an equals(...) method that is used to determine equivalence. There are two outputs for the comparison:

1. When we find two equal consecutive strings, we increment the variable counter and test if it is equal to MIN_OCCURRENCES. In that case, there are four equal consecutive strings, and we can exit the method with return true.
2. If currentSign and nextSign are not equal, we must reset the counter to 1.

If at the end of the loop, no string has been detected that occurs four times in a row, the method is exited with return false.

The whole if-else block can be shortened if you are willing to always test, even if the counter has been reset:

```
count=currentSign.equals( nextSign ) ? count+1 : 1;
if ( count == MIN_OCCURRENCES ) return true;
```

Reverse an Array

com/tutego/exercise/array/ArrayReverser.java

```
public static void reverse( double[] numbers ) {
  final int middle=numbers.length / 2;

  for ( int left=0; left<middle; left++ ) {
    int right=numbers.length - left - 1;
    swap( numbers, left, right );
  }
}

private static void swap( double[] numbers, int i, int j ) {
  double swap =numbers[ i ];
  numbers[ i ]=numbers[ j ];
  numbers[ j ]=swap;
}
```

The reverse(...) method gets an array as a parameter. So, we get a reference to an object from another place. Changes do not take place on a copy, but we operate on exactly the array passed by the caller. Since arrays are objects that are accessed by references, the caller may have passed null. In that case, the coming numbers.length will lead to a NullPointerException, and that is fine.

The algorithm itself is not difficult. We need to swap the first element with the last, then the second with the second last, and so on. We move the swapping of the elements to a separate method swap(...).

To avoid overwriting the elements in reverse(...), we must only run halfway. The variable middle represents the half. Although the variable is used only once in the loop, a variable of this kind helps to document the meaning of this expression more precisely. Our loop starts with the loop counter left at 0 and runs to the middle. The variable right runs in the opposite direction.

Find the Nearest Cinema

com/tutego/exercise/array/MinDistance.java

```java
static double minDistance( Point[] points, int size ) {

  if ( points.length == 0 || size>points.length )
    throw new IllegalArgumentException(
        "Array is either empty or size out of bounds" );

  double minDistance=points[ 0 ].distance( 0, 0 );

  // Index variable i starting at 1, second element
  for ( int i=1; i<size; i++) {
    double distance=points[ i ].distance( 0, 0 );
    if ( distance<minDistance )
      minDistance=distance;
  }

  return minDistance;
}
```

First, we check in the method if the parameters `points` and `size` are correct. We expect at least one element, and the number of elements to be considered must not be greater than the number of elements in the array. If the passing was `null`, a `NullPointerException` follows automatically by accessing `length`.

When asking for the largest or smallest element of a list, the algorithms always look the same. We start with a candidate and then check if this candidate needs to be corrected. Our candidate is `minDistance`. We initialize it with the distance of the first point to the zero point. We don't have to calculate the distance to the zero point ourselves, here the `Point` method `distance(x,y)` conveniently helps us. We pass the coordinates 0, 0, relative to which the point should calculate its distance.

So that all points are considered, we run through the array and use `size` as a length constraint. From the new point, we also calculate the distance to the zero point, and if we found a point closer to the zero point, we have to correct our choice.

At the end of the method, we return the minimum distance to the origin. If the method should now return a `Point` rather than the distance itself, we rewrite the method to remember `Point nearest` in addition to `double minDistance`; if we were to omit `minDistance`, the distance would have to be recalculated each time, which would waste performance unnecessarily.

com/tutego/exercise/array/MinDistance.java

```java
static Point minDistance2( Point[] points, int size ) {
  Point  nearest=points[ 0 ];
  double minDistance=nearest.distance( 0, 0 );

  for ( int i=1; i<size; i++) {
    double distance=points[ i ].distance( 0, 0 );
    if ( distance<minDistance ) {
      minDistance=distance;
      nearest=points[ i ];
    }
  }
  return nearest;
}
```

Raid the Candy Store and Share Fairly

com/tutego/exercise/array/FairSharing.java

```java
public static int findSplitPoint( int[] values ) {

  if ( values.length<2 )
    return -1;

  int sumLeft=values[ 0 ];

  int sumRight=0;
  for ( int i=1; i<values.length; i++)
    sumRight += values[ i ];
  for ( int splitIndex=1; splitIndex<values.length; splitIndex++) {
    int relativeDifference=relativeDifference( sumLeft, sumRight );

    Logger.getLogger( "MuggingFairly" )
          .info( "splitIndex="+splitIndex
                  +",sum left/right="+sumLeft+"/"+sumRight
                  +",difference="+relativeDifference );

    if ( relativeDifference <= 10 )
      return splitIndex;

    int element=values[ splitIndex ];
    sumLeft  += element;
    sumRight -= element;
  }
  return -1;
}

// https://en.wikipedia.org/wiki/Relative_change_and_difference
private static int relativeDifference( int a, int b ) {
  if ( a ==b ) return 0;
  int absoluteDifference=Math.abs( a - b );
  return (int) (100. * absoluteDifference / Math.max( a, b ));
}
```

The algorithm for the solution can be implemented either iteratively or recursively. However, in this case, the decision has been made to utilize the iterative approach due to its simplicity and ease of comprehension.

Let's start with a simple consideration of how to solve the problem. We could

1. Take an index that divides the array into two halves.
2. Calculate the sum of the right and left parts.
3. Compare them, and if the two sides are approximately equal, end the program with a result.

The index moves from front to back, and the sums are always recalculated. This algorithm is simple, but we have to go over the array several times, so eventually, the runtime is quadratic. This works better.

If we split the array in two and the cursor moves one position to the right, the sum changes according to a simple pattern: what is added to the sum on the left is subtracted on the right. This is the core idea of the solution.

At the beginning of the method, we check if one or no element was passed. If so, there can be no fair division, and we return -1. If the null reference is passed, the program throws a NullPointerException, which is a good reaction.

In the next step, we declare two variables that store the sums of the left and right halves. Initially, the left sum only comprises the first element of the array, while the right sum includes elements from the second position (index 1) through the end.

We will adjust these two variables, sumLeft and sumRight, in the following. The loop runs from the first to the last element. Since we have already completely formed the left and right sum before the loop run, we can now already calculate the relative difference, and if it is <= 10, then we actually already have a result. If the distance between the values was greater, we add to the left element and subtract from the right element. Finally, we go further into the loop, and if at any time the relative difference becomes less than or equal to 10, we jump out with splitIndex, and otherwise the method is terminated with -1.

Draw Mountains

com/tutego/exercise/array/MountainVisualizer.java

```java
private static String mountainChar() { return "*"; }
public static void printMountain( int[] altitudes ) {

  int maxAltitude=altitudes[ 0 ];

  for ( int currentAltitude : altitudes )
    maxAltitude=Math.max( maxAltitude, altitude );
  // include height 0, so it's >= 0
  for ( int height=maxAltitude; height >= 0; height-- ) {
    System.out.print( height+" " );
    for ( int altitude : altitudes )
      System.out.print( altitude == height ? mountainChar() : ' ' );
    System.out.println();
  }
}
```

The printMountain(int[] altitudes) method takes a whole array of altitude information, and for the graphical representation, we need to find the highest value in the first step. This is the task of the first loop, but it must not run until the array has any entries at all. maxAltitude stores the maximum.

The next step is to draw lines. Each line represents a height. The writing of all lines is done by a for loop with a loop counter height. Since it starts with the maximum height, the loop starts with maxAltitude and goes down to 0. The task states that it does not go below zero, which means we do not need to complete a second search for the smallest number.

In the body of the height loop, we first output the height followed by a space. (We write height + " " and not height + ' ', why?) An inner for loop takes care of the line. It runs repeatedly over the height information altitudes passed to the method. For each element in altitudes, we query whether it matches the height height, and if so, we draw the symbol over mountainChar(); otherwise we draw a blank. A blank line is written at the end of the line.

The drawing of the mountain symbol is done by the mountainChar() method; it returns a *. We could have drawn the character directly or referenced it using a constant, but the method is a preparation for the next task ...

Optional Extension

In the first proposed solution, the `mountainChar()` method always returns `*`; if the method is to return other symbols, it needs a bit more context because it must be able to look back and forward. So let's extend the signature: `mountainChar(int[] altitudes, int index)`. The method gets access to the array and to the current position. The call looks like this:

com/tutego/exercise/array/MoreMountainVisualizer.java

```java
for ( int height=maxAltitude; height >= 0; height-- ) {
  System.out.print( height+" " );
  for ( int x=0; x<altitudes.length; x++ )
    System.out.print( altitudes[ x ] == height ?
                      mountainChar( altitudes, x ) : ' ' );
  System.out.println();
}
```

This way, `mountainChar(...)` can decide for itself what the correct symbol is.

com/tutego/exercise/array/MoreMountainVisualizer.java

```java
private static char mountainChar( int[] altitudes, int index ) {
  int previous=index == 0 ? 0 : altitudes[ index - 1 ];
  int current =altitudes[ index ];
  int next    =index<altitudes.length - 1 ? altitudes[ index+1 ] : -1;

  if ( previous<current && current>next )
    return '^';
  if ( current<next )
    return '/';
  if ( current>next )
    return '\\';
  // current == next )
  return '-';
}
```

In the first step, the variables `previous`, `current`, and `next` are initialized with the heights from the array; this way it is possible to look at the height of the current element but also at the height of the predecessor and successor. Before the first element of the array, the height should be 0, as well as after the last element.

Depending on the relations, a choice can be made for the character at the height `current`:

- If `previous` and `next` are lower than `current`, we have a peak and draw a `^`.
- If we are lower than the right neighbor, we are going uphill and draw /.
- If we are higher than the right neighbor, it is going downhill, the symbol is \.
- Otherwise, the right neighbor is at the same height as we are, and this is indicated by -.

Check Mini-Sudoku for Valid Solution

com/tutego/exercise/array/Sudoku3x3Checker.java

```java
final int DIMENSION=3;
for ( int i=1; i <=DIMENSION * DIMENSION; i++ ) {
  boolean found=false;
  matrixLoop:
```

```
  for ( int row=0; row<DIMENSION; row++ ) {
    for ( int col=0; col<DIMENSION; col++ ) {
      int element=array[ row ][ col ];
      if ( element == i ) {
        found=true;
        break matrixLoop;
      }
    }
  }
  if ( !found )
    System.out.printf( "Missing %d%n", i );
}
```

We declare the array for the task with elements in advance. Therefore, we create a variable, DIMENSION, for the dimensions of the array. We assume that the 3×3 array has exactly nine elements.

We want to look at two alternative solutions. If it is necessary to test whether the numbers 1 to 9 occur in the two-dimensional array, a loop can produce the values from 1 to 9, and then it is possible to test whether each of these numbers occurs in the two-dimensional array. To accomplish this, we create a boolean variable found, which we initialize with false at the beginning and set to true whenever the element occurs in the array; in that case, we can also cancel the loops. In principle, we could, of course, continue searching, but this is unnecessary. To break the loop, we have to resort to a special construction in Java, the jump labels. If we simply use break in the condition statement, it will terminate the innermost loop, but not the outer loop. With a jump label, we can also exit the outer loop with break. At the end of the loops, we query the found flag, and if the flag is still false because it was not set to true in the condition statement, the number is missing. We print it out.

The disadvantage of the solution is the relatively high execution time; moreover, a break with the label makes the code unreadable and harder to understand. We have to run the 3×3 array nine times. This works better. However, we have to remember whether we have seen a number before or not.

com/tutego/exercise/array/Sudoku3x3Checker.java

```
boolean[] numberExisted=new boolean[ DIMENSION * DIMENSION ];

for ( int row=0; row<DIMENSION; row++ ) {
  for ( int col=0; col<DIMENSION; col++ ) {
    int element=array[ row ][ col ];
    if ( element >= 1 && element <= DIMENSION * DIMENSION )
      numberExisted[ element - 1 ]=true;
  }
}

for ( int i=0; i<numberExisted.length; i++ ) {
  boolean found=numberExisted[ i ];
  if ( !found )
    System.out.printf( "Missing %d%n", i+1 );
}
```

The second solution declares a boolean array numberExisted as memory. The handy thing about Sudoku numbers is that they range from 1 to 9, so we can easily map that to index 0 to 8. When we get a number from the array and compute an index for the array from it, we need to guard against getting an ArrayIndexOutOfBoundsException. Therefore, we check before if the number element is in the right range. If it is, then we set the value true on the position element - 1.

After the single pass, we examine the array. If we find a position that has never been written to, we know that the number is missing. Whether a position in the array has been written to more than once is not relevant.

Enlarge Image

com/tutego/exercise/array/ArrayMagnifier.java

```java
static int[][] magnify( int[][] array, int factor ) {
  int originalWidth = array[ 0 ].length;
  int originalHeight = array.length;
  int magnifiedWidth = originalWidth * factor;
  int magnifiedHeight = originalHeight * factor;

  int[][] magnifiedArray = new int[ magnifiedHeight ][ magnifiedWidth ];

  for ( int row = 0; row < magnifiedHeight; row++ )
    for ( int col = 0; col < magnifiedWidth; col++ )
      magnifiedArray[ row ][ col ] = array[ row / factor ][ col / factor ];

  return magnifiedArray;
}
```

To improve clarity, new variables are declared at the beginning of the method. These variables store the width and height of both the two-dimensional original array and the array being created. The subsequent step involves constructing a new two-dimensional array that is larger in width and height by a factor of factor compared to the old array.

The main task is performed by the two nested loops. In the first outer loop, we use row to loop overall new rows. Since two-dimensional arrays are nothing more than arrays within arrays, the outer array holds all the references to the inner arrays, the rows. The inner loop, controlled by the counter col then run from 0 up to the width of the current row, handling each column in the row.

The interesting part is in the inner loop. We have the variables row and col in the value ranges of the new enlarged two-dimensional array. We need to initialize the position magnifiedArray[row] [col]. For this, we get the values from the old small array. We calculate the position down with row / factor for the row and col / factor for the column. Remember: row goes from 0 to height * factor and col to width * factor. The row / factor and col / factor divisions divide integers, and the result is again an integer; this has the effect of getting the same number out of the small source array several times.

Create SVG Polygons with Variable Number of Coordinates

com/tutego/exercise/array/SvgVarargPolygon.java

```java
/**
 * Prints an SVG polygon. Example output:
 * <pre>
 * <polygon points="200,10 250,190 160,210 " />
 * </pre>
 * @param points of the SVG polygon.
 */
public static void printSvgPolygon( int... points ) {

  if ( points.length % 2 == 1 )
    throw new IllegalArgumentException(
      "Array has an odd number of arguments: "+points.length );

  System.out.print( "<polygon points=\"" );
```

```
for ( int i=0; i<points.length; i += 2 )
    System.out.printf( "%d,%d ", points[ i ], points[ i+1 ] );

System.out.println( "\" />" );
}
```

Two errors may occur:

1. In a vararg, the compiler itself builds an array from the passed arguments, but we can also pass a reference to an array. Since references can be `null`, there could be a call to `printSvgPolygon(null)`. Passing `null.length` will automatically lead to a `NullPointerException`.
2. When `printSvgPolygon()` is called, the compiler builds an empty array; this contains no elements, which is fine in principle for our method. But there is another requirement for the length: the method itself always expects pairs of x and y coordinates. It would be an error to pass only one coordinate and not two. Unfortunately, the compiler can't test something like that, you can't make any requests on the number of varargs like: "at most 102 elements", "the number of elements must be divisible by 10", etc. We have no choice but to perform the test at runtime. We can easily detect the error by checking whether the number of elements in the array is even or odd. If the number is even, pairs were always passed, for x and y. If the number is odd, a coordinate is missing. We penalize erroneous calls with an `IllegalArgumentException`. It would still be worth considering making two condition statements out of the two checks, and then including the number of elements in the exception message in the case of the odd passing.

Generating the output consists of three parts:

1. In the first part, the prologue, we set the start tag for the polygon.
2. In the second part, a loop runs over all the elements of the array and always picks out two elements that come to the console separated by commas—there is a space after the pair. Since we always pick two elements from the array at a time, the index is incremented by 2 in the `for` loop's increment expression. Since the number of elements in the array is even, there won't be any `ArrayIndexOutOfBoundsExcepion`.
3. The method ends with the epilogue, closing the tag.

Check for Approval

com/tutego/exercise/array/AllTrue.java

```java
private static boolean allTrue( boolean first, boolean... remaining ) {

    for ( boolean b : remaining )
        if ( b == false )
            return false;

    return first;
}
```

With variable argument lists, it is not possible to expect a minimum number of arguments. The solution to this problem is to introduce a minimum number of fixed parameters and then use a vararg for the rest at the end.

The method has two paths that return `true` or `false`:

1. First, we traverse the array. If one of the `boolean` values in the array is `false`, we can exit the method directly with `return false`. If the array is empty, nothing happens. There are authors who do not test `boolean` values with `== false` but negate the expression, but I think that `if ( b == false )` reads better than `if ( !b )`; it also depends on the variable name. It may be that `null` was passed as an argument, in which case the enhanced `for` loop will throw a `NullPointerException`, which is intentional.
2. If the loop does not terminate, all elements in the array must have been `true`, and the first parameter `first` decides the result.

Help, Tetraphobia! Put All Fours Last

com/tutego/exercise/array/Tetraphobia.java

```java
private static boolean numberContainsNoFour( int number ) {
  return !String.valueOf( number ).contains( "4" );
}

public static int[] fourLast( int... numbers ) {

  if ( numbers.length<2 )
    return numbers;

  for ( int startIndex=0; startIndex<numbers.length; startIndex++) {

    if ( numberContainsNoFour( numbers[ startIndex ] ) )
      continue;

    // from right to left search the first number without a 4
    for ( int endIndex=numbers.length - 1;
          endIndex>startIndex; endIndex-- ) {
      if ( numberContainsNoFour( numbers[ endIndex ] ) ) {
        // Swap number at startIndex (with '4') and
        // number at endIndex (without '4')
        int swap=numbers[ startIndex ];
        numbers[ startIndex ]=numbers[ endIndex ];
        numbers[ endIndex ]=swap;
      }
    }
  }
  return numbers;
}
```

For our solution, in addition to the desired `fourLast(...)` method, we write an additional private method `boolean numberContainsNoFour(int)`, which answers whether the number passed does not contains a 4. In the implementation, we make it simple and convert the number to a string, and `contains(String)` checks whether the string `"4"` is in the string representation. We could have done the check numerically, of course, but that would have been much more complicated. We would always have to divide that number by 10 and then look at the remainder and test if it is 4. That would require more code than just this one one-liner.

The method `fourLast(…)` gets passed an array, which again could be `null` and in such a case lead to a `NullPointerException` by `numbers.length`. Moreover, the array could contain only one element, in which case we directly return the passed array to the caller.

Our algorithm is implemented in a simple way: we run in a loop from left to right, and when we find something containing a 4, we run in a second loop from right to left, looking for the first free space without a 4. Then, we swap the contents of the array.

The proposed solution is not quite optimal and should be improved by the readers.

1. The first thing that should be improved is the loop with `startIndex` that always runs to `numbers.length`. This is unnecessary because if the inner loop should find a number with a 4, then this number will go to the back, and we can subtract one from the length because we don't have to look at the last element.
2. Second, the inner loop is not optimal because it always starts from right to left, looking for the first number without a 4. However, the block of fours only grows to the left, so we could remember in a second variable where we placed our last 4. If the inner loop runs again, we could continue at this position and do not have to find it again from the right.
3. Third, we can combine the two improvements. In the case where there is no swap in the inner loop, we would be done.

Quiz: Copy Arrays

The `arraycopy(…)` method can be used to move ranges in an array or copy parts of an array to another array. Let's look from the Javadoc at the parameter variables of `arraycopy(…)`, which are self-explanatory:

```
static void arraycopy(Object src, int srcPos, Object dest, int destPos, int
length).
```

In our case, we do not move something in an array, but copy parts of an array twice into a new array. `hooey` is the source and `shuck` the destination. The following results if the constants are set and the words `hooey` and `shuck` are renamed:

```
int[] src={1, 2, 3, 4 };
int[] dest=new int[ 3 ];
System.arraycopy( src, 0, dest, 0, 2 );
System.arraycopy( src, 3, dest, 2, 1 );
```

The result is [1, 2, 4], i.e., a new array with element 3 missing at index 2 (bushwa). The first copy operation transfers from the source starting at the first location 0 to the new array starting at location 0, a total of 2 elements. The second copy operation moves from location 3 (so skips location 2) everything to the end of the destination array starting from location 2. The number of copied elements is one.

With the nonsensical variable names, it should also have become clear that clean code—here variable identifiers—saves human processing time and reduces errors.

Quiz: Compare Arrays

The `==` operator checks whether the objects referenced by the two reference variables are identical. The two variables `array1` and `array2` do not because they are two completely separate objects in memory. Therefore, the output will be `false`.

Arrays are objects, and as objects, they have all the methods that the base type java.lang.Object also provides. However, we can't do anything with any of these methods, which we quickly notice when we call the toString() method on an array object. The equals(...) method of an array comes from Object, and there we have an identity comparison, which, as explained in the first point, results in the output false.

To compare arrays, we are quite right with the class java.util.Arrays and the method equals(...). In general, we can compare arrays with this method, but our two arrays have a little peculiarity: they contain strings and an inner array with integers. If this sub-referenced array were not present, true would indeed appear in this output. However, Array.equals(...) works flat, meaning that the referenced inner array would have to be identical. But since this integer array is also a new array in each case, the two references to the integer array are not equal and thus Array.equals(...) returns false on our array.

Only with the method Array.deepEquals(...) will true appear on the screen. deepEquals(...) also keeps track of the referenced sub-arrays and looks to see if the values are equivalent. The identity of the sub-arrays is not essential for deepEquals(...). The two integer arrays are equivalent, and therefore the return value of deepEquals(...) is true.

Character and String Processing

5

For storing characters and strings, Java provides the types char, Character, String, and StringBuilder. The use of the data types must be practiced because each type has its justification. The exercises help the readers to understand the advantages and disadvantages of each data type.

Prerequisites

- Be able to use API of String and StringBuilder safely,
- Recognize when String and StringBuilder is more appropriate,

Data types used in this chapter:

- java.lang.Character
- java.lang.String
- java.lang.StringBuilder

THE STRING CLASS AND ITS MEMBERS

String is not only a data type that stands for immutable strings, but the class also provides many methods. If you know the methods and how to use them, you can save yourself a lot of work.

Quiz: Is String a Built-In Keyword? ★

Java has built-in data types, including int, double, boolean. Is String also a primitive built-in data type? Is String a keyword in Java?

Building HTML Elements with Simple Concatenation ★

As a reminder, tags are used in HTML for markup, an example is Emphasized and Italics.
Task:

1. Write a new method htmlElement(String tag, String body) that encloses a string body with a start and end tag tag and returns it as a new String. There is extra handling:
   - If tag is equal to null or empty (""), then only the body is considered and no start-end tags are written.
   - If body is equal to null, then it is considered like a passed empty string.

DOI: 10.1201/9781003454502-6

2. Write two new methods, `strong(String)` and `emphasized(String)` that work in the background with `htmlElement(...)` and create a `<strong>` and `<em>`, respectively.

Example:

- `htmlElement( "strong", "strong is bold" )` → `"<strong>strong is bold</strong>"`.
- `strong( emphasized( "strong+emphasized" )` → `"<strong><em>strong+emphasized</em></strong>"`.
- `htmlElement( "span", null )` → `"<span></span>"`.
- `htmlElement( "", "no" )` → `"no"`.
- `htmlElement( null, "not strong" )` → `"not strong"`.
- `htmlElement( null, null )` → `""`.

Note: There are several restrictions on tag names that a good program could check. For example, tag names may only contain the digits 0–9 and upper and lower case letters. These cases can be ignored.

Check Safe Transmission by Doubling Characters ★

Bamboo Blobfish uses a type-print telegraph to communicate important messages to Bonny Brain. Since every character is crucial, Bamboo sends each character twice in a row for safety.

Task:

- Write a method `int isEveryCharacterTwice(String)` that checks if each character in the string occurs twice in a row.
  - If the number of symbols is odd, the message is wrong and the method returns 0.
  - If each character occurs twice, the answer is any positive number. - If a character does not occur twice in a row, the method returns the position with the first wrong digit but negated it.

Examples:

- `isEveryCharacterTwice("jjoovveellyynn")` → `1`.
- `isEveryCharacterTwice("ccapptttaaiinn")` → `-3`.
- `isEveryCharacterTwice("222")` → `0`.
- `isEveryCharacterTwice(null)` → `NullPointerException`.

The fact that a negative index marks certain locations can also be found in the Java library. The `Arrays` class provides `binarySearch(…)`, which searches for something in a sorted array, and if the method finds the element, returns the location; if `binarySearch(…)` does not find the entry, it returns the negated position where the element could be inserted.

Swap Y and Z ★

Captain CiaoCiao types a longer text on his keyboard, and quite late he notices that instead of the English keyboard layout, the German one is activated. Now "y" and "z", or "Y" and "Z" are swapped. The text has to be corrected.

Task:

1. Create a new class `YZswapper`.
2. Set a new static method `void printSwappedYZ(String string)`, which prints a given `string` to the screen, but prints the letter "y" as "z", "z" as "y", "Y" as "Z" and "Z" as "Y". The point is not to return a string from the method!
3. Do not write only one variant, but try to program at least two variants. There is, for example, the possibility to check the characters with `if-else` or with `switch-case`.

Examples:

- `printSwappedYZ("yootaxz")` gives the output `zootaxy` on the screen and
- `printSwappedYZ("yanthoxzl")` gives the output `zanthoxyl`.

Give Defiant Answers ★

Tony the Defiant is responsible for Captain CiaoCiao's black market activities, but he gets caught and questioned by the police. To annoy the cops, he repeats everything they say and puts a "No idea!" at the end. If the policeman asks, "Where is the illegal whiskey distillery?", Tony says, "Where is the illegal whiskey distillery? No idea!"

Task:

1. Create a new class, and ask for input from the command line.
2. Depending on the input, distinguish three cases:

   - If the input ends with a ?, then output to the screen whatever is coming from the input, but append " No idea!" at the end.
   - If no question is asked by the police—the input does not end with ?
   - —Tony the Defiant keeps his mouth shut completely.
   - If the input is "No idea!", and regardless of the case, Tony defiantly replies "Aye!".

Quiz: String Comparisons with == and Equals(...) ★

Strings are objects, and therefore there are two ways to compare them:

- By comparing the references via ==.
- Using the method equals(Object), which is typical for objects.

What difference does this make?

Quiz: Is Equals(...) Symmetric? ★

Assuming s is a string: is there a difference between s.equals("tutego") and "tutego".equals(s)?

Test Strings for Palindrome Property ★

A palindrome is a word that reads the same from the front as from the back, such as "Otto" or even "121".

The fact that such words and even sentences exist at all amuses Captain CiaoCiao since he can entertain the audience with it. However, he is always presented with strings that are not palindromes. Therefore, all words must be tested beforehand.

Task:

- Write a Java program that examines whether a string is a palindrome.
  - Create a new class PalindromeTester.
  - Implement a static method boolean isPalindrome(String s).
  - Enhance the program with a class method boolean isPalindromeIgnoring-Case(String s), so that the test becomes case-insensitive.
  - Now, all characters that are not letters or digits should also be ignored. Character.isLetterOrDigit(char) helps to detect this. This can be used to check sentences like A man a plan a canal Panama or Pepe in Tahiti never has pep or Be mean - always be mean! Let's call the method isPalindromeIgnoringNonLettersAndDigits(String).

Check if Captain CiaoCiao is in the Middle ★

Captain CiaoCiao is the center of the world, so he expects to be in the center in all texts as well.

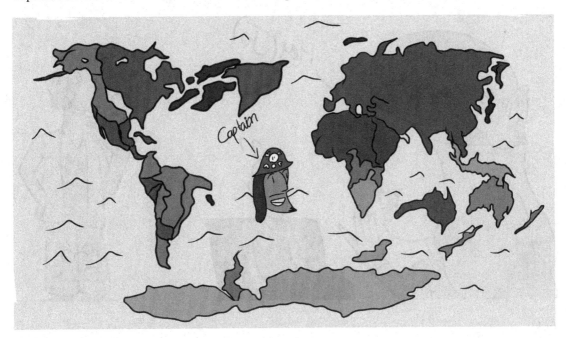

Task:

- Write a method boolean isCiaoCiaoInMiddle(String) that returns true if the string "CiaoCiao" is in the middle.

Examples:

- isCiaoCiaoInMiddle("CiaoCiao") → true.
- isCiaoCiaoInMiddle("!CiaoCiao!") → true.
- isCiaoCiaoInMiddle("SupaCiaoCiaoCute") → true.
- isCiaoCiaoInMiddle("x! _ CiaoCiaoabc") → true.
- isCiaoCiaoInMiddle("\tCiaoCiao ") → true.
- isCiaoCiaoInMiddle("BambooCiaoCiaoBlop") → false.
- isCiaoCiaoInMiddle("Bernie und Ert") → false.

Find the Shortest Name in the Array ★

Bonny Brain uses only the shortest call name for a person.

Task:

- Write a method `String shortestName(String... names)` that returns the shortest partial string of all full names. The string can also contain exactly one space if the name is composed of parts. In other words, there are strings with one name or strings with two names.
- If there are no names, the answer is an empty string.
- The vararg array must not be `null`, and no string in the array must be `null`.

Example:

- `shortestName("Albert Tross", "Blowfish", "Nick Olaus", "Jo Ker")` → `"Jo"`.

Count String Occurrences ★

Captain CiaoCiao eliminated the developer Dev David in a careless action. He was in the process of writing a method; the Javadoc is ready, but the implementation is missing.

```
/**
 *Counts how many times the substring appears in the larger string.
 *
 *A {@code null} or empty ("") String input returns {@code 0}.
 *
 * <pre>
 *StringUtils.countMatches(null, *)    = 0
 *StringUtils.countMatches("", *)      = 0
 *StringUtils.countMatches("abba", null) = 0
 *StringUtils.countMatches("abba", "")   = 0
```

```
* StringUtils.countMatches("abba", "a")  =2
* StringUtils.countMatches("aaaa", "aa") =2
* StringUtils.countMatches("abba", "ab") =1
* StringUtils.countMatches("abba", "xxx")=0
* </pre>
*
* @param string  the String to check maybe null
* @param other   the substring to count maybe null
* @return the number of occurrences, 0 if either String is {@code null}
*/
public static int countMatches( String string, String other ) { return null; }
```

Note: The * in the Javadoc symbolizes an arbitrary argument.

Task:

- Implement the method.

Determine the Larger Crew Size ★

Bonny Brain is studying old logbooks that show the strength of her crew and captured ships:

```
|-|||
|-||
|||-|||
|||||-||
```

Each crew member is symbolized by a dash; a minus sign separates the crew size. On the left is the number of people on their ship, on the right is the number on the raided ship.

Task:

- The dashes are hard to read for Bonny Brain. Write a program that makes the coding clear:
  ```
  |-||    => Raided ship had a larger crew, difference 2
  |-||    => Raided ship had a larger crew, difference 1
  ||-||   => Ships had the same crew size
  |||||-|| => Pirate ship had a larger crew, difference 3
  ```

Build Diamonds ★★

Captain CiaoCiao likes diamonds, the bigger, the better.

Task:

- Write a program that generates the following output:
  ```
     A
    ABA
   ABCBA
  ABCDCBA
   ABCBA
    ABA
     A
  ```
  Using a prompt on the console, it should be possible to specify the maximum width of the diamond. In our example, this is 7—the length of the string ABCDCBA. The only input for the width that can be achieved with strings of ascending and descending uppercase letters should be accepted, i.e., at most the length of ABCDEFGHIJKLMNOPQRSTUVWXYZYXWVU...BA.

Check for a Good Password ★

All the dirty secrets are encrypted by Captain CiaoCiao, but too often his password was too simple and was guessed. He has learned that a secure password is important for his business, but he can't quite remember the rules: a good password has a certain length, contains special characters, etc.

Task:

1. Create a new class PasswordTester.
2. Write a method isGoodPassword(String) that tests some criteria. The method should return false if the password is weak, and true if the password has a proper syntax. If a test fails, a message should appear via System.err and no further checks should take place.

Bake Peanut Butter Cookies ★★

Just before the holiday, the crew gathers around Captain CiaoCiao to bake peanut butter cookies. The amateur bakers bring peanut butter, sugar, or eggs. When they arrive, they sit down at a table one by one and want to start baking.

Given is a list of all the ingredients that the amateur bakers have brought. The list is represented as a string, where P stands for peanut butter, S for sugar, and E for egg. The string could be: PSESEPESP or also PPPEEESSS.

As long as there are three amateur bakers sitting next to each other and have peanut butter, sugar, and eggs, baking can be carried out regardless of the order of the ingredients.

Task:

- Determine how many times peanut butter cookies can be baked, that is, the three ingredients come together directly next to each other in any order.
- Amateur bakers who have failed to listen carefully may bring entirely different ingredients, such as rum, licorice, or marinated eel, which cannot be used to bake peanut butter cookies.

Examples:

- "PSESEPESP" → 3
- "PPPEEESSS" → 0
- "SEPEPLSEE" → 1

Calculate Sum of Digits ★

As Bonny Brain is often responsible for issuing payments and is concerned that someone may alter the amounts, she employs a trick whereby she sends the cross sum along with the amount through a separate channel.

The cross sum of a number is formed by adding each digit of the number. For example, if the number is 10938, the cross sum is $1 + 0 + 9 + 3 + 8 = 21$.

Task:

1. Create a new class `SumOfTheDigits`.
2. Write a class method `int digitSum(long value)` that calculates the cross sum of a number.
3. Add an overloaded class method `int digitSum(String value)` that takes the digits in a string.

Which method is easier to implement? Which method should call the other as a subroutine?

Decolumnize Texts ★★

Captain CiaoCiao is scanning old logbooks, but they were originally in columns. After OCR text recognition, the columns are preserved.

Since this is hard to read, the two columns should be recognized and translated into a regular continuous text without columns.

Task:

- Write a method `decolumnize(String)` that searches for the column and returns a text with one column from a text with two columns.

    Example:

```
I'm dishonest, and a to watch out for,
dishonest man you    because you can
can always trust to  never predict when
be dishonest.        they're going to do
Honestly, it's the   something incredibly
honest ones you want stupid.
```

→

```
I'm dishonest, and a
dishonest man you
can always trust to
be dishonest.
Honestly, it's the
honest ones you want
to watch out for,
because you can
never predict when
they're going to do
something incredibly
stupid.
```

Each column is separated by at least one space. Note that the right and left columns can have incomplete blank lines!

Draw a Meadow with Favorite Flowers ★★

Captain CiaoCiao wants to beautify his ship and decorate it with flowers. He finds a graphic by Joan G. Stark to use as a template and thinks about how to tell the painters and decorators what patterns he wants in the cabin.

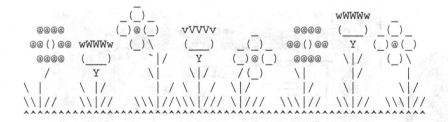

Task:

1. Copy the flowers into a string. Tip: Create a string like `String flower="";`, put the flower string on the clipboard, and paste it between the quotes in the IDE; IntelliJ and Eclipse will then independently encode the special characters like \ and \n. Java text blocks can also be used effectively for this multiline string."

2. There are eight kinds of flowers, and we can number them from 1 to 8. We encode the order as a string, for example, `"12345678"`. It should now be possible to change the order and have flowers appear more than once, for example, by encoding `"8383765432"`. If an identifier is wrong, the first flower will always appear automatically for it.

Examples:

- `"838"` leads to

```
  _       _(_)_        _
 _(_)_   (_)@(_)    _(_)_
(_)@(_)   (_)\     (_)@(_)
 (_)\      `|/      (_)\
  |         \|        |
  \|/       | /      \|/
  \\\|/    \\\|//   \\\|/
^^^^^^^^^^^^^^^^^^^^^^^^^^
```

- `"ABC9"` leads to

```
 @@@@    @@@@    @@@@    @@@@
@@()@@  @@()@@  @@()@@  @@()@@
 @@@@    @@@@    @@@@    @@@@
  /       /       /       /
 \ |     \ |     \ |     \ |
 \\|//   \\|//   \\|//   \\|//
^^^^^^^^^^^^^^^^^^^^^^^^^^^^^^^
```

Hold the locations for the transition between the flowers in an array.

Detect Repetitions ★★★

Captain CiaoCiao flips through a book and finds patterns of the sort ✿❀✿❀✿❀✿❀✿❀✿❀✿❀✿❀. How reassuring for him. He wants to make stamps for printing, so he can print such sequences of patterns himself. Of course, the cost should be reduced, but the stamp itself should not contain any repetitions of symbols. For a given pattern sequence, a program needs to be developed that determines the minimum sequence of symbols that need to be on the stamp.

Task:

- Write a method `String repeatingStrings(String)` that returns the repeating string in case of repetition, otherwise `null` if no substring repeats.

Examples:

- `repeatingStrings("✿✿✿")` returns `"✿"`.
- `repeatingStrings("✿❀"+"✿❀"+"✿❀")` returns `"✿❀"`.
- `repeatingStrings("Ciao"+"Ciao")` returns `"Ciao"`.
- `repeatingStrings("Captain CiaoCiaoCaptain CiaoCiao")` returns `"Captain CiaoCiao"`.
- `repeatingStrings("○◐◑●")` returns `null`.
- `repeatingStrings("CaptainCiaoCiaoCaptain")` return `null`.
- `repeatingStrings("✿")` returns `null`.
- `repeatingStrings("")` return `null`.
- `repeatingStrings(null)` return `null`.

Note: `repeatingStrings(…)` should return the shortest repeating string.

Constrain Line Boundaries and Wrap Lines ★★

Bonny Brain is switching to carrier pigeons for communication, and there isn't too much space on the paper. Now all texts must be reduced in width.

Task:

- Write a class WordWrap with a static method String wrap(String string, int width) that splits a string without line breaks into small substrings of maximum width width and returns them separated by \n. Inside words—and punctuation marks belong to the word—should not be forcibly wrapped!

Example:

- The call to

```
String s="Live now; make now always the most precious time. "
        +"Now will never come again.";
System.out.println( wrap( s, 10 ) );
```

returns the following output with a maximum line length of 30:

```
Live now; make now always the
most precious time. Now will
never come again.
```

Quiz: How Many String Objects? ★

How many string objects are present in the following program code?

```
String str1="tutego";
String str2=new String( "tutego" );
String str3="tutego";
String str4=new String( "tutego" );
```

Test If the Fruit Is Wrapped in Chocolate ★★

Captain CiaoCiao likes fruit skewers covered in chocolate. Sara gets the job of frosting the fruit, making different layers of dark and white chocolate.

Bambi checks to make sure the layers are correct. If she sees dhFhd, she knows that the fruit F got first a layer of white chocolate, then a layer of dark chocolate. At dhhd the fruit is missing, and this does not match Captain CiaoCiao's expectation. At ddhFh the layer is broken, which is also not right. And at F, the chocolate is completely missing, what a disappointment!

Task:

- Write a recursive method checkChocolate(String) that checks if the string is symmetric, that is, on the left and the right is the same type of chocolate, and in the middle is the fruit F.

From Top to Bottom, from Left to Right ★★★

In a cave Bonny Brain discovers a text, however, the text does not run from left to right, but is written from top to bottom.

```
s u
ey!
ao
```

Written vertically, this is the string sea you!—and it's much easier to read!

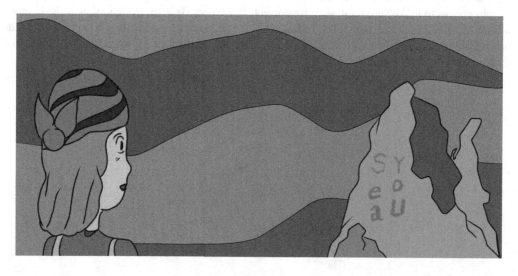

Task:

- Write a method `printVerticalToHorizontalWriting(String)` that returns a string to its horizontal position and prints it. The argument is a string in which line feeds separate the lines.

Example:

- Let's stick with the string from above:

  ```
  String s="s u\ney!\nao ";
  printVerticalToHorizontalWriting( s );
  ```

  The output on the screen will be `sea you!`.

Three important assumptions should hold:

1. Lines are separated only with \n.
2. Each line is the same length; for example, the last line has space so that all lines are three characters (in this example) long (not counting line breaks).
3. There is no \n at the end of the string.

DYNAMIC STRINGS WITH STRINGBUILDER

While `String` objects are immutable, objects of `java.lang.StringBuilder` can be modified. The same is true for `StringBuffer`, but this class is API-like and not relevant for the exercises.

Fill Strings ★

Captain CiaoCiao loves freedom, and spacing is essential to him. Even with texts, he thinks, the letters could have a little more spacing.

Task:

- Write a method mix(String, String) that spreads a string and puts fill characters between all characters.
- The parameters may be null.

Examples:

- mix("We're out of rum!", "-") → "W-e-'-r-e- -o-u-t- -o-f- -r-u-m-!"
- mix("Blimey", "👻") → "B👻l👻i👻m👻e👻y"
- mix("HI", "♥") → "H♥I"
- mix("♥", "!!") → "♥"
- mix("", "👻") → ""

Practicing the Alphabet with a Parrot ★

Captain CiaoCiao is teaching his parrot the alphabet. To save himself time and effort, he uses a program that generates the alphabet for him.

Given is the following method:

```java
static String abcz() {
  String result;
  result = "ABCDEFGHIJKLMNOPQRSTUVWXYZ";
  return result;
}
```

The method returns a string with all characters in the alphabet from 'A' to 'Z'. So Captain CiaoCiao can copy the string to an input field at https://ttsreader.com/de/ and let it read aloud. However, there must then be spaces between the letters to make the sound better.

The method is performant in its task, but not very flexible, for example, when it comes to generating only certain ranges, such as from '0' to '9'. Because the parrot can already do ABC very well, but from G to Z it gets tough.

Task:

- Change the method abcz() so that the String is dynamically generated via a loop.
- Add a method String abcz(char start, char end) that generates a string with all symbols between the start character start and the end character end; the end character is included and belongs to the string.
- Write a method String abcz(char start, int length) which returns length characters starting from start. Can one of the methods be mapped to the other?
- Consider how to handle incorrect parameters, such as when the end index is before the start index.

The primitive data type char is nothing more than a numeric positive data type that can be converted to the data type int. Consequently, we can calculate with a char, and if we take the letter 'A' and add 1 to it, we come out with 'B'.

Quiz: Lightly Attached ★

If you want to build strings dynamically, you have two options in Java:

1. via the class String and the String concatenation with +.
2. via StringBuilder (we do not want to explicitly mention StringBuffer here—the two classes are API-identical).

In code:

```
String s="";
s += "Ay ";
s += "Captain";

StringBuilder sb=new StringBuilder();
sb.append( "Ay " ).append( "Captain" );
String t=sb.toString();
```

How do the two solutions differ? How many objects are generated?

Convert Number to Textual Unary Encoding ★

Captain CiaoCiao is worried about the safety of his crew, and therefore he wants to disguise the amount of loot from the raids. Only two symbols are supposed to be used for this purpose.

The *unary encoding* represents a natural number *n* as follows:

N	UNARY ENCODING
0	0
1	10
2	110
3	1110
4	11110

A positive integer *n* is represented by *n* ones followed by a zero. By the way, a code of this kind is called *prefix-free* because no word is the prefix of another word. In the encoding, we could also swap 0s and 1s without any problem, and the prefix characteristic does not change.

Unary encoding results in codes of different lengths.

Task:

- Write a method `String encode(int... values)` that creates a string from a vararg array with integers, in which all unary encoded values from the array are concatenated.
- Add a method `int[] decode(String value)` that turns a unary encoded string back into an `int` array.

Example:

- `encode( 0, 1, 2, 3, 0, 1 )` → `"0101101110010"`
- `encode( 0, 0, 0 )` → `"0000"`
- `encode()` → `""`
- `Arrays.toString( decode("0101101110010") )` → `[0, 1, 2, 3, 0, 1]`

Lose Weight by Moving Digits ★

Bonny Brain has noticed that it's great to cheat on freight charges. The people in charge in the office often forget the exact weight, but they can remember the occurring digits perfectly, and it is not noticed if at most two digits are swapped. Bonny Brain uses this to its advantage by putting the smallest digit in the number forward to achieve a smaller weight, but 0 must be ignored, otherwise the length of the number changes, and this is noticeable.

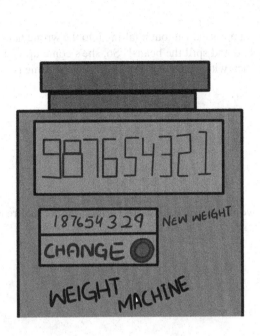

Task:

- Write a method `int cheatedWeight(int weight)` that does exactly this transformation.

Examples:

- `cheatedWeight(0)` → 0
- `cheatedWeight(1234)` → 1234
- `cheatedWeight(4321)` → 1324
- `cheatedWeight(100)` → 100
- `cheatedWeight(987654321)` → 187654329

Remove Vowels ★

Captain CiaoCiao is spitting out his memoir faster than a cannonball, and poor Kiko Kokopu can't keep up with the note-taking. What if we just leave out all the boring old vowels? A wise linguist once claimed that even without the A, E, I, O, U's, a text can still be understood. Common vowel letters are: A, E, I, O, U. Is it true what the scientists say and can we understand this captain's salty tale without any vowels?
Task:

1. Create a new class `RemoveVowel`.
2. Write a class method `String removeVowels(String string)` that removes the vowel letters from a passed `String`.
3. Solve the task with at least two different variants.

Examples:

- `"Hello Javanese"` → `"Hll Jvnsn"`.
- `"BE NICE"` → `"B NC"`.

Don't Shoot the Messenger ★

Bonny Brain is cooking up a devious plan to send a secret message without it falling into the wrong hands. She's so paranoid that the messenger might get ambushed and spill the beans! So, she's come up with a cunning scheme—she's sending multiple messengers, each with a part of the message. The scheme is like this:

- A text is broken down into letters.
- Messenger 1 gets the 1st letter.
- Messenger 2 gets the 2nd letter.
- Messenger 1 gets the 3rd letter.
- Messenger 2 gets the 4th letter.

The recipient of the message must now wait for the two messengers: know the original order and reassemble the message.

Task:

- Write a method `String joinSplitMessages(String...)` that takes any number of the split messages and returns the assembled string.
- If message parts are missing, this should not cause an error.

Examples:

- `joinSplitMessages("Hoy", "ok")` → `"Hooky"`.
- `joinSplitMessages("Hooky")` → `"Hooky"`.
- `joinSplitMessages("Hk", "oy", "o")` → `"Hooky"`.
- `joinSplitMessages("H", "", "ooky")` → `"Hooky"`.

Compress Repeated Spaces ★★

Bubbles listens in on a conversation for Captain CiaoCiao and then transcribes it. But because she's so busy munching on peanuts that she accidentally jams the space bar on her transcription machine! Before she knows it, spaces start doubling up. Poor Bubbles, she can't give the captain a garbled message like this.

Task:

- Write a static method `StringBuilder compressSpace(StringBuilder string)` that merges more than two spaces in the passed `string` into one space.
- The passed `string` should be returned with `return string;` the change should be done directly at `StringBuilder`.

Example:

- `"Will  you  shut  up,  man!  This  is  the  way!"` → `"Will you shut up, man! This is the way!"`

Insert and Remove Crackles and Pops ★

Messages over the radio often have crackling, which is distracting Captain CiaoCiao.

Task:

- Write two methods:
  - `String crackle(String)` should insert "♫CRACK♪" at arbitrary intervals and return the crackle string.
  - `String decrackle(String)` shall remove the crackle again.

Split CamelCase Strings ★

To save volume when transmitting text by telegraph, Funker Frogfish uses a trick: he capitalizes the next character after space and then deletes the space. `ciao  ciao` becomes `ciaoCiao`. If the next character is already an uppercase letter, only space is removed, thus `Ciao  Ciao` becomes `CiaoCiao`. Since the uppercase letters within the series of lowercase letters look like humps, the spelling was named CamelCase.

Captain CiaoCiao receives the strings, but it is hard to read such a text.

Task:

- Write a new method `String camelCaseSplitter(String)` that separates all CamelCase segments again.

Examples:

- `camelCaseSplitter("List")` → `"List"`.
- `camelCaseSplitter("CiaoCiao")` → `"Ciao Ciao"`.
- `camelCaseSplitter("numberOfElements")` → `"number Of Elements"`.
- `camelCaseSplitter("CiaoCiaoCAPTAIN")` → `"Ciao Ciao CAPTAIN"`.

If words are completely in uppercase, as in the last case, only the change between lowercase and uppercase applies.

Underline Words ★★

Sporadically, Bonny Brain has to call the crew's attention to rules. She does this by writing a message and underlining the important words. Bonny Brain has underlined the word "treasure" in the following message:

```
There is more treasure in books than in all the pirates' loot on Treasure
Island
              --------  --------
```

Task:

1. Create a new class `PrintUnderline`.
2. Write a new static method `printUnderline(String string, String search)` that underlines each string `search` in `string` as shown in the example above. Keep in mind that `search` can occur more than once in the string or not at all.
3. The case of the search string should not matter, as also shown in the example.

Implement Caesar Encryption ★★★

Captain CiaoCiao discovered the ancient art of encryption that is supposed to have already been used by Gaius Julius Caesar. The captain is so impressed by the Roman general that he's decided to use the same encryption method for his own texts. But can he really outsmart his enemies with this ancient code?

The *Caesar encryption* involves shifting each character three positions in the alphabet. For instance, A is replaced by D, B by E, and so on. Once the end of the alphabet is reached, the sequence starts over, resulting in X becoming A, Y becoming B, and Z becoming C.

Task:

1. Create a new class `Caesar`.
2. Implement a method `String caesar(String s, int rotation)` that does the encryption. `rotation` is the shift, which could be arbitrary, not only 3 as from the input example.
3. Write a method `String decaesar(String s, int rotation)` which takes back the encryption.
4. Caesar encryption falls into the class of *decryption ciphers*. Would you recommend it for Captain CiaoCiao?

Example:

- `caesar( "abxyz. ABXYZ!", 13 )` → `"noklm. NOKLM!"`
- `decaesar( caesar( "abxyz. ABXYZ!", 13 ), 13 ) )` → `"abxyz. ABXYZ!"`

SUGGESTED SOLUTIONS

Quiz: Is String a Built-In Keyword?

String is not a built-in data type. All keywords in Java are lowercase, and all reference types are upper-case according to the naming convention. java.lang.String is a class, and String objects exist as instances at runtime. The String class inherits from java.lang.Object like all other classes.

Building HTML Elements with Simple Concatenation

com/tutego/exercise/string/HtmlBuilder.java

```java
public static String htmlElement( String tag, String body ) {
  if ( tag == null )
    tag="";
  if ( body == null )
    body="";
  if ( tag.isEmpty() )
    return body;
  else
    return "<"+tag+">"+body+"</"+tag+">";
}

public static String strong( String body ) {
  return htmlElement( "strong", body );
}

public static String emphasized( String body ) {
  return htmlElement( "em", body );
}
```

The general method String htmlElement(String tag, String body) can be used by the other methods.

Tag and body may be null according to the assignment, then they are treated as an empty string. Then comes the main check: if the tag is empty, only the body is returned; if the tag is not empty, our method creates a start tag, concatenates the body, and appends an end tag.

For the strong(...) and emphasized(...) methods, we fall back to our previously defined method, fill the tag name with strong and em, respectively, and pass the body.

Check Safe Transmission by Doubling Characters

com/tutego/exercise/string/RepeatingCharacters.java

```java
private static int isEveryCharacterTwice( String string ) {
  int FAILURE_CODE=0;
  int SUCCESS_CODE=1;

  if ( string.length() % 2 != 0 )
    return FAILURE_CODE;
  for ( int i=0; i<string.length(); i += 2 ) {
    char first =string.charAt( i );
```

```
      char second=string.charAt( i+1 );
      if ( first != second )
        return -(i+1);
  }

  return SUCCESS_CODE;
}
```

The method gets a string and first tests if the input is correct. The number of characters must be even because if the number is odd, it is not possible that each character occurs twice. If null is passed, there will be a NullPointerException when trying to retrieve the length; this is to be expected.

In the next step, we run two steps over the array. We extract the character at location i and the following character at location i + 1. If the two characters do not match, then i + 1 is where the character is not like the character before it. We negate the expression and report the location. This always gives a negative return value because we do not invert i (the index starts at 0), but i + 1, which leads to -1 in the result. The negative returns are always odd.

If there is no exit from the loop, the method returns 1.

Swap Y and Z

Java provides several options for comparisons: if-else, switch-case and the conditional operator. This reflects the solutions:

com/tutego/exercise/string/YZswapper.java

```java
static void printSwappedYZ1( String string ) {
  for ( int i=0; i<string.length(); i++ ) {
    char c=string.charAt( i );
    if ( c == 'y' ) c='z';
    else if ( c == 'z' ) c='y';
    else if ( c == 'Y' ) c='Z';
    else if ( c == 'Z' ) c='Y';
    System.out.print( c );
  }
}
```

In the first proposed solution, we run the string from front to back. We can query the number of characters with length() and each character at a position with chatAt(...). If we have the character at a position, it can be checked and replaced by another character, which we finally output. This variant contains a screen output, and we do not temporarily create a new string.

com/tutego/exercise/string/YZswapper.java

```java
static void printSwappedYZ2( String string ) {
  for ( int i=0; i<string.length(); i++ ) {
    switch ( string.charAt( i ) ) {
      case 'y': System.out.print( 'z' ); break;
      case 'z': System.out.print( 'y' ); break;
      case 'Y': System.out.print( 'Z' ); break;
      case 'Z': System.out.print( 'Y' ); break;
      default:  System.out.print( string.charAt( i ) );
    }
  }
}
```

The second variant also runs over the string manually. However, instead of comparing the individual characters via ==, this solution uses a switch-case construction. The fact that System.out. print(char) occurs many times is not nice.

com/tutego/exercise/string/YZswapper.java

```java
static void printSwappedYZ3( String string ) {
  for ( int i=0; i<string.length(); i++ ) {
    char c=string.charAt( i );
    System.out.print( c == 'y' ? 'z' :
                      c == 'Y' ? 'Z' :
                      c == 'z' ? 'y' :
                      c == 'Z' ? 'Y' :
                      c );
  }
}
```

The third variant uses a nested conditional operator to compare if the letter is Y or Z.

As of Java 14, there are also new switch notations with a ->, which allows for more variations. Option 1:

com/tutego/exercise/string/YZswapper.java

```java
static void printSwappedYZ5( String string ) {
  for ( int i=0; i<string.length(); i++ ) {
    switch ( string.charAt( i ) ) {
      case 'y' -> System.out.print( 'z' );
      case 'z' -> System.out.print( 'y' );
      case 'Y' -> System.out.print( 'Z' );
      case 'Z' -> System.out.print( 'Y' );
      default  -> System.out.print( string.charAt( i ) );
    }
  }
}
```

Option 2:

com/tutego/exercise/string/YZswapper.java

```java
static void printSwappedYZ6( String string ) {
  for ( int i=0; i<string.length(); i++ ) {
    System.out.print(
        switch ( string.charAt( i ) ) {
          case 'y' -> 'z'; case 'Y' -> 'Z';
          case 'z' -> 'y'; case 'Z' -> 'Y';
          default  -> string.charAt( i );
        } );
  }
}
```

Some readers may wish for a method to swap characters, but there is no such method for strings. There is a replace(...) method, but it doesn't help us because if we replace for example "y" with "z", later the "original" "z" characters are no longer recognizable and must then be converted to "y". In principle, we could proceed in three steps and use, for example, a special character as a placeholder:

1. Replace all "y" with "$".
2. Replace all "z" with "y".
3. Replace all "$" with "z".

This is not elegant, especially since we have to make sure that a placeholder symbol like "$" is free.

We have seen that there are several ways to solve the task. Whenever we need to check a variable against various constants known at compile-time, `switch` is a good choice. If you can use the current Java versions, you should use the notation with `switch` and arrow. It is not only shorter but also prevents unintentional fall-throughs.

Give Defiant Answers

com/tutego/exercise/string/TonyTheDefiant.java

```java
String input=new Scanner( System.in ).nextLine().trim();
if ( input.equalsIgnoreCase( "no idea?" ) )
  System.out.println( "Aye!" );
else if ( input.endsWith( "?" ) ) {
  System.out.println( input+" No idea!" );
}
```

We query for a line from the command line using `Scanner`, and then cut white space at the front and back. If the input is `No idea?` the output is `Aye!`. For case-insensitive testing, we rely on `equalsIgnore-Case(...)`, which is faster than an `input.toLowerCase().equals("no idea?")` because `equal-sIgnoreCase(...)` can compare directly, while `toLowerCase()` first creates a new `String` object to compare with `equals(...)`. But the `String` object is garbage after the `equals(...)` check. It is advisable to refrain from creating new objects unnecessarily as it can increase memory usage and runtime.

If the input wasn't `No idea?`, we test if the input ends with a question mark. If so, we repeat the input and append `No idea!` at the end. Nothing happens if none of the cases applies.

We must not do the first test whether the input ends with a question mark. If we reverse the case distinctions, the program would recognize the question mark at the back when `No idea?` is entered and the output would be `No idea? No idea!`, which is not correct.

Quiz: String Comparisons with == and Equals(...)

In principle, strings can be compared with `==`, but usually, this will not work because that would require that the `String` objects are only built internally in the virtual machine. Normally, however, we build objects ourselves, e.g., by reading a file line by line or by reading from the command line. Then each line and input is a new `String` object. Java developers should make it a habit to always compare strings with the `equals(...)` method. There are also variants here, e.g., `equalsIgnoreCase(...)`.

Newcomers from other programming languages have difficulties at the beginning. Most programming languages allow comparing strings with `==`.

Quiz: Is Equals(...) Symmetric?

Comparisons with the `equals(Object)` method should be symmetric, that is, there should be no difference whether it says `a.equals(b)` or `b.equals(b)`. However, the symmetry is broken by `null`. Thus, `String s=null; s.equals("tutego")` leads to a `NullPointerException`, but `"tutego".equals(s)` leads to `false`. In practice, therefore, it is more robust to call `equals(...)` on a string literal and pass another string.

If `null` can occur in the comparison and `NullPointerException` is to be prevented, `Objects.equals(…)` can be used well:

OpenJDK's implementation of `Objects.equals(…)`.

```java
public static boolean equals(Object a, Object b) {
    return (a == b) || (a != null && a.equals(b));
}
```

Test Strings for Palindrome Property

com/tutego/exercise/string/PalindromeTester.java

```java
public static boolean isPalindrome( String string ) {

  for ( int index=0; index<string.length() / 2; index++ ) {
    char frontChar=string.charAt( index );
    char backChar =string.charAt( string.length() - index - 1 );
    if ( frontChar != backChar )
      return false;
  }
  return true;
}

public static boolean isPalindromeIgnoringCase( String string ) {
  return isPalindrome( string.toLowerCase() );
}

public static boolean isPalindromeIgnoringNonLettersAndDigits(String string) {

  for ( int startIndex=0, endIndex=string.length() - 1;
        startIndex<endIndex;
        startIndex++, endIndex-- ) {
    while ( ! Character.isLetterOrDigit( string.charAt( startIndex ) ) )
      startIndex++;
    while ( ! Character.isLetterOrDigit( string.charAt( endIndex ) ) )
      endIndex--;

    char frontChar=Character.toLowerCase( string.charAt( startIndex ) );
    char backChar =Character.toLowerCase( string.charAt( endIndex ) );
    if ( frontChar != backChar )
      return false;
  }
  return true;
}

public static boolean isPalindromeRecursive( String string ) {

  if ( string.length()<2 )
    return true;
```

```
if ( string.charAt( 0 ) != string.charAt( string.length() - 1 ) )
    return false;

return isPalindromeRecursive( string.substring( 1, string.length() - 1 ) );
}
```

The task of testing with palindromes is a classic in computer science. There are different approaches to this task; it can be answered relatively easily with a Java library method in a one-liner, or it can be solved iteratively via a loop and also recursively.

The solution shown here is simple and performant. If we want to test whether a string is a palindrome, all we have to do is compare the first character with the last, then the second with the second to last, and so on. We loop from 0 to half of the string and do exactly that: with `string.charAt(index)` we run from the left to the middle and with `string.charAt( string.length() - index - 1 )` from the right to the middle. Once we have extracted the characters, we compare them; if the characters are not equal, we exit the method with `return false`. If the program survives the loop, `string` is a palindrome. The solution works for strings with an even and also odd number of characters.

Our method `isPalindromeIgnoringCase(String)` tests whether the string is also a palindrome regardless of case. In this case, we first convert the string to lowercase and pass it to our existing method `isPalindrome(String)` for testing.

For the `isPalindromeIgnoringNonLettersAndDigits(String)` method, we could proceed as we did for the `isPalindromeIgnoringCase(String)` method. We could use a Java method to delete everything that is not a letter or digit, or we could dispense with an extra pass to clean up the string and do the query directly. This is the approach taken by the implementation shown. We iterate through each character of the string from left and right and define two loop counters `startIndex` and `endIndex` for it. The start index becomes larger and the end index smaller. We start with the start index on the first character and with the end index on the last character. One of the two characters may not be a letter or a digit. So, we have to search from the left until we come to a valid symbol, and we have to do the same from the right. This is what the two `while` loops do. Since the check can now be case-insensitive, we convert the two characters to lowercase and then compare them. If the characters are not equal, `return false` terminates the method. If each comparison is true, the method's response is `return true`.

Finally, we look at the recursive implementation. Here there are two possibilities. Here we show the possibility that first a test checks if there is no or a character in the string. In that case, we have reached the end of the recursion and can return `true`. Next, we extract the first and the last characters and compare them. If the characters are not the same, we exit the method with `false`. If the characters match—case-insensitive here—we extract a substring and go down one recursion level. Since the recursion here is at the end, we also call it an end recursion, which in principle can be optimized by runtime environments, although the standard JVM does not do this optimization yet.

An alternative solution with a recursion would be to parameterize the method with a start and end index, which is then moved within the method each time, without generating temporary strings. That is, instead of forming a partial string, only the start and end index are adjusted. However, this solution is no longer very far from an iterative solution.

Finally, let's look at a one-liner with the Java method `reverse(…)`:

```
String s="otto";
boolean isPalindrome=new StringBuilder(s).reverse().toString().equals(s);
```

Alternatively, even a bit shorter:

```
boolean isPalindrome=s.contentEquals(new StringBuilder(s).reverse());
```

Check if Captain CiaoCiao is in the Middle

com/tutego/exercise/string/InMiddle.java

```java
public static boolean isStringInMiddle( String string, String middle ) {

  if ( middle.length() > string.length() )
    return false;

  int start=string.length() / 2 - middle.length() / 2;
  return string.regionMatches( start, middle, 0 /* middle offset */, middle.
length() );
}

public static boolean isCiaoCiaoInMiddle( String string ) {
  return isStringInMiddle( string, "CiaoCiao" );
}
```

The core idea of the algorithm is to determine the midpoint of the main string, then subtract half the length from the string you want in the middle, and compare whether the middle string is located from that position.

Finally, whether the string "CiaoCiao" occurs is quite specific. Therefore, we generalize the question and write a general method isStringInMiddle(String string, String middle) that works for any string that should be in the middle.

In the first step, we check the parameters. If null was passed for one of the parameters, it throws a NullPointerException when accessing the length. The reaction is good. If both are valid String objects, the lengths are determined and compared. If the middle string is longer than the main string itself, this is an error, and we return false directly.

The following lines follow the described algorithm. regionMatches(...) is useful in this case. The signature of the method is:

```java
boolean regionMatches(int toffset, String other, int ooffset, int len).
```

This is a better approach than using substring(...) to first cut out the string and then comparing it with equals(...).

Find the Shortest Name in the Array

com/tutego/exercise/string/ShortName.java

```java
private static final int INDEX_NOT_FOUND=-1;

private static String shortest( String s1, String s2 ) {
  return s1.length() <= s2.length() ? s1 : s2;
}

private static String shortestName( String... names ) {

  if ( names.length == 0 )
    return "";

  String result=names[ 0 ];
```

```
  for ( String name : names ) {
    int spacePos=name.indexOf( ' ' );
    if ( spacePos == INDEX_NOT_FOUND )
      result=shortest( result, name );
    else {
      String part1=name.substring( 0, spacePos );
      String part2=name.substring( spacePos+1 );
      result=shortest( result, shortest( part1, part2 ) );
    }
  }
  return result;
}
```

To simplify the algorithm, we extract the task of determining the shortest of two strings into a separate method, shortest(String, String), which will be called multiple times later. This method returns the shorter of the two strings passed in. If both strings are of equal length, the method returns the first string; however, the choice is arbitrary.

The actual shortestName(…) method gets a vararg of strings, and as usual, the parameter can be null. By accessing length it will throw a NullPointerException if null is passed—the desired behavior. If no element was passed to the method, the method can do nothing and returns the empty string.

Since there is at least one string in the array, we use it to initialize the variable result, which we will also return at the end. The extended for loop runs through all the strings in the array, and in the body result may be updated. First, let's see if there is a space in the string. Now there are two alternatives:

1. If there is no space in the string, then shortest(result, name) returns the shorter string, and overwrites result with the result.
2. If there is a space in the name, substring(…) splits the name into two parts, part1 and part2. Here we nest the shortest(…) method. First, it determines the shorter string between part1 and part2. Then, it compares this result with result to identify the shortest string, which is then stored in result.

At the end of the loop, we have determined the shortest string, which we return.

Count String Occurrences

com/tutego/exercise/string/StringUtils.java

```
private static final int INDEX_NOT_FOUND=-1;

public static int countMatches( String string, String other ) {

  if ( string == null || other == null || string.length() == 0 || other.
length() == 0 )
    return 0;

  int result=0;
  for ( int index=0;
        (index=string.indexOf( other, index )) != INDEX_NOT_FOUND;
        index += other.length() )
    result++;

  return result;
}
```

The countMatches(...) method must return 0 for incorrect values. It is erroneous if a string is null or contains no characters. This check is done at the beginning.

The variable result will later indicate the number of matches and form the return. In the for loop, we repeatedly search for this partial-string other with the String method indexOf(...). For this purpose, the loop initializes a variable index, which always contains the last found locations, and if there are no more found locations, this is also a termination condition of the for loop. This index is then always incremented by the length of other so that the indexOf(...) method can continue searching behind the substring other at the next iteration.

If such a method is needed in real Java programs, developers could get it from Apache Commons. The implementation itself is at https://commons.apache.org/proper/commons-lang/apidocs/src-html/org/apache/commons/lang3/StringUtils.html.

Determine the Larger Crew Size

First, let's summarize what we need to accomplish: in a string, we need to find the separator character (a minus sign) and determine how many dashes are to the left and right of the minus sign. These values must be compared. There are three outputs for the comparison: the right value can be larger or smaller than the left one, or both values can be the same.

There are two simple solutions:

- Split the input with split("-") into two strings, and then query this string length with length().
- Get the position of the minus sign in the string with indexOf(...) and then calculate the length left and right of the separator character.

Here is a special solution for friends with the motto: "why do simple when it can be complicated?" In practice, this is of little use and is only justified if the profiler indicates that a code position is a bottleneck that needs to be optimized. Otherwise, clarity always comes first!

Let us assume for a moment that we have found the separator character at the position i and delete it because we want to avoid counting the one separator character. The total length shrinks thereby by one.

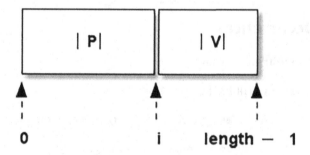

FIGURE 5.1   Relationship between location of the minus sign and team sizes.

If P (pirates) and V (victims) are sets, then let $|P|$ be the number of pirates and $|V|$ the number of raiders. These three pieces of information (0, i, and *length* - 1) give us answers:

- How many pirates are there? There are i – 0, so i many.
- How many raiders are there? There are *length* – 1 – i many.

We could find these values and compare them, and the problem would be solved.

However, more can be done with the information. The task asks for the difference in team strengths. Wouldn't it be possible to calculate the difference and use the sign to find out which team is stronger? You can.

- $|P| < |V|$ it follows $|P| - |V| < 0$.
- $|P| > |V|$ from this follows $|P| - |V| > 0$.
- $|P| = |V|$ from this follows $|P| - |V| = 0$.

When comparing two numbers, the difference can always be formed and the sign observed.

In the expression $|P| - |V|$ repeats, we can calculate that:

- $|P| - |V| = i - (length - 1 - i) = i - (-i + length - 1) = i + i - (length - 1) = 2 \times i - (length - 1)$.

This is the difference in team size, and the sign tells us which team is larger.

It's time for the Java program:

com/tutego/exercise/string/CrewSize.java

```java
public static void printDecodedCrewSizes( String string ) {
  int index=string.indexOf( '-' );
  if ( index< 0 )
    throw new IllegalArgumentException( "Separator - is missing in "+string );
  System.out.print( string+" => " );
  int diff=2 * index - (string.length() - 1);
  switch ( Integer.signum( diff ) ) {
    case -1 -> System.out.printf(
        "Raided ship had a larger crew, difference %d%n", -diff );
    case  0 -> System.out.println( "Ships had the same crew size" );
    case +1 -> System.out.printf(
        "Pirate ship had a larger crew, difference %d%n", diff );
  }
}
```

First, the location i is determined; if there is no minus sign, an exception follows. Then, the difference is calculated. Now a case distinction with if-else can be added, but the program does something else: It maps all negative numbers to -1, all positive numbers to 1, and 0 remains 0. This leaves three possibilities that switch-case can handle. The last thing to do is to reverse the sign of the output in the case of a negative difference.

Build Diamonds

com/tutego/exercise/string/DiamondPrinter.java

```java
private static void printDiamondCore( char character, char stopCharacter ) {
  if ( character == stopCharacter ) {
    System.out.print( character );
    return;
  }
  System.out.print( character );
  printDiamondCore( (char) (character+1), stopCharacter );
  System.out.print( character );
}
```

```java
public static void printDiamond( int diameter ) {
  if ( diameter<1 )
    return;

  diameter=(diameter <= 2 * 26 - 1) ? diameter : 2 * 26 - 1;

  int radius=diameter / 2;
  for ( int indentation=radius; indentation >= -radius; indentation-- ) {
    int absIndentation=Math.abs( indentation );
    System.out.print( " ".repeat( absIndentation ) );
    printDiamondCore( 'A', (char) ('A'+radius - absIndentation) );
    System.out.println();
  }
}
```

The actual solution of the task is in the method `printDiamond(int)`, but we want to use a second method to write a line of the diamond. For the indentation with spaces, we fall back on the method `repeat(int)`.

`printDiamondCore(char, char)` draws a diamond line on the screen, where the method gets a start character and a stop character. For example, if the start character is A and the stop character is C, then the method prints the sequence ABCBA on the screen. The implementation is recursive. There are two scenarios: if the start character is equal to the stop character, then the character is not set twice, but only once. Otherwise, the character is set, and then the method is recursively called with the next character, leaving the end character the same. After the recursive call descends, the character is set once again. We could in principle reverse the case distinction to first ask if the character does not match the stop character and enter recursion earlier, but termination conditions of recursions are more common at the beginning of the method.

The actual method `printDiamond(int)` first checks if the circumference of diamonds is valid, and exits if not. Since we pass the diameter, but we are interested in the radius, we divide the diameter by 2. Now the actual program flow can start. Prior to commencing the actual program flow, we examine a unique characteristic: the correlation between the indentation and diamond size. The diamond with diameter 7 shall serve as an illustration, and we give the diamond size as radius. The indentation by spaces is symbolized by the underscore _ :

Relationship of diamond lines, indentation, and diamond radius.

LINES	INDENTATION	RADIUS
A	3	1
ABA	2	2
ABCBA	1	3
ABCDCBA	0	4
ABCBA	1	3
ABA	2	2
A	3	1

We can read that the sum of radius and indentation is always the same, 4 in our example. We can now use a loop to count down from 3 to 0 and back up to 3 and derive the radius. Or we can loop over the radius of the diamond from 1 to 4 and back to 1 and derive the indentation.

The proposed solution uses the indentation `indentation` as the loop counter. And a trick is used so that two loops are not necessary: The loop lets `indentation` start with the radius and end at the negative radius. We run once through the zero points with it. Inside the loop, we are not interested in the negative numbers, so we choose the absolute value and thus have a descending and ascending indentation. From these indentation values, as we have just seen, we can calculate the radius and thus output the line. At the beginning, indentation is equal to radius, which means radius - indentation is 0 at the beginning. So, the method printDiamondCore('A', 'A') writes only the A. In the next pass, the indentation is decreased by one, that is, the difference between the radius, which does not change, and indentation is A + 1`= B, so we draw the core ABA.

Check for a Good Password

com/tutego/exercise/string/PasswordTester.java

```java
public static final int MIN_PASSWORD_LEN=8;

public static boolean isGoodPassword( String password ) {

  if ( password.length()<MIN_PASSWORD_LEN ) {
    System.err.println( "Password is too short" );
    return false;
  }
  if ( ! containsUppercaseLetter( password ) ) {
    System.err.println( "Must contain uppercase letters" );
    return false;
  }

  if ( ! containsLowercaseLetter( password ) ) {
    System.err.println( "Must contain lowercase letters" );
    return false;
  }

  if ( ! containsDigit( password ) ) {
    System.err.println( "Must contain a number" );
    return false;
  }

  if ( ! containsSpecialCharacter( password ) ) {
    System.err.println( "Must contain special characters like .," );
    return false;
  }

  return true;
}

private static boolean containsUppercaseLetter( String string ) {
  for ( int i=0; i<string.length(); i++ ) {
    char c=string.charAt( i );
    if ( Character.isUpperCase( c ) )
      return true;
  }
  return false;
}
```

```java
private static boolean containsLowercaseLetter( String string ) {
  for ( int i=0; i<string.length(); i++ ) {
    char c=string.charAt( i );
    if ( Character.isLowerCase( c ) )
      return true;
  }
  return false;
}

private static boolean containsDigit( String string ) {
  for ( int i=0; i<string.length(); i++ ) {
    char c=string.charAt( i );
    if ( Character.isDigit( c ) )
      return true;
  }
  return false;
}

private static boolean containsSpecialCharacter( String string ) {
  for ( int i=0; i<string.length(); i++ ) {
    char c=string.charAt( i );
    if ( c == '.' || c == ',' )
      return true;
  }
  return false;
}

public static void main( String[] args ) {
  System.out.println( isGoodPassword("toshort") );
  System.out.println( isGoodPassword("justlowercase" ) );
  System.out.println( isGoodPassword("noDigits") );
  System.out.println( isGoodPassword("1specialChar") );
  System.out.println( isGoodPassword("MoreSpecialChars.$#&") );
}
```

Our method performs various tests one after the other. If a test fails, `return false` terminates the method. If all tests are positive, the method ends with `return true`.

Except for the first test, the individual tests are separated into methods. This increases the clarity. Each method receives a string, processes it from start to end, and checks for specific properties. The approach here is also that if we found what we were looking for, we can directly exit the method with a corresponding `return true`. Let's take `containsUppercaseLetter(String)` as an example. The method runs the string from front to back and checks with `Character.isUpperCase(char)` if there is an uppercase letter. If so, we don't need to test any more characters, we can exit the method immediately.

Bake Peanut Butter Cookies

The task is solved with two methods. The first method `countCookies(...)` loops over the string, and the other method `hasRecipeIngredients(...)` tests if a substring contains the baking ingredients.

com/tutego/exercise/string/PeanutButterCookies.java

```java
static void countCookies( String input ) {
  int cookies=0;
  for ( int i=0; i< input.length() - 2; ) {
    String triplet=input.substring( i, i+3 );
    if ( hasRecipeIngredients( triplet ) ) {
      cookies++;
      i += 3;
    }
    else
      i++;
  }

  System.out.printf( "Cookies: %d, Ingredients remaining: %d%n",
                     cookies,
                     input.length() - 3 * cookies );
}

private static boolean hasRecipeIngredients( String triplet ) {
  return triplet.length() == 3
        && triplet.contains( "P" )
        && triplet.contains( "S" )
        && triplet.contains( "E" );
}
```

Let's start with the main method. The string is processed and then substring of length 3 will be extracted. The method hasRecipeIngredients(...) determines if the substring contains the valid baking ingredients. If yes, the variable cookies is incremented and the position is advanced by three digits because the baking ingredients are "used up". If the substring does not contain valid ingredients, the program moves the position only one step to the right. The for loop does not contain a continuation expression. Finally, the number of cookies is output, and we can calculate how many ingredients are left in total that did not occur for one baking operation in a row.

The second method hasRecipeIngredients(...) only has to test if the letters P, E, S occur in any order in the string. Of course, we could, for example, use a switch expression to query all combinations, such as case "PES", "PSE", "EPS", ... and so on. Alternatively, we can question whether the substring contains the letters P, S, and E in any case. If yes, and the string is exactly three characters long, only the three letters occur in any combination. Since there is no method contains(char), the solution uses the method boolean contains(String), also allows indexOf(char) >= 0 the test. Since we call the method exclusively with strings of length 3, the length query can, of course, be omitted, but this is an example of defensive programming that one cannot trust the caller ...

Calculate Sum of Digits

com/tutego/exercise/string/SumOfTheDigits.java

```java
static int digitSum( long value ) {
  return digitSum( String.valueOf( value ) );
}

static int digitSum( String value ) {
  int sum=0;
```

```
for ( int i=0; i<value.length(); i++ )
  // sum += value.charAt( i ) - '0';
  sum += Character.getNumericValue( value.charAt( i ) );

  return sum;
}
```

The first thing to note is that only one of the two methods needs to be implemented because we can always call the other method. If we call digitSum(long), we can turn the integer into a string, and then call digitSum(String). Vice versa: if we call digitSum(String), we can convert the string to an integer with Long.parseLong(String) and call digitSum(long).

It is a bit of a matter of taste which of the two methods you implement. The approach is different. If we implement the method with the long parameter type, we always have to divide by 10 to decompose the number step by step. Here, we need some mathematics, and this solution has a second disadvantage, namely, that we get the result from right to left. This doesn't matter for the sum of the digits, for some conversions it is rather impractical. So, we implement digitSum(String).

As usual, we run the string from left to right with the for loop. We must now consider each character as a digit. To convert a Unicode character with a digit into a numeric value, we can use the method Character.getNumericValue(char). A char like '1' becomes 1, and '7' becomes 7. In principle, we could do this calculation ourselves by subtracting '0' from the Unicode character, but getNumericValue(...) works in general on all Unicode characters. For example, getNumericValue('٢') returns the result 2.

Decolumnize Texts

The algorithm must do the following: in the first step, it must determine where there is a space in the same place in all the lines, which is an indication of the column. In the next step, we have to separate at this place and first put all the rows of the left columns under each other, then all the rows of the right column.

The actual method decolumnize(...) falls back on the internal method find-ColumnIndex(String[]), which finds the column with the blank for an array of strings. Furthermore, findColumnIndex(...) accesses another internal method isSpaceAt(...), which we want to start with.

com/tutego/exercise/string/Decolumnizer.java

```
private static boolean isSpaceAt( String string, int index ) {
  if ( index >= string.length() )
    return true;
  return string.charAt( index ) == ' ';
}
```

The method isSpaceAt(String, int) checks if there is a space in the passed string string at the position index or not. In addition, this method evaluates everything that is "behind" the string as white space. That means that there is an infinite number of white spaces behind the actual string.

This method is used for the actual method findColumnIndex(String[]):

com/tutego/exercise/string/Decolumnizer.java

```
private final static int COLUMN_NOT_FOUND=-1;

private static int findColumnIndex( String[] lines ) {
  int length=lines[ 0 ].length();
  for ( String line : lines )
    length=Math.max( length, line.length() );
```

```
mainLoop:
for ( int column=1; column< length - 1; column++ ) {
  for ( String line : lines )
    if ( ! isSpaceAt( line, column ) )
      continue mainLoop;
  return column;
}


  return COLUMN_NOT_FOUND;
}
```

Before we run through all the lines and ask if each line has space at some point, we need to figure out how far we are allowed to run. Therefore, the first step is to find the longest line. It must be the longest line because some lines may be empty, and some lines may be short, in which case there is white space behind these short lines again.

Once we have determined the longest line, we run through all possible columns with a loop. It cannot be the column with index '0', nor can it be the last column because there cannot be a real column to the left or right of these positions. Regardless of this, it makes little sense if the columns are only one symbol ready, so one could certainly start with another index, perhaps in the neighborhood of the center.

The function of the two nested loops is the following: the outer loop runs all possible columns, while the inner loop makes sure that for each column all possible rows are examined. If there is no space in a row in the column column, then we don't even need to consider the other rows, but continue with the next column. This possibility is achieved with the keyword continue—we have to use a jump label here because without it continue would only continue in the inner loop, but we want to continue in the outer loop.

If the program overcomes the inner loop, we have found a place for all lines where there is a space. The variable column contains the found position, which is returned. The program doesn't care if this location is in the middle, maybe there is a column with blanks at the beginning, then a column is recognized that shouldn't be a column. If we run over all columns and rows and there are no blanks among them, the return is COLUMN _ NOT _ FOUND, i.e., -1.

Now we can get to the actual method decolumnize(String):

com/tutego/exercise/string/Decolumnizer.java

```
public static void decolumnize( String string ) {
  String[] lines=string.split( "\n" );
  if ( lines.length< 2 ) {
    System.out.println( string );
    return;
  }

  int column=findColumnIndex( lines );

  if ( column == COLUMN_NOT_FOUND ) {
    System.out.println( string );
    return;
  }

  // Left column
  for ( String line : lines ) {
    int a=line.length();
    System.out.println(
        line.substring( 0, (a <= column) ? a : column ).trim() );
  }
```

```
    // Right column
  for ( String line : lines )
    if ( column<line.length() )
      System.out.println( line.substring( column+1 ).trim() );
    else
      System.out.println();
}
```

It first splits the large string into many lines using the `split(...)` method. Splitting into columns only makes sense if there are at least two lines, so if there is one line, it will be output as such without starting the search for a column.

Otherwise, the real work begins, the search for the column. If the method `findColumnIndex(...)` does not find a column, then we output the string and end the method.

If we have found a column index, a first loop outputs the left column and the second loop outputs the right column. So, the two loops run the overall lines twice, but consider in the first case only everything to the left of the column index, and in the second case only everything to the right of the column index.

For the left column, consider that the rows can be shorter than the column index because the rows as a whole can be shorter; we remember: `isSpaceAt(...)` is programmed so that everything after the actual string is considered white space. If we output the line of the left column, the `substring(...)` method must not go from 0 to the column index, but from the smaller value, the line length, and the column index. We still cut possible blanks at the back and front for the output.

For the right column, we proceed similarly. Only now do we have to check if the right row exists at all. If yes, `substring(...)` returns a substring starting at the column index to the end of the line. Otherwise, we output an empty line.

The program doesn't prioritize removing superfluous blank lines at the end. When the number of lines on the left and right columns is uneven, the right column will have as many blank lines as the left column has lines.

Draw a Meadow with Favorite Flowers

com/tutego/exercise/string/Flowers.java

```
private static final String FLOWERS="""

                      _(_)_                        wWWWw
      @@@@           (_)@(_)   vVVVv        _    @@@@    (___)  _(_)_
     @@()@@ wWWWw   (_)\\     (___)   _(_)_  @@()@@    Y   (_)@(_)
      @@@@   (___)     `|/     Y    (_)@(_)  @@@@    \\|/    (_)\\
       /      Y       \\|    \\|/    /(_)     \\|     |/       |
      \\\\ |     \\\\ |/      | / \\\\ | /  \\\\|/       |/     \\\\|     \\\\|/
       \\\\\\|//     \\\\\\\\|//   \\\\\\\\\\\\|//\\\\\\\\\\\\|///  \\\\|///  \\\\\\\\\\\\|//    \\\\\\\\\\|//
     \\\\\\\\\\\\\\|//
        ^^^^^^^^^^^^^^^^^^^^^^^^^^^^^^^^^^^^^^^^^^^^^^^^^^^^^^^^^^^^

      """;

private static final int[] FLOWER_START_POS={0, 7, 13, 22, 29, 37, 44, 50,
57};

private static final String[] FLOWER_LINES=FLOWERS.split( "\n" );
private static final int FLOWER_HEIGHT=FLOWER_LINES.length;
private static final int LONGEST_LINE_LEN=FLOWER_LINES[FLOWER_HEIGHT-1].length();
```

```java
private static String flowerLine( int flower, int line ) {
   String s=FLOWER_LINES[ line ]+" ".repeat( LONGEST_LINE_LEN );
   return s.substring( FLOWER_START_POS[flower], FLOWER_START_POS[flower+1] );
}

private static int flowerFromId( char id ) {
   return id >= '1' && id <= '8' ? Character.getNumericValue( id ) - 1 : 0;
}

public static void printFlowers( String string ) {
   for ( int line=0; line<FLOWER_HEIGHT; line++ ) {
      for ( int i=0; i<string.length(); i++ )
         System.out.print( flowerLine( flowerFromId( string.charAt( i ) ), line
) );
      System.out.println();
   }
}
```

For the flowers, we use multiline strings, which are available since Java 15. The string is in a static variable in the proposed solution; a local variable is also possible in principle, but it is inconvenient.

We want to declare a few additional static variables. So that we can refer to the individual flowers later, we keep the positions at which the flowers start in a separate array FLOWER _ START _ POS. For example, the first flower starts from index 0, the second flower from index 7, and so on. Another constant FLOWER _ LINES results from the flower string and stores the lines of all flowers in an array—so we can easily ask for a line later. The number of lines also tells us the height of the flowers. The last line is also the longest line, which we also want to remember in a constant LONGEST _ LINE _ LEN. If the flowers should ever change, we would have to adjust or recalculate some of these constants.

Let's look at the individual methods. String flowerLine(int flower, int line) internally accesses the array FLOWER _ LINES and extracts from a desired flower exactly this partial string from the line with all flowers. To achieve this, the method considers a peculiarity, namely, some lines may be shorter than the longest line (i.e., not all lines are the same length), and then forming a substring would quickly lead to an exception. The trick is to first append spaces to each line. We know the number of spaces because there are at most LONGEST _ LINE _ LEN many. The string with many spaces is formed by the repeat(...) method of the String class.

The flowerLine(...) method thus returns the individual line for each flower. Now we have to do decoding from a character to the flower. Flower 1 must be mapped to 0. This is done by a new method int flowerFromId(char id). We translate a character with the flower ID to an integer, so we can access the array internally later.

The last method is printFlowers(String). It falls back on the other two methods, so only a few lines are needed for the actual algorithm. The basic idea is simple: we go over all the lines and then set the partial string for each flower and each line in turn. This means we have to nest two loops. The outer loop goes over all the lines. For each line, we then split the string with the order into individual characters, which gives us the flower identifiers in id. toCharArray() returns an array of all the characters that the extended for loop can run. Now we run over all the flower identifiers through the inner loop and all the lines through the outer loop. In the inner loop, we first convert the flower identifier to the internal position and then get the partial string of the flower for the line, which we output with System.out. print(...). After the internal loop, we end the line with a line feed.

Detect Repetitions

Before we look at the solution in code, the algorithm that solves the problem must be clear. Let us take the simple string aaa as an example. As humans, we have no problem immediately recognizing the pattern that a repeats three times. A program could do the following: it could take the first character of aaa—that is, a—and repeat it until the string has length 3. Then we compare whether it resembles the initial string aaa. It does! What about ababab? If the program also starts repeating the first character a, aaaa is created, and the comparison with the original ababab turns out negative. In the next step, the program can take the first two characters ab and repeat them, and the result is ababab, which matches the original. We have a match.

With the simple algorithm, we can test strings of any length: form repetitions of substrings of length 1, 2, 3, 4. … However, it helps us to consider what format the valid solutions will have (Table 5.1).

From the table, we can see that ab, for example, cannot be used to create strings of length 3, and abcd cannot be used to create strings of length 2.

If we have a substring with two characters, then the strings generated from it can be a multiple of two, so can be two characters long, can be four characters long, can be six characters long, and so on. If we have a string with three characters, we can build repeats from it with three characters, six characters, nine characters, and so on.

Let's turn the game around. We don't know what the substring looks like and how long it is, but we know the output string. For example, if the output string is 12 characters long, what are the possible repeating strings?

```
aaaaaaaaaaaa
abababababab
abcabcabcabc
abcdabcdabcd
abcdefabcdef
```

These are repetitions of a, ab, abc, abcd, abcdef; the length of these strings are the divisors of 12, which are 1, 2, 3, 4, and 6. Other combinations are not possible. In particular, the substring cannot be longer than half the string length because otherwise, the duplication is longer than the original string. So, in a naive approach, we could go up from one to $n/2$ for a total string length of n; if we want to do better, we go up only the divisors.

TABLE 5.1   Valid repetitions of length 1, 2, 3, 4, 5, 6

PARTIAL SEQUENCE	OF LENGTH 1	2	3	4	5	6
a	a	aa	aaa	aaaa	aaaaa	aaaaaa
ab	—	ab	—	abab	—	ababab
abc	—	—	abc	—	—	abcabc
abcd	—	—	—	abcd	—	—
abcde	—	—	—	—	abcde	—
abcdef	—	—	—	—	—	abcdef

com/tutego/exercise/string/RepeatingStrings.java

```
public static String repeatingStrings( String string ) {

  if ( string == null || string.length() < 2 )
    return null;

  for ( int i = 1; i <= string.length() / 2; i++ ) {
    if ( string.length() % i == 0 ) {
      String substring        = string.substring( 0, i );
      String repeatedSubstring = substring.repeat( string.length() / i );

      if ( string.equals( repeatedSubstring ) )
        return substring;
    }
  }

  return null;
}
```

If the method receives a `null` reference or strings consisting of a single character, it returns `null` directly. Furthermore, we can assume that the strings are longer than two characters.

The for-loop generates all numbers i from 1 to n/2; whether they are divisors of the string length is not known yet. The remainder operator `%` helps to check if the length of the string is divisible by `i` without remainder. If so, we have found a multiple, and the strings can be formed.

Inside the block, `string.substring(0,  i)` creates the substring that is repeated `string.length()  /  i` times. If this generated repetition matches the original string, we have found a match. If the two strings do not match, we return to the loop.

If the for-loop is fully executed and no match is found, the method returns `null`.

Constrain Line Boundaries and Wrap Lines

com/tutego/exercise/string/WordWrap.java

```
public static String wrap( String string, int width ) {
  if ( string.length() <= width )
    return string;
  int breakIndex=string.lastIndexOf( ' ', width );
  if ( breakIndex == -1 )
    breakIndex=width;
  String firstLine=string.substring( 0, breakIndex );
  String remaining=wrap( string.substring( breakIndex ).trim(), width );
  return firstLine+"\n"+remaining;
}
```

The method `wrap(...)` has two parameters: the text and the maximum line width. At the beginning of the method, we test if the string fits entirely into one line. If it does, we don't need to wrap and can return the line as is. Only if the text is longer than the maximum width we need to do something. We start searching from the maximum width toward the left for a space character. The `lastIndexOf(char,  int)` method is perfect for this because the second parameter indicates the starting position for the search.

The search may or may not find a space character. The space character may not be in the line because of an extremely long word, or we may find a space character. Let's call the position where we need to wrap the text `breakIndex`.

We must decide what to do with words that are too long for a line. One solution would be to not break up words and allow them to be longer than the width, or we can forcibly break the word. We choose (according to the task) to forcibly break the word. If the `breakIndex` is equal to -1, which means that no space character was found, we set the `breakIndex` to the maximum line width.

Now that we have our wrapping position, we create two variables, one for the first line and one for the remaining text. The first line is easy to calculate: we create a substring from the beginning of the text to the `breakIndex`. From the `breakIndex` to the end of the string, we have another possibly very long string that also needs to be wrapped. We can realize this with loops, but recursion is also very practical in our case. We pass these new substrings again into the `wrap(...)` method, which step by step delivers new first lines.

Recursions always need a stopping criterion. In our case, it is a string that is smaller than the maximum width. Then we return from the recursion to the caller. The last caller of `wrap(...)` thus receives the last line from the string in `remaining`. Let's imagine ourselves at the end of the string. We need to connect the next-to-last and last lines with a line break and then return to the caller of the `wrap(...)` method. Since this is recursive, the caller gets the last two lines and can concatenate them with the third last line. The game continues until the recursion is resolved.

Recursion is not easy for many people. It is challenging to imagine the individual steps nested. Also, mutable data structures can quickly become a problem, and you lose track of where exactly something is being read or written. The recommendation at this point is to set breakpoints or console outputs behind the assignment of `firstLine` and behind the assignment of `remaining`, as well as at the beginning of the `wrap(...)` method when the string enters the method.

Quiz: How Many String Objects?

All double-quoted strings are automatic `String` objects. The Java Virtual Machine stores strings of this type in a so-called *constant pool*. Such strings exist as objects only once. That is, `str1`, `str3`, and the string passed to the constructor are identical. If we command the runtime environment to build a new object with `new`, we end up with a new object as well, that is, `str2` and `str4` are new objects. In total, in the scenario we would have one string object in the constant pool and two newly built objects by the `new` keyword, which would also disappear by the GC if not referenced; the strings in the constant pool remain until the end of the runtime.

Test if the Fruit is Wrapped in Chocolate

com/tutego/exercise/string/ChocolateCovered.java

```java
private static final String FRUIT="F";

public static boolean checkChocolate( String string ) {
  return checkChocolate( string, 0 );
}

private static boolean checkChocolate( String string, int layer ) {

  if ( string.isEmpty() )
    return false;

  if ( string.length() == 1 )
    return string.equals( FRUIT ) && layer != 0;
```

```
if ( string.charAt( 0 ) != string.charAt( string.length() - 1 ) )
  return false;

return checkChocolate( string.substring( 1, string.length() - 1 ),
                       layer+1 );
}
```

A recursive solution is perfect for the task. We have a public method, as requested by the task, checkChocolate(string), and a second private method checkChocolate(String, int), which is used by the recursion. Additionally, we declared a variable FRUIT for the fruit itself, so we could change the symbol.

The internal method is called with a string and with an integer that is incremented at each nesting. We need this variable so that we can distinguish if the string contains only the fruit, but no chocolate.

In the method checkChocolate(String, int), we check if the string is empty, in which case the chocolate, fruit, and all are missing, and we return false. Passing null escalates to a NullPointerException. If the string is one character long, there are two things to test: first, whether it is the desired fruit—please no nuts—but also whether the method has been called recursively at least once, that is, at least one layer of chocolate exists. Because if the very first call is with a string of length 1, the method must return false.

If the string is more than one character long, we check the first and last character, similar to a palindrome test. If the characters do not match, false is returned. Whenever the first and last characters are identical, the recursion continues with the next round. We build a substring that goes from the second to the second last character, increase the nesting depth by 1, and use it to call checkChocolate(...) recursively.

From Top to Bottom, from Left to Right

To solve the task, we study the given string again:

```
s u
ey!
ao
```

There are several possible solutions. One would be to split the string into lines, for example, with String[] lines=string.split("\n"); and then run two nested loops first over all columns (width lines[0].length()), then over the lines (Table 5.2).

Here we will show another way. Let's put the lines next to each other and look at which symbol is at which index:

In the end, we want to see the result sea you!, so the question is which indexes we need to address for this. The answer is:

```
0, 3, 6, 1, 4, 7, 2, 5
```

TABLE 5.2   Characters at an index

index	0	1	2	3	4	5	6	7
character	s		u	e	y	!	a	o

The sequence is not arbitrary, it follows a pattern. We need to find a mapping that transfers a number to the index so that we can read the character under the index:

TABLE 5.3   Derivation of $i/3 + i\%3 * 3$

I	0	1	2	3	4	5	6	7
$i/3$	**0**	**0**	**0**	**1**	**1**	**1**	**2**	**2**
$i \% 3$	0	1	2	0	1	2	0	1
$i \% 3 \times 3$	**0**	**3**	**6**	**0**	**3**	**6**	**0**	**3**
$i/3 + i \% 3 \times 3$	0	3	6	1	4	7	2	5

Now we have everything together to program the solution. The solution consists of two steps:

com/tutego/exercise/string/VerticalToHorizontalWriting.java

```java
static void printVerticalToHorizontalWriting( String string ) {
  String oneliner   =string.replace( "\n", "" );
  int numberOfLines=string.length() - oneliner.length()+1;
  for ( int i=0; i<oneliner.length(); i++ ) {
    char c=oneliner.charAt(    (i / numberOfLines)
                            +(i % numberOfLines) * numberOfLines );
    System.out.print( c );
  }
}
```

The line break (new line) is encoded by the escape sequence \n. Since the string consists of several lines separated by \n, we have to remove these \n characters in the first step.

For the algorithm, we need another metric: the number of lines. Here we can resort to a nice trick. If we have deleted the \n characters, the string is shorter by exactly the number that there are \n characters. So if we take the difference between the original length and the length of the string without \n characters, we have the number of lines. Since the last line is not terminated with a \n, we have to add one. For our string from the example, that would be two \n characters + 1, so three lines.

The for loop creates a counter, which we transfer to the position of the character via the formula. The character is read and output to the screen.

Fill Strings

com/tutego/exercise/string/StringFiller.java

```java
private static boolean hasText( String string ) {
  return string == null || string.isEmpty();
}

private static String mix( String string, String fill ) {

  if ( hasText( string ) ) return "";
  if ( hasText( fill ) )   return string;

  StringBuilder result=new StringBuilder();
```

```
for ( int i=0; i<string.length() - 1; i++ ) {
  char c=string.charAt( i );
  result.append( c ).append( fill );
}

result.append( string.charAt( string.length() - 1 ) );

return result.toString();
}
```

Let's start by checking the parameters. If the string is null, or empty, we return an empty string. If the string is not null and it has at least one character, but the fill string is null or empty, there is nothing to do, and we take a shortcut by returning string directly. In principle, a NullPointerException would also be appropriate if string or fill were equal to null because if no valid objects are passed in, methods had better throw an exception. Since the test for null and for the existence of characters is done twice, this functionality is outsourced to an extra method hasText(String).

We start with an empty string, which we fill in a loop. After we have extracted a character, we append this character and the string fill to the previous result. However, we do not run with the index to the very last character, but only to the second to last, so that we can always put the filling string, just not after the last element. Therefore, the termination condition is < string.length() - 1. We append the last character to result at the end after the loop, and then return result to the caller.

In the first conditional statement, we have verified that the string has a length of at least one character. Consequently, we can loop from index 0 up to < string.length() - 1. In case the string length is equal to 1, 1 - 1 equals 0, and only the last character will be appended to the result without any loop iteration.

The fact that the filling string is placed between the characters can also be solved differently: we could query the index and see if it does not stand for the last character, and only then append the filling characters. If the index is on the last character, the filling characters are not appended. Another solution would be to first build a StringBuilder with the original string and then loop over the StringBuilder from right (end) to left (beginning) and insert the substring with insert(...).

Practicing the Alphabet with a Parrot

com/tutego/exercise/string/ABCZ.java

```
static String abcz() {
  StringBuilder result=new StringBuilder();

  for ( char c='A'; c <= 'Z'; c++ )
    result.append( c );

  return result.toString();
}

static String abcz( char start, char end ) {

  if ( end<start )
    return "";

  StringBuilder result=new StringBuilder( end - start+1 );
  for ( char c=start; c <= end; c++ )
    result.append( c );
```

```
  return result.toString();
}

static String abcz( char start, int length ) {
  return abcz( start, (char) (start+length - 1) );
}
```

For the solution of the abcz() method, we resort to the convenient feature of Java that char is a numeric data type that can be used to count. A loop can thus generate 'A' to 'Z', and the entire alphabet is created. All characters are first concatenated in a StringBuilder until finally the StringBuilder is converted to a String via toString() and returned. StringBuilder as the return type is unusual and rather impractical, since other places usually expect String objects again.

In the second method, abcz(char start, char end), we simply parameterize start and end, and now we could even rewrite the first method abcz() to internally call abcz('a', 'z'). Since abcz(char start, char end) could be passed incorrect arguments, we check them in the first step: end must not be lesser than start. The assignments could be equal because if, for example, the method abcz('a', 'a') is called, an 'a' should appear at the end. In case of incorrect values, we could also throw an exception; here we decide to use an empty string as a return. We build the StringBuilder with an int parameterized constructor. The constructor is passed a starting size of the internal buffer; in our case, the total length is known.

The third method delegates to the second method by adding the length to the start character and subtracting one because the last character is already included. The call to abcz('a', 1) should result in "a" and not in "ab".

The last two methods are related. In fact, it doesn't matter which of the two methods we implement; one method can always be mapped to the other. Here, we have implemented the method with the two characters in the parameter list, and the other method merely delegates to that implementation.

In principle, methods that do not differ significantly in the number of parameters and whose parameter types are very close to each other are error-prone. char and int are both numeric data types. Developers must be cautious not to accidentally call the wrong method. Therefore, the implementation of abcz(char, int) also has a type conversion to char because the addition of a char and an int yields an int and not a char. If we didn't use the type conversion there, we would starve endlessly in a recursion. Callers of the method may not have this in mind and write, for example, abcz('a', 'b' + 1)—the call is unlikely to be intentional. With a good API design, we can reduce errors.

Quiz: Lightly Attached

Concatenation of String objects always creates new String objects temporarily. String objects internally reference another object, an array of characters. This means that there is always another object behind a String object, which is also created and must be removed again by the garbage collector. If you have loops with many passes, you should avoid using the + operator for concatenation.

The situation is different with the StringBuilder method append(...). It also uses an array internally for the characters, but no new objects are built when appending (in the best case). Of course, the internal buffer of the StringBuilder object may not be enough, so a new internal array must be built for the characters, but if you can estimate the size from the StringBuilder, no temporary objects are created during concatenation. Of course, if there has to be a String object at the end, toString() has to be called again, which again leads to a new object. In total, there are three objects in our scenario: we build a StringBuilder object ourselves with new, internally the StringBuilder builds an array for the symbols, and finally, we have a third object with toString().

Convert Number to Textual Unary Encoding

com/tutego/exercise/string/UnaryCoding.java

```java
private static int ensurePositive( int value ) {
  if ( value<0 )
    throw new IllegalArgumentException(
        "Value is negative, but must be positive" );
  return value;
}

static String encode( int... values ) {
  StringBuilder codes=new StringBuilder( values.length );
  for ( int value : values )
    codes.repeat( "1", ensurePositive( value ) ).append( '0' );
  return codes.toString();
}
```

To notify developers of erroneous input, each entry in the array is checked to see if it is positive. This is handled by the helper method `ensurePositive(int)`, which raises an exception if the value is negative; otherwise, the method returns the passed value.

encode(int... values) builds an internal `StringBuilder`. It is unclear how large the compound string will grow because it grows depending on the values passed. However, we know that it is at least as large as the number of array elements, which means we can use that as the starting capacity of the `StringBuilder` object. The outer extended `for` loop runs over the array and extracts each `value`. In Java 21, the `StringBuilder` class was enhanced with a new method, `repeat(CharSequence, int)`. In our application, this method appends the string `"1"` to the `StringBuilder` for a designated number of repetitions. As this method returns a `StringBuilder`, it facilitates further `append(...)` operations, like appending a `'0'` to complete the sequence.

com/tutego/exercise/string/UnaryCoding.java

```java
static int[] decode( String string ) {
  if ( string.isEmpty() )
    return new int[0];

  if ( ! string.endsWith( "0" ) )
    throw new IllegalArgumentException(
        "String must end with 0 but did end with "
      +string.charAt( string.length() - 1 ) );

  int arrayLength=0;

  for ( int i=0; i<string.length(); i++ ) {
    if ( string.charAt( i ) == '0' )
      arrayLength++;
    else if ( string.charAt( i ) != '1' )
      throw new IllegalArgumentException(
          "String can only contain 0 or 1 but found "+string.charAt( i ) );
  }

  int[] result=new int[ arrayLength ];
  int resultIndex=0;

  int count=0;
```

```
    for ( int i=0; i<string.length(); i++ ) {
      if ( string.charAt( i ) == '1' )
        count++;
      else {
        result[ resultIndex++ ]=count;
        count=0;
      }
    }


    return result;
}
```

The decode(String) method first checks the incoming string. If it is empty, we don't even need to start our algorithm and can return with an empty array. Furthermore, the string must be terminated with a zero—we check this as well and throw an exception otherwise.

If the incoming string is correct, we are faced with the problem that by looking at the string, we don't know how big the array is for the return. Therefore, the first loop counts the number of zeros because it matches the number of entries in the array to be created. Character by character, the for loop runs over the string and counts up arrayLength whenever a zero is found. If the other character is not a one, the method raises an exception.

After the first loop pass, the size of the array is known, and the array can be created with that size. Another for loop follows, which counts the number of ones. If zero follows, the sequence of ones finds its termination, and the counter count is written into the array. The counter is reset, and a new search for the ones begins.

Lose Weight by Moving Digits

com/tutego/exercise/string/WeightCheater.java

```java
private static void swap( StringBuilder string, int i, int j ) {
  if ( i == j ) return;
  char temp=string.charAt( i );
  string.setCharAt( i, string.charAt( j ) );
  string.setCharAt( j, temp );
}

public static int cheatedWeight( int weight ) {
  StringBuilder weightString=new StringBuilder().append( weight );
  char smallestDigit=weightString.charAt( 0 );
  int  smallestDigitIndex=0;
  for ( int i=1; i<weightString.length(); i++ ) {
    char c=weightString.charAt( i );
    if ( c != '0' && c<smallestDigit ) {
      smallestDigit=c;
      smallestDigitIndex=i;
    }
  }
  swap( weightString, smallestDigitIndex, 0 );

  return Integer.parseInt( weightString, 0, weightString.length(), 10 );
}
```

The cheatedWeight(...) method accepts an integer parameter and returns an integer value. In theory, the problem could be solved using arithmetic operations, but this would be a cumbersome approach. It is easier to convert the integer to a string, find the smallest digit, and put it in front. As we can swap symbols in a string, we resort to a mutable `StringBuilder`. We declare a helper method `swap(...)`, which swaps two symbols at the given positions. Although in our case we always swap with the first place, this utility method could perhaps become relevant for later fields of application. Therefore, the method is generic. It first checks if the two positions are identical; if they are, no swapping is necessary. Otherwise, the character at position `i` is extracted and stored in an intermediate variable, then the character at position `j` is placed at position `i`, and then the cached symbol is placed at position `j`.

With the method `cheatedWeight(...)`, we find the digit with the smallest value in the loop and also remember the position. However, we have to ignore 0; it is of course smaller than all other digits, but the task prohibits the prefixing of 0.

After running the loop, we swap the digit at the position `smallestDigitIndex` with the first digit. Finally, we need to convert the `StringBuilder` to an integer; the Integer class provides the method for this:

```
static int parseInt(CharSequence s, int beginIndex, int endIndex, int radix)
throws NumberFormatException
```

`StringBuilder` is a special `CharSequence`. The method says the following: Give me any string, a start position, an end position, and a radix—10 for the ordinary decimal system—and I'll convert that region to an integer for you.

Remove Vowels

Different approaches to the solution are to be listed:

com/tutego/exercise/string/RemoveVowel.java

```java
public static String removeVowels1( String string ) {
  string=string.replace( "a", "" ).replace( "A", "" );
  string=string.replace( "ä", "" ).replace( "Ä", "" );
  string=string.replace( "e", "" ).replace( "E", "" );
  string=string.replace( "o", "" ).replace( "O", "" );
  string=string.replace( "ö", "" ).replace( "Ö", "" );
  string=string.replace( "u", "" ).replace( "U", "" );
  string=string.replace( "ü", "" ).replace( "Ü", "" );
  string=string.replace( "i", "" ).replace( "I", "" );
  string=string.replace( "y", "" ).replace( "Y", "" );
  return string;
}
```

The first solution is not only simple but also with a high amount of code duplication. The `replace(...)` method is overloaded: with one variant we can replace characters with other characters, with the other variant we can substitute strings with strings. The `replace(char, char)` method can't remove a character. However, with the second variant that allows for string replacement, we can substitute a string of any length with an empty string, effectively deleting it.

Variant number 2:

com/tutego/exercise/string/RemoveVowel.java

```java
public static String removeVowels2( String string ) {
  char[] chars=new char[ string.length() ];
  int len=0;

  for ( int i=0; i<string.length(); i++ ) {
    char c=string.charAt( i );
```

```
    if ( "aeiouöäüyAEIOUÄÖÜY".indexOf( c ) < 0 )
      chars[ len++ ] = c;
  }

  return new String( chars, 0, len );
}
```

The second method builds a temporary `char` buffer by first collecting all characters that are not vowels. This buffer of characters can be smaller than the string, but not larger. To start, we, therefore, build a `char[]` with the maximum number of characters expected, and that is the length of the incoming string. In a new variable `len`, we note the size of the new resulting array. A loop now runs over all characters of the string. In the next step, we have to test whether the character is a vowel or not. This solution, as well as the following ones, uses quite different approaches here. A good way is to test with `indexOf(char)`. We first collect all the characters we want to find in a string. Then `indexOf(char)` tests whether the character we are looking at is in that substring or not. If `indexOf(...)` answers with a positive result, we know that the character was in the string, that is, it was a vowel. Since we would like to remove all vowels, we simply turn the condition around; `indexOf(char)` returns -1 if the character was not in the string. And if the character was not in the string, we put the character in the array and increment the position. A small performance optimization would be to sort the characters by frequency. At the end of the loop, we have gone over the input string once and put selected characters into the array. Now we need to convert the array back to a string. For this, the `String` class provides a suitable constructor.

The third variant differs in two details from the previous variant:

com/tutego/exercise/string/RemoveVowel.java

```
public static String removeVowels3( String string ) {
  StringBuilder result = new StringBuilder( string.length() );
  for ( int i=0; i < string.length(); i++ ) {
    char c = string.charAt( i );
    switch ( c ) {
      case 'a', 'e', 'i', 'o', 'u', 'y', 'ä', 'ö', 'ü' -> { }
      default -> result.append( c );
    }
  }
  return result.toString();
}
```

The first difference is that no array is used as a buffer, but a `StringBuilder`, to which `append(...)` is used to append the character that is not a vowel. The second change concerns whether the character is a vowel. Here we resort to the modern `switch` statement with the arrow notation.

The fourth solution resorts to a custom method `isVowel(char)` that tests whether a character is a vowel.

com/tutego/exercise/string/RemoveVowel.java

```
private static boolean isVowel( char c ) {
  return "aeiouyäöüAEIOUYÄÖÜ".indexOf( c ) >= 0;
}

public static String removeVowels4( String string ) {
  StringBuilder result = new StringBuilder( string.length() );
  for ( int i=0; i < string.length(); i++ ) {
    char c = string.charAt( i );
    if ( ! isVowel( c ) )
      result.append( c );
  }
```

```
  return result.toString();
}
```

Indeed, the consideration is whether a method that removes vowels should also decide what a vowel is. If we want to program well, then a single method should not be able to do too much. Therefore, it is reasonable to have one method that tests whether a character is a vowel and another method that can remove vowels from a string. Both have different tasks.

The following two solutions anticipate a bit thematically and use regular expressions quite cleverly.

com/tutego/exercise/string/RemoveVowel.java

```
public static String removeVowels5( String string ) {
  return string.replaceAll( "[aeiouyäöüAEIOUYÄÖÜ]", "" );
}
```

With the corresponding `replaceAll(...)` method, the task can be solved with a one-liner. `replaceAll(String, String)` gets as first argument a regular expression, which here stands for a group of characters. If the regular expression matches a character, the character is replaced by an empty string, i.e., removed.

The last solution goes a different, quite creative way.

com/tutego/exercise/string/RemoveVowel.java

```
public static String removeVowels6( String string ) {
  String result="";
  String[] tokens=string.split( "[aeiouyäöüAEIOUYÄÖÜ]" );
  for ( String value : tokens )
    result += value;
  return result;
}
```

Instead of replacing the characters with nothing, the vowels here are separators. The `split(...)` method consequently returns us all substrings before or after a vowel. We can reassemble these substrings into a result string.

Don't Shoot the Messenger

com/tutego/exercise/string/Messenger.java

```
private static String charAtOrEmpty( String string, int index ) {
  return index<string.length() ? string.substring( index, index+1 ) : "";
}

private static String joinSplitMessages( String... parts ) {
  int maxStringLength=0;

  for ( String part : parts )
    maxStringLength=Math.max( maxStringLength, part.length() );

  StringBuilder result=new StringBuilder();
  for ( int index=0; index<maxStringLength; index++ )
    for ( String part : parts )
      result.append( charAtOrEmpty( part, index ) );
```

```
    return result.toString();
}
```

Later, when we run over all parts of the messenger, characters might be missing because the transfer is incomplete; an example is "H", "", "ooky", where the second string has no character at the 0 position. To counter possible exceptions, we introduce a separate method charAtOrEmpty(String, int), which will fall back from a String to a character at a position; if the character does not exist at that position because the string is not that long, an empty string will be returned.

The charAtOrEmpty(...) method mimics the behavior of JavaScript. There is also a charAt(...) function here; it returns an empty string if the character at that index does not exist.

The actual joinSplitMessages(...) method takes a vararg of strings. We do not check for null, but let it come to a NullPointerException, which will follow when the extended for loop accesses the array.

The algorithm consists of two steps. In the first step, the maximum string length is determined from all parts. The background is that messengers might transmit fewer data, so we go by the messenger that has the largest number of characters. So, the query is meant for a scenario like joinSplitMessages("H", "", "ooky"). At the end of the loop, the variable maxStringLength contains the length of the longest string.

In the second step, we ask for the first character of the first part, then the first character of the second part, the first character of the third part, and so on. In the next step, we learn the second character of the first part, the second character of the second part, and so on. The outer loop generates indices from 0 to the maximum length of all the strings, and the inner loop runs over all the parts of the messengers. To request a character of the part's string, we resort to our method, which ensures that no exception occurs if no character exists at the index position.

After passing the loops, we convert the StringBuilder to a String and return the String.

Compress Repeated Spaces

com/tutego/exercise/string/CompressSpace.java

```
public static final String TWO_SPACES="  ";

static String compressSpace( String string ) {
  return compressSpace( new StringBuilder( string ) ).toString();
}

static StringBuilder compressSpace( StringBuilder string ) {
  int index=string.lastIndexOf( TWO_SPACES );

  while ( index >= 0 ) {
    string.deleteCharAt( index );
    index=string.lastIndexOf( TWO_SPACES );
  }
  return string;
}
```

For practical reasons, we write an overloaded compressSpace(...) method, one variant with the String parameter type and the String return type, a second time with the StringBuilder parameter type, and this variant returns a StringBuilder. The String variant is more convenient for users because strings are more common as a type than StringBuilder. The variant with the String parameter then takes the trouble of converting to a StringBuilder and back. In addition to the two methods, we create a constant TWO _ SPACES that contains two spaces.

If we need to modify a string, we have two options: One is to rebuild a new string character by character, in our case including all characters but not two spaces in a row. The other option is to modify an existing string. This is the solution we choose.

We go with `lastIndexOf(...)` from right to left, thus from back to front over the `StringBuilder`, and search for two blanks. If we have a result greater than or equal to 0, then we delete exactly one character at the position where the two spaces occurred so that the first space disappears. We are now also searching for the next instance of two spaces using `lastIndexOf(...)`. Eventually, we will have searched the entire `StringBuilder` from right to left, and we won't find any more instances of two spaces. This is the point at which we should stop.

It is perhaps strange that the `lastIndexOf(...)` method is used and not `indexOf(...)` which runs from left to right. Both work. However, for delete operations, it is more performant if fewer data are deleted. So, if we were to run over the string from the left and would find two spaces, we would have to move everything behind it one position to the left. But since there may be another two spaces on the right, we would move them too, even if they disappear later anyway. If we run from right to left, we won't find two more spaces to the right of our current position, which means we won't move any unnecessary spaces.

Insert and Remove Crackles and Pops

com/tutego/exercise/string/Crack.java

```java
private static final String CRACK="♪CRACK♪";

public static String crackle( String string ) {
  int capacity=string.length()+string.length() * CRACK.length() / 10;
  StringBuilder result=new StringBuilder( capacity );
  result.append( string );

  for ( int i=string.length() - 1; i >= 0; i-- )
    if ( Math.random()<0.1 )
      result.insert( i, CRACK );
  return result.toString();
}

public static String decrackle( String string ) {
  return string.replace( CRACK, "" );
}
```

We first declare a private final constant CRACK with the crackle string, so we can easily change the string. Later, two places refer to CRACK, when inserting the crackle and also when deleting the crackle.

The crackle(...) method gets a `String` and returns a `String`. There are different approaches to the task. The solution here copies the passing string into a dynamic `StringBuilder` to insert the crackle at appropriate places. We generate potential insertion positions with a for loop and decide randomly whether to insert the crackle or not. There are two special features to the program. The first is that we do not generate the indexes from left to right, that is, not from the beginning to the end, but we go from right to left and work our way forward. The reason for this approach is that it allows us to avoid having one crackle overwrite another crackle. This is because if we insert a crackle at one point, the string will grow to the right as seen from the index, but not to the left. If we continue to run to the left with the index and insert a crackle there later, there can never be an overlap. Of course, if we run from left to right and insert a crackle, we could also increase the index by the length of CRACK.

The second trick is to decide to insert a crackle. A case decision with Math.random() < 0.1 is executed with a 10% probability. The insertion is done by the insert(...) method of the StringBuilder object.

The decrackle(...) method is simpler because here we can fall back on the well-known replace(...) method of the String class. We let search for the crackle string and replace it with the empty string.

Split CamelCase Strings

com/tutego/exercise/string/CamelCaseSplitter.java

```java
private static String camelCaseSplitter( String string ) {
  StringBuilder result=new StringBuilder( string );

  for ( int i=1; i<result.length(); i++ ) {
    char previousChar=result.charAt( i - 1 );
    char currentChar =result.charAt( i );
    boolean isPreviousCharLowercase=Character.isLowerCase( previousChar );
    boolean isCurrentCharUppercase =Character.isUpperCase( currentChar );
    if ( isPreviousCharLowercase && isCurrentCharUppercase ) {
      result.insert( i, " " );
      i++;
    }
  }

  return result.toString();
}
```

There are various alternative solutions for this task. The approach used here involves copying the string into a StringBuilder and inserting spaces where necessary. This approach does not involve converting upper case to lower case letters, but only requires the insertion of spaces in appropriate locations. The specific location that needs to be identified is a transition between a lowercase and uppercase letter. If a lowercase letter follows another lowercase letter or an uppercase letter follows another uppercase letter, it can be ignored.

If we have built the StringBuilder results with the original string, then the constructor will throw a NullPointerException if the passed string was null. This is an acceptable response. We then start to run the string, but since the length of the string changes due to the added spaces, we do not walk the string parameter, but result instead, the StringBuilder. Now we always consider pairs. The loop generates us indices i and at the place i is the current character and at the place i - 1 is the previous character. Therefore, the loop must also start at 1. Otherwise, we would have generated an index of -1, which leads to an error at the beginning. If the argument is none or one character long, the loop body is not entered.

The two characters previousChar and currentChar are now tested to see if the previous character was a lowercase letter and the following character was an uppercase letter. We rely on the answer of the Character methods, which provide correct answers for all Unicode characters. Case discrimination checks the criterion that an uppercase letter must follow a lowercase letter. In this case, we put a space at that position. This shifts the whole following block of characters from one place to the right. If we have detected a shift, then the index 'i' points to the upper case letter. If we have inserted a space at this position, the index will point to space afterward. However, we do not have to check spaces via our algorithm. We can therefore increase the index for space by one so that the index is then on the following uppercase letter. Since it continues afterward in the continuation expression of the loop, the index is increased once again. Thus, the index goes behind the capital letter, and the test continues for the following characters. If i++ is missing, this will not be noticed, since spaces are not letters, but by incrementing i, the algorithm saves a comparison.

At the end of the loop, the dynamic `StringBuilder` is converted to a `String` and returned.

Alternative implementations may be to build a `StringBuilder` first and not modify it later, there is also a regular expression solution.

A solution with a regular expression is possible, but not trivial:

```
String regex="(?<=\p{javaLowerCase})(?=\p{javaUpperCase})";
String s=String.join( " ", "CiaoCiaoCAPTAINCiaoCiao".split( regex ) );
```

\p{javaLowerCase} and \p{javaUpperCase} stand for the `character` methods. ?<= is called "zero-width positive look behind" and ?= is a "zero-width positive look ahead". "Look ahead" says already quite well what it is about: Just look, don't touch anything! We can use it to find characters, but they don't become part of the match; the number of matched characters is 0. The spelling determines the transition from a lowercase letter to an uppercase letter, but since it's not a match, no characters are missing in the `split(...)` result.

In Java, the usual notation for identifiers is CamelCase; each new segment starts with an uppercase letter. Examples are: `ArrayList`, `numberOfElements`.

Underline Words

com/tutego/exercise/string/PrintUnderline.java

```
public static void printUnderline( String string, String search ) {
  System.out.println( string );

  string=string.toLowerCase();
  search=search.toLowerCase();

  StringBuilder secondLine=new StringBuilder();
  for ( int index=0;
        (index=string.indexOf( search, index )) >= 0;
        index += search.length() ) {
    secondLine.append( " ".repeat( index - secondLine.length() ) )
              .append( "-".repeat( search.length() ) );
  }
  System.out.println( secondLine );
}
```

The task has an interesting logic, which at first sight makes it difficult to understand. We have to manage the following: find all substrings and then put spaces wherever the search string does not appear and minus signs under all substrings.

The `printUnderline(...)` method first prints the text followed by the new line. To make the search case-insensitive, we convert `string` and `search` to lowercase. `indexOf(...)` then searches a lowercase string for a lowercase substring.

With `secondLine` we have a variable that grows over time so that it can be output at the end. The advantage is that once we want the `printUnderline(...)` method to return `String`, we don't have to change much code. The second advantage is the possibility to query the length—so we can find out how many characters have already been written.

A loop finds all positions with the searched string `search`. The `for` loop is complex because there is also an assignment in the conditional expression for breaking the loop. The idea is the following: we update the variable `index` with the found location, and if this is greater than or equal to 0, we have a found location and execute the body of the loop. We end the loop when `indexOf(...)` states that there are no more finds. As a result, there are exactly as many runs as there are finds of `search`.

The body of the loop needs to do two things:

- Produce spaces, and as many as we need to get from the last location (`secondLine.length()`) to the current find location (`index`). In other words: we put `index - secondLine.length()` many spaces.
- Append as many minus signs to the `secondLine` as the `string search` is long.

Both can be implemented nicely with the `repeat(...)` method, which quickly multiplies the desired character (or string).

Finally, we update the variable `index` in the `for` loop's continuation expression by the length of the string to be searched because after the last find we have to continue directly after the search string. In other words, `indexOf(...)` starts the next search at the end of the last string, starting from `index`.

Implement Caesar Encryption

The proposed solution consists of the methods `caesar(...)` for encryption and `decaesar(...)` for decryption and another private method named `rotate(...)`:

com/tutego/exercise/string/CaesarCipher.java

```java
public static final int ALPHABET_LENGTH=26;

private static int rotate( int c, int rotation ) {
  if ( rotation< 0 )
    throw new IllegalArgumentException(
        "Rotation is not allowed to be negative, but was "+rotation );

  if ( c >= 'A' && c <= 'Z' )   // Character.isUpperCase( c ) is too broad
    return 'A'+(c - 'A'+rotation) % ALPHABET_LENGTH;
  else if ( c >= 'a' && c <= 'z' )
    return 'a'+(c - 'a'+rotation) % ALPHABET_LENGTH;
  else
    return c;
}
```

The private method `int rotate(int c, int rotation)` moves a character a certain number of positions—we also call this *distance*. Since we want to consider upper as well as lower case characters, there are two case distinctions. Furthermore, the character may be neither an uppercase nor a lowercase letter, and then the original character is returned unchanged. In the constant `ALPHABET_LENGTH` we store the length of the alphabet, i.e., 26. Negative shifts are not allowed and lead to an exception.

The program logic is the same for uppercase and lowercase letters, so let's look at the expression representative of uppercase letters. At first glance, the solution is simple: we add the distance to the Unicode position of the character `c`. If we have a character like `'W'` and add three, we end up with `'Z'`. We have problems with the wrapping, so that after `'Z'` we have to continue with `'A'` again. Of course, a case distinction could check whether we run beyond `'Z'`, and then subtract the length of the alphabet, i.e., 26, but there is another solution to the problem which does not require a case distinction: In this solution, we do not add the distance to the character `c`. The consideration is rather what we have to add to the starting letter `'A'` to get to the letter `c`, and then also shifted by the distance. These are two parts. With `c - 'A'` we have calculated exactly the distance we have to add to get from the starting letter `'A'` to `c`. `'A' + (c - 'A')` is equal to `c`. Since we want to have a distance of `rotation` from the start letter, we add the distance, so `'A' + (c - 'A'+rotation)`. This looks shortened like `c + rotation`, but there is a subtle difference, namely, that we can now take the parenthesized expression % ALPHABET _ LENGTH, so that 'Z' +1 leads us back to 'A'.

com/tutego/exercise/string/CaesarCipher.java

```java
public static String caesar( String s, int rotation ) {
  StringBuilder result=new StringBuilder( s.length() );

  for ( int i=0; i<s.length(); i++ )
    result.append( (char) rotate( s.charAt( i ), rotation ) );

  return result.toString();

  // Freaky solution
  // IntUnaryOperator rotation=c -> rotate( c, rotation );
  // return s.chars().map( rotation ).mapToObj( Character::toString )
  //          .collect( Collectors.joining() );
}

public static String decaesar( String s, int rotation ) {
  return caesar( s, ALPHABET_LENGTH - rotation );
}
```

The String caesar(String s, int rotation) method is then itself without surprise. We build an internal StringBuilder in which we collect the result, then run over the input string once from front to back, grab each character and rotate it, then put it in those containers. Finally, we convert the StringBuilder to a String and return it.

The method decaesar(...) uses a nice property, and that is that and after a certain number of shifts we end up back at the original character. And this number of shifts is just the size of the alphabet, so 26. What happens if we don't shift the character by 26 positions, but only by 25? Then we would not have shifted the character to the "right", but to the "left"; a B would then no longer become a C, but the B would become an A. We can therefore decode with the position ALPHABET_LENGTH - rotation, which moves the character back to the left to its original position. One difference to caesar(...) is, however, that we must not go into the negative by the subtraction because otherwise, an exception threatens. This is of course not symmetrical to caesar(...) because the distance may be arbitrary..1

Writing Your Own Classes

6

We've already created multiple classes. However, these classes have only utilized static fields and methods, and we haven't leveraged them to create instances yet. While we have crafted objects using classes from the Java standard library, we aim to broaden our understanding. We're now looking to design our own classes and create instances of these custom types.

This chapter is about electronic consumer devices, and most of the exercises build on each other. We will first build simple electrical devices such as radios and televisions; later we will realize abstractions and collect these electrical devices on a ship. And when Captain CiaoCiao and Bonny Brain go on vacation, everything must be turned off nicely. In this way, the topics of associations and inheritance can be practiced. As a reminder, an association is what we refer to as a "has" or "knows" relationship; an inheritance is an "is-a-kind-of" relationship.

Prerequisites

- Be able to create new classes.
- Be able to set instance variables in classes.
- Be able to implement methods.
- Know visibilities `private`, package visible, and `public`.
- Be able to use static methods and fields.
- Be able to declare and use enumeration types.
- Know how to implement simple and overloaded constructors.
- Know types of associations.
- Be able to implement 1:1 association.
- Be able to use a `List`.
- Be able to use delegation of operations.
- Be able to implement inheritance relations with `extends`.
- Be able to override methods.
- Understand the two meanings of `super`.
- Be able to use dynamic binding.
- Be able to use and declare interfaces.
- Use default methods in interfaces.

Data types used in this chapter:

- `java.util.ArrayList`
- `java.util.Timer`
- `java.util.TimerTask`
- `java.util.Comparator`
- `java.util.function.Predicate`

DOI: 10.1201/9781003454502-7

CLASS DECLARATION AND OBJECT PROPERTIES

For a new type, we write a new class in Java. Let's create a few classes in this section and give the classes instance variables and methods.

Declare Radio with Instance Variables and a Main Program ★

The first type of our collection of electrical devices is a radio. Radio has a state that we want to store. Task:

- Create a new class `Radio`.
- Provide the radio with the following instance variables:
    - `isOn`, is the radio on or off?
    - `volume`, how loud does the radio play music?
- What types of variables are useful? Make sure that the instance variables are not static!
- Write an additional class `Application`, which creates a `Radio` object in its `main(...)` method. Assign and access the variables for testing.

Consider the naming conventions: classes start with an uppercase letter and variables and methods with a lowercase letter; only constants are in uppercase.

Implementing Methods of a Radio ★

Methods are to be put into the new class `radio` so that the object "can" do something. Task:

- Add the following nonstatic methods:
    - `void volumeUp()`/`void volumeDown()`: change the instance variable volume by 1 and −1, respectively. The volume may only be in the range of 0–100.
    - `void on()`/ `void off()`/ `boolean isOn()`: access the instance variable `isOn`; it is okay if a method is named like an instance variable. The `on()`/`off()` methods are supposed to print messages like "on"/"off" on the screen.
    - `public String toString()`: it should return information about the internal state as a string, where the string should take a form like `Radio[volume=2, is on]`.
- In the `main(...)` method of the `Application` class, the object methods of the radio can be tested like this, for example:

excerpt from Application.java

```
Radio grandmasOldRadio=new Radio();
System.out.println( grandmasOldRadio.isOn() );      // false
grandmasOldRadio.on();
System.out.println( grandmasOldRadio.isOn() );      // true
System.out.println( grandmasOldRadio.volume );      // 0
grandmasOldRadio.volumeUp();
grandmasOldRadio.volumeUp();
grandmasOldRadio.volumeDown();
grandmasOldRadio.volumeUp();
```

```
System.out.println( grandmasOldRadio.volume );      // 2
System.out.println( grandmasOldRadio.toString() ); // Radio[volume=2,
is on]
System.out.println( grandmasOldRadio );            // Radio[volume=2,
is on]
grandmasOldRadio.off();
```

Private Parts: Make Instance Variables Private ★

The private details of implementation must not be public so that you can change the insides at any time. Task:

- Make all instance variables from Radio private.
- Decide if the methods can be made public.
- Are there any internal methods that should be private?

Create Setters and Getters ★

In the Java world, getters and setters are commonly utilized to define *properties*. These properties can be automatically accessed by many frameworks through their corresponding getter and setter methods. Task:

1. Add a new private double instance variable frequency to the Radio so that you can set the frequency.
2. Modify the toString() method so that it takes the frequency into account.
3. Writing these setters and getters is often tedious, so either generate them automatically using an integrated development environment (IDE) or use tools to put them in the bytecode automatically. Generate setters and getters for frequency using the IDE.
4. If you want to implement read-only operations and prevent properties from being modified externally, use getters without setters. If a variable is final, only getters will work. Generate only one getter for the state volume.

Setters and getters are an important naming convention. If a property XXX is of type boolean, the prefix is generally isXXX(), not getXXX(). So, our existing method isOn() is also a getter.

STATIC VARIABLES METHODS

Class variables and static methods often lead to confusion for novice programmers. Yet, it is simple: either state is stored within individual objects or within the class object itself. If we have different objects with instance variables, the object methods can access the individual properties. A static method can only access class variables without explicitly specifying an object.

Convert Station Names to Frequencies ★

So far, the radio has only instance variables and instance methods. Let's add a static method that has no link to a concrete radio object.

Task:

- Implement a static method double stationNameToFrequency(String) in the class Radio that maps a station as a string to a frequency (for example, the well-known pirate radio station "Walking the Plank" has the frequency 98.3).
- If null is passed to the method, then the result shall be 0.0. Furthermore, for unknown station names, the return should be 0.0.

Example:

- In the main program, we can write:
  ```
  System.out.println( Radio.stationNameToFrequency( "Walking the Plank" )
  ); // 98.3
  ```

String comparisons with stations can be implemented with switch-case or with equals(...).

Write Log Output with a Tracer Class ★

You use loggers to log program output and be able to trace it later—much like Captain CiaoCiao records in his logbook everything that happened on the seas, in the ports, and within the crew.

Task:

1. Create a new class Tracer.
2. Add a static method void trace(String) that prints a passed string on the screen.
3. Extend the program with two static methods on() and off(), which remember in an internal state whether trace(String) leads to output or not. At the beginning, the tracer shall be switched off.
4. Optional: add a method trace(String format, Object... args) that internally calls System.out.printf(format, args) when tracing is turned on.

Example:

    We can then use the class like this:

```
Tracer.on();
Tracer.trace( "Start" );
int i=2;
Tracer.off();
Tracer.trace( "i="+i );
//  Tracer.trace( "i=%d", i );
Tracer.on();
Tracer.trace( "End" );
```

The expected output is:

```
Start
End
```

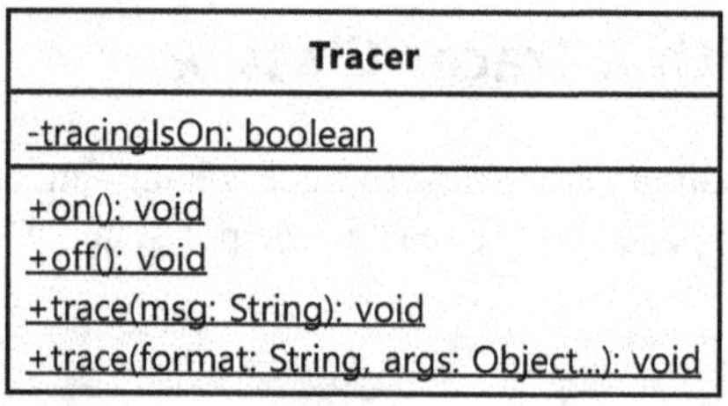

Tracer
-tracingIsOn: boolean
+on(): void +off(): void +trace(msg: String): void +trace(format: String, args: Object...): void

FIGURE 6.1   UML diagram with static properties.

Quiz: Nothing Stolen ★

Given the following class declaration:

```
public class StolenGoods {
  int value=1_000_000;
  static void print( int Value ) {
    System.out.println( value );
  }

  public static void main( String[] args ) {
    int value=2_000_000;
    new StolenGoods().print( value );
  }
}
```

Can the program be translated? If so, what is the output on the screen?

SIMPLE ENUMERATIONS

Enumerations are closed sets built in Java using the keyword enum.

Give Radio an AM–FM Modulation ★

Modulation is vital in radio transßmissions; there is AM (amplitude modulation) and FM (frequency modulation).[1]
Task:

- Declare a new enumeration type Modulation with the values AM and FM in its own file.
- Add a private instance variable Modulation modulation to Radio where the radio keeps the modulation.
- Set the Modulation via a new Radio method void setModulation(Modulation modulation), a getter can also exist.
- Customize the toString() method in Radio.

Set Valid Start and End Frequency for Modulation ★

For broadcasting, three frequency ranges (called frequency bands) are classified, which encode over AM:

- Longwave: 148.5–283.5 kHz.
- Mediumwave: 526.5–1,606.5 kHz.
- Shortwave: shortwave broadcasting uses several bands between 3.2 and 26.1 MHz.

Coded over FM:

- Ultra-shortwave (FM): 87.5–108 MHz.

Task:

- Add two new private instance variables:
  - minFrequency
  - maxFrequency
- When calling setModulation(Moduluation), the instance variables minFrequency and maxFrequency are to be set to their minimum and maximum value ranges, namely, for AM 148.5 kHz to 26.1 MHz and for FM 87.5–108 MHz.

CONSTRUCTORS

Constructors are special initialization routines that are automatically called by the virtual machine when an object is created. We often use constructors to assign states when creating objects, which we then store in the object.

Writing Radio Constructors ★

So far, our radio has had only a default constructor generated by the compiler. Let's replace it with our own constructors:

Task:

- Write a constructor for the class `Radio` so that you can initialize a radio with a frequency (`double`). But you should still be able to create radios with the parameterless constructor!
- Alternatively, a `Radio` object should be able to be initialized with a station name (as `String`) (use `stationNameToFrequency(..)` internally for this). The station name is not stored, only the frequency.
- How can we use the constructor delegation with `this(…)`?

Example: We should be able to construct radios in the following way:

```
Radio r1=new Radio();
Radio r2=new Radio( 102. );
Radio r3=new Radio( "BFBS" );
```

Implement Copy Constructor ★

If an object of the same type is assumed to be a template in the constructor of a class, we refer to this as a *copy constructor*.

Task:

- Implement a copy constructor for `Radio`.

Realize Factory Methods ★

In addition to constructors, some classes provide an alternative variant to create objects, called *factory methods*. The following applies:

- Constructors exist in principle, but they are private, and consequently, outsiders cannot create instances.
- So that objects can be built, there are static methods, which internally call the constructor and return the instance.

Task:

1. Create a new class `TreasureChest` for a treasure chest.
2. A treasure chest can contain gold doubloons and gemstones; create two public final instance variables `int  goldDoubloonWeight` and `int  gemstoneWeight`. So, the object is immutable, the states cannot be changed later. Getters are not necessary.
3. Write four static factory methods that return a `TreasureChest` object:

   - `TreasureChest newInstance()`
   - `TreasureChest newInstanceWithGoldDoubloonWeight(int)`

- `TreasureChest newInstanceWithGemstoneWeight(int)`
- `TreasureChest    newInstanceWithGoldDoubloonAndGemstoneWeight (int, int)`

Where would be the problem here with a usual constructor?

ASSOCIATIONS

An association is a dynamic connection between two or more objects. We can characterize association in several ways:

- Does only one side know the other, or do both sides know each other?
- Is the lifetime of one object related to the lifetime of another object?
- With how many other objects does an object have an association? Is there a connection to only one other object or several? For 1:n or n:m relationships, we need containers, like arrays or dynamic data structures like the `java.util.ArrayList`.

Connect Monitor Tube with TV ★

So far, we have had one electrical appliance: a radio. It's time to add a second electrical device and includes a 1:1 association.

Task:

- Create a new class TV.
- The TV should get methods `on()`/`off()` which write short messages to the console (an instance variable is not necessary for the example for now).
- Create a TV in the `main(...)` method of `Application`.
- Create a new class `MonitorTube`.
  - The `MonitorTube` shall also get `on()`/`off()` methods with console messages.
- A TV shall reference a `MonitorTube` via a private instance variable. How can this be done in Java?
  - Implement a unidirectional relationship between the TV and the monitor tube. About the life cycle: when the TV is built, the monitor tube should also be created, you don't need to be able to replace the monitor tube.
- When the TV is switched on/off, the monitor tube should also be switched on/off.
- Optional: how can we implement a bidirectional relationship? There might be a problem?

In the end, this relation should be implemented:

FIGURE 6.2   UML diagram of the directed association.

Quiz: Association, Composition, and Aggregation ★

Associations can be divided into three groups:

- Normal association.
- Composition.
- Aggregation.

What is meant by this?

Add Radios with a 1:n Association to the Ship ★★

Captain CiaoCiao owns a whole fleet of ships, and they can take cargo. In the beginning, Captain CiaoCiao only wants to load radios onto his ship.

Task:

1. Create a new class `Ship` (without `main(...)` method).
2. To enable `Ship` to hold radios, we use the data structure `java.util.ArrayList`. As private instance variable, we include in `Ship`:
   `ArrayList<Radio> radios=new ArrayList<Radio>();`
3. Write a new `load(...)` method in `Ship` to allow the ship to hold a radio.
4. Build two ships in the `main(...)` method of `Application`.
5. Assign multiple radios to a `ship` in the `main(...)` method.
6. Write a `Ship` method `int countDevicesSwitchedOn()` that returns how many radios are switched on. Attention: it is not about the total number of radios on the ship, but about the number of radios switched on!
7. Optional: Give the ship also a `toString()` method.
8. What do we need to do if the ship also wants to load other electrical devices, such as ice machines or televisions?

Implementation goal: a ship references radios.

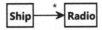

FIGURE 6.3   UML diagram of the 1:n association.

INHERITANCE

Inheritance models an is-a-type-of relationship and ties two types together very directly. The modeling is critical to form groups of related things.

Introduce Abstraction into Electrical Devices via Inheritance ★

Until now, radios and televisions have been disconnected. But there is one thing they have in common: they are all electronic consumption devices.
Task:

1. Create a new class `ElectronicDevice` for electronic devices.
2. Derive the class `Radio` from the class `ElectronicDevice`—leave TV out of it for now.
3. Pull into the superclass the common features of the potential electrical devices.
4. Write a new class `IceMachine` which is also an electrical device.

Nowadays, a development environment can automatically move properties into the superclass via refactoring; find out how.

Task Objective: implement the following inheritance relationship.

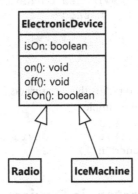

FIGURE 6.4   UML diagram of the inheritance relationship.

Quiz: Three, Two, and One ★

Given the following declarations in a file *Numbers.java*, can the compiler translate the compilation unit? If you can run the program, what is the result?

```
class One {
  public One() { System.out.print( 1 ); }
}

class Two extends One {
  public Two() { System.out.print( 2 ); }
}

class Three extends Two {
  public void Three() { System.out.print( 3 ); }
}

public class Numbers {
  public static void main( String[] args ) { new Three(); }
}
```

Quiz: Private and Protected Constructor ★

- If a class has a private constructor, can you make an instance of the class?
- If a class has a protected constructor, who can make an instance of the class?

Determine the Number of Switched on Electrical Devices ★

Inheritance can be used to declare a parameter with a supertype, which then addresses a whole group of types with it, namely, all subtypes as well.
Task:

- Declare a new static method in the class ElectronicDevice:
```
public static int numberOfElectronicDevicesSwitchedOn(
ElectronicDevice... devices ) {
  // Returns the number of switched on devices,
  // that were passed to the method
}
```

Example:

- If, for example, r1 and r2 are two radios that are turned on, and ice is an ice machine that is turned off, main(...) may say, for example:
```
int switchedOn =
  ElectronicDevice.numberOfElectronicDevicesSwitchedOn( r1, ice, r2 );
System.out.println( switchedOn ); // 2
```

Ship Should Hold Any Electronic Device ★

So far, the ship can only store the type Radio. Now, general electrical devices should be stored.
Task:

1. Change the type of the dynamic data structure from Radio to ElectronicDevice:
```
private ArrayList<ElectronicDevice> devices =
    new ArrayList<ElectronicDevice>();
```
2. Furthermore, the method to add electrical devices has to change—why?

Task objective: ships store all types of electrical devices.

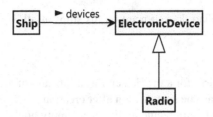

FIGURE 6.5   UML diagram.

Take Working Radios on the Ship ★

When radios are taken onto the ship, a message should appear on the console. Moreover, Captain CiaoCiao dislikes taking broken radios onto the ship.
Task:

- When a radio is passed to the load(...) addition method, it should be checked if it has volume 0; in that case, it should not be included in the data structure.
- When a radio is added, the console output should be: Remember to pay license fee!

Solve Equivalence Test with Pattern Variable ★

Java 14 introduces "pattern matching for instanceof" which can shorten the code nicely.
Task:

- Given is an older class Toaster with an equals(...) method for a test for equivalence:
  com/tutego/exercise/oop/Toaster.java

```
public class Toaster {
  int capacity;
  boolean stainless;
  boolean extraLarge;

  @Override public boolean equals( Object o ) {
    if ( !(o instanceof Toaster) ) return false;
    Toaster toaster=(Toaster) o;
    return    capacity == toaster.capacity
          && stainless ==toaster.stainless && extraLarge ==toaster.
extraLarge;
  }
  @Override public int hashCode() {

    return Objects.hash( capacity, stainless, extraLarge );
  }
}
```

- Rewrite the equals(...) method to use instanceof with a pattern variable.

Fire Alarm Does Not Go Off: Overriding Methods ★

Fire is something Captain CiaoCiao doesn't need on his ships at all. If there is a fire, it must be extinguished as soon as possible.
Task:

- Implement a class `Firebox` for a fire detector as a subclass of `ElectronicDevice`.
- Fire detectors should always be switched on after creation.
- The `off()` method should be implemented with an empty body or with console output so that a fire detector cannot be turned off.

Example:

- Task target: an overridden `off()` method that does not change the `isOn` state. This can be tested like this:
```
Firebox fb=new Firebox();
System.out.println( fb.isOn() );   // true
fb.off();
System.out.println( fb.isOn() );   // true
```

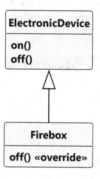

FIGURE 6.6   UML diagram.

Calling the Methods of the Superclass ★★

A radio has `on()`/`off()` methods, and the TV class also already has `on()`/`off()` methods. However, the TV is not yet an `ElectronicDevice`. The reason is that the TV needs special treatment because of the monitor tube.

If TV also extends the class `ElectronicDevice`, a TV, therefore, overwrites the methods of the superclass `ElectronicDevice`. But a problem arises:

- If we omit the two methods, the tube would not be turned off, but the TV would pass as an electrical device when inherited.
- If we leave the methods in the class, only the tube will be turned off, but the device is no longer switched on or off. After all, this state was managed by the superclass via the `on()`/`off()` methods.

Task:

- Fix the problem that a `TV` is an `ElectronicDevice`, but the monitor tube is turned on/off.

POLYMORPHISM AND DYNAMIC BINDING

A central feature of object-oriented programming languages is the dynamic resolution of method calls. This form of calls can be decided thereby not at compile-time, but at runtime, if the object type is known.

Holiday! Switch Off All Devices ★

Before Captain CiaoCiao lies down in the hammock with a Tropical Storm cocktail and enjoys his vacation, all electrical appliances on the ship must be turned off.

Task:

- Implement a method `holiday()` in the `Ship` class that turns off all the electrical devices in the list.
  ```
  public void holiday() {
      // call off() for all elements in the data structure
  }
  ```

- The main(...) method of `Application` may contain, for example:
  ```
  Radio bedroomRadio=new Radio();
  bedroomRadio.volumeUp();
  Radio cabooseRadio=new Radio();
  cabooseRadio.volumeUp();
  ```

```
TV mainTv=new TV();
Radio crRadio=new Radio();
Firebox alarm=new Firebox();
Ship ship=new Ship();
ship.load( bedroomRadio );
ship.load( cabooseRadio );
ship.load( mainTv );
ship.load( crRadio );
ship.load( alarm );
ship.holiday();
```

The Big Move ★

The fearless Captain CiaoCiao has decided to abandon his old ship and move onto a fresh barge. Since not all of his fellow pirates are capable of reading, a graphical loading list should be created with little pictures representing various items.

Task:

- Copy the following class `AsciiArt` as a nested class into the class `Ship`:

```
public static class AsciiArt {
  public static final String RADIO=" .-.\n|o.o|\n|:_:|";
  public static final String BIG_TV="""
```
```
     .---..------------------------------------.---.
     |   ||.------------------------------------.|| |
     |.-.||||                                  |||.-.|
     | o ||||                                  ||| o |
     |`-'||||                                  |||`-'|
     |.-.||||                                  |||.-.|
     | o ||||                                  ||| o |
     |`-'|||`----------------------------------'|||`-'|
     `---'`------------------------------------'`---'
          _||_                              _||_
         /____\\                           /____\\""";
  public static final String TV=" \\   /\n _\\\/_\n|    |\n|____|";
  public static final String SOCKET="""
```
```
          ____
         |    \\
      ___|     \\
     (___|      `.____
         |       _|__
      ___|      .'
     (___|     .'
         |____/""";
}
```

- Implement a new method `printLoadingList()` in `Ship` which iterates over all devices of the ship and implements the following rules for the output:
  - If the device is a `Radio` and the wattage is positive, a radio will be printed to the screen by accessing `AsciiArt.RADIO`. Broken radios have 0 watts and must not be printed.
  - If the device is a TV and the wattage is above 10,000, the image of a big TV (`AsciiArt.BIG _ TV`) will be printed.
  - If the device is a TV (regardless of the wattage), the image of a normal TV (`AsciiArt.TV`) is printed.
  - If none of the above cases applies, the image of a socket (`AsciiArt.SOCKET`) will be printed.
- Solve the task with the language feature *Pattern Matching for switch*.

Quiz: Bumbo Is a Great Drink ★★

Bonny Brain finds a recipe for Bumbo in the weekly issue of "BETTER BOARDED". But can she possibly view it?

Does the following program compile? If so, what output does it give? If not, what compiler error is there?

```java
class Drink {
  public Drink getInstance() {
    return this;
  }
  public void printIngredients() { }
}
class YummyDrink extends Drink { }
class Bumbo extends YummyDrink {
  public YummyDrink getInstance() {
    return this;
  }

  @Override public void printIngredients() {
    System.out.println(
      "2 ounces rum, 1 ounce water, 2 sugar cubes, cinnamon, nutmeg"
    );
  }

}
public class DrinkBumbo {
  public static void main( String... args ) {
    new Bumbo().getInstance().printIngredients();
  }
}
```

Quiz: Vodka with Taste ★

Given two classes, a superclass, and a subclass. The program translates correctly; what is output to the screen?

```java
class AlcoholicDrink {
 public void seasoned() {
   System.out.println( "-none-" );
 }
}

public class Vodka extends AlcoholicDrink {
 public void seasoned() {
   System.out.println( "blackcurrant" );
 }

 public static void main( String[] args ) {
   ((AlcoholicDrink) new Vodka()).seasoned();
 }
}
```

Quiz: Rum-Paradise ★★

Given the following program with two classes. Does the program compile, or is there a compiler error? If the program compiles and executes, what is the result?

```java
class AlcoholicDrink {
  int aged=1;
  AlcoholicDrink() { aged++; }
  int older() { return aged++; }
}

public class Rum extends AlcoholicDrink {
  int aged=3;
  Rum() { aged += 4; }
  int older() { return aged++; }

  public static void main( String[] args ) {
    AlcoholicDrink lakeGay=new Rum();
    System.out.println( lakeGay.older() );
    System.out.println( lakeGay.aged );
  }
}
```

ABSTRACT CLASSES AND ABSTRACT METHODS

Abstract classes are something strange at first sight: What to do with classes you can't make objects of? And what about abstract methods? A class without implemented methods has nothing to offer, after all!

Both concepts are crucial. Supertype and subtype always have a contract; a subtype must have at least what a supertype specifies and must not break semantics. If a superclass is abstract or if methods are abstract, the subclasses from which objects can be built promise to provide that functionality.

Quiz: Consumer Devices as an Abstract Superclass? ★

Can we create exemplars of `ElectronicDevice`? Do we have to be able to create instances of `ElectronicDevice`? What would be the consequences if `ElectronicDevice` was an abstract class?

TimerTask as an Example for an Abstract Class ★★

Captain CiaoCiao records each robbery by video and analyzes the sequences in the debriefing. However, the finest 8K quality videos quickly fill the hard drive. He wants to determine in time whether he needs to buy a new hard drive.

A `java.util.Timer` can perform tasks repeatedly. To achieve this, the `Timer` class has a schedule(...) method for adding a task. The task is of type `java.util.TimerTask`.
Task:

- Write a subclass of `TimerTask` that prints a message on the screen whenever the number of free bytes on the file system falls below a certain limit (e.g., less than 1000 MB).
  Returns the free bytes:
  ```
  long freeDiskSpace=java.io.File.listRoots()[0].getFreeSpace();
  ```

- The `Timer` should execute this `TimerTask` every 2 seconds.

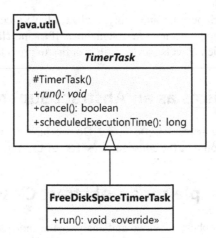

FIGURE 6.7   UML diagram of `TimerTask` and its own subclass.

Bonus: Integrate a message in the tray with:

```java
import javax.swing.*;
import java.awt.*;
import java.awt.TrayIcon.MessageType;
import java.net.URL;
try {
  String url =
    "https://cdn4.iconfinder.com/data/icons/common-toolbar/36/Save-16.png";
  ImageIcon icon=new ImageIcon( new URL( url ) );
  TrayIcon trayIcon=new TrayIcon( icon.getImage() );
  SystemTray.getSystemTray().add( trayIcon );

  trayIcon.displayMessage( "Warning", "Hard drive full", MessageType.INFO );
}
catch ( Exception e ) { e.printStackTrace(); }
```

SUGGESTED SOLUTIONS

Declare Radio with Instance Variables and a Main Program

com/tutego/exercise/device/bmxtuz/Radio.java

```java
public class Radio {
  boolean isOn;
  int     volume;
}
```

The variable `isOn` expresses whether radio is on or off; here a `boolean` variable is suitable. For the volume, we resort to a numeric data type, where we have the choice between an integer data type like `int` and a floating-point data type like `double`. It all depends on the requirements; in the following, we will use the `int` data type.

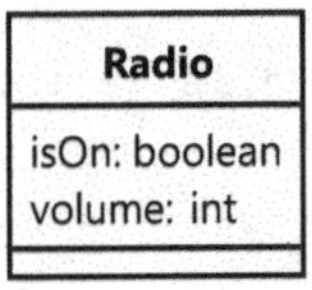

```
         Radio
  isOn: boolean
  volume: int
```

FIGURE 6.8   UML diagram of Radio with instance variables.

A Radio cannot be started, so it must not contain a main(…) method. We put the start method into the new class Application. It builds the radio and assigns states.

com/tutego/exercise/device/bmxtuz/Application.java

```java
public class Application {

  public static void main( String[] args ) {
    Radio grandmasOldRadio=new Radio();
    grandmasOldRadio.isOn   =true;
    grandmasOldRadio.volume=12;
    System.out.println( "Current volume: "+grandmasOldRadio.volume );
  }
}
```

Implementing Methods of a Radio

com/tutego/exercise/device/xcafnd/Radio.java

```java
public class Radio {

  boolean isOn;
  int      volume;
  void changeVolume( int value ) {
    volume=Math.clamp( volume+value, 0, 100 );
  }

  void volumeUp() {
    changeVolume( 1 );
  }

  void volumeDown() {
    changeVolume( -1 );
  }

  void on() {
    isOn=true;
  }

  void off() {
    isOn=false;
  }

  boolean isOn() {
    return isOn;
  }
```

```
  public String toString() {
    return "Radio[volume="+volume+",is "+(isOn ? "on" : "off")+"]";
  }
}
```

The methods can be divided into three groups:

- Methods that access the variable `volume`.
- Methods that access `isOn`.
- The `toString()` method, which accesses both instance variables in read-only mode.

To check the value range and set the `volume` variable, a new `changeVolume(...)` method has been created that sets the volume directly; it must be private later. This frees our methods responsible for slightly increasing or decreasing the radio's volume from directly handling the variable setting. The implementation ensures that the new volume remains between 0 and 100. What we've implemented here is also called saturation arithmetic (https://en.wikipedia.org/wiki/Saturation_arithmetic); all operations must remain within a fixed range and cannot exceed it. Java 21 introduces a new method `clamp(long, int, int)` which our implementation utilizes; before Java 21, one could solve the range restriction with `volume=Math.min( Math.max( volume+value, 0 ), 100 )`.

The `toString()` method follows a common structure: After the type name, which is a kind of prefix, key-value pairs follow. Instead of just taking the instance variable `isOn` as a `boolean` representation `true` or `false` in the string, the condition operator returns an individual identifier `on` or `off`.

Extra assignment in assignment: The `toString()` method can be generated by the development environment. Find out how to do this.

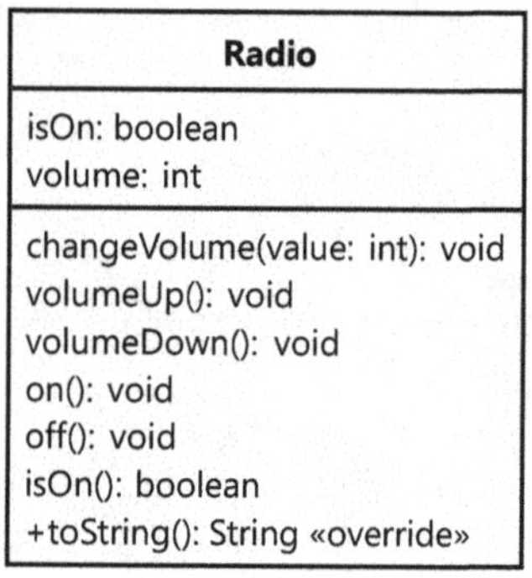

Radio
isOn: boolean volume: int
changeVolume(value: int): void volumeUp(): void volumeDown(): void on(): void off(): void isOn(): boolean +toString(): String «override»

FIGURE 6.9 UML diagram of `Radio` with instance variables and methods.

Private Parts: Make Instance Variables Private

We put the keyword `private` in front of the instance variables and in front of the method `changeVolume(int)`:

```
private boolean isOn;
private int volume;

private void changeVolume( int value ) {
  volume=Math.min( Math.max( volume+value, 0 ), 100 );
}
```

We can make the other properties explicitly public with the keyword `public`. If no visibility modifier is set, the properties are package-visible, that is, visible only to the types in the same package, but not outside the package.

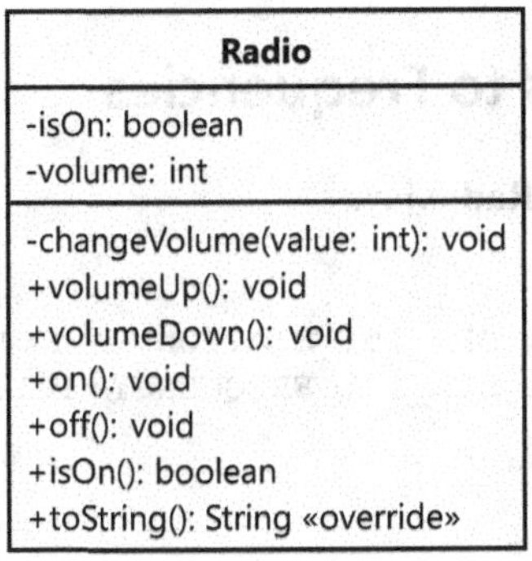

```
┌─────────────────────────────────────────┐
│                  Radio                   │
├─────────────────────────────────────────┤
│ -isOn: boolean                           │
│ -volume: int                             │
├─────────────────────────────────────────┤
│ -changeVolume(value: int): void          │
│ +volumeUp(): void                        │
│ +volumeDown(): void                      │
│ +on(): void                              │
│ +off(): void                             │
│ +isOn(): boolean                         │
│ +toString(): String «override»           │
└─────────────────────────────────────────┘
```

FIGURE 6.10   UML diagram of `Radio` with public and private properties.

Create Setters and Getters

com/tutego/exercise/device/sgxrwy/Radio.java

```java
private boolean isOn;
private int volume;
private double frequency;

public void setFrequency( double frequency ) {
  this.frequency=frequency;
}

public double getFrequency() {
  return frequency;
}

public int getVolume() {
  return volume;
}

public String toString() {
  return "Radio[volume="+volume+", isOn="+isOn+", frequency="+frequency+']';
}
```

A modern development environment can generate getters/setters automatically.

IntelliJ
In the editor, press Alt+Ins, and a small menu will appear. Choose *Getters and Setters* there. In the dialog, you can now select the instance variables.

Eclipse
Go to *Source* in the context menu and select *Generate Getters and Setters*. In the following dialog, you can select the instance variables and determine whether only getters/setters should be generated.

NetBeans

Press Alt+Ins, and select *Getters and Setters* from the context menu. Alternatively, activate *Source > Insert Code*.

Convert Station Names to Frequencies

com/tutego/exercise/device/oxujap/Radio.java

```java
class RadioStations {
  public static final String SEA_101_STATION_NAME="sea 101";
  public static final double SEA_101_FREQUENCY=101.0;
}

class Radio {
  public static double stationNameToFrequency( String station ) {
    if ( station == null )
      return 0.0;

    return switch ( station.trim().toLowerCase() ) {
      case "walking the plank" -> 98.3;
      case RadioStations.SEA_101_STATION_NAME -> RadioStations.
SEA_101_FREQUENCY;
      default -> 0.0;
    };
  }

  // other methods omitted
}
```

The method `stationNameToFrequency(String station)` first tests the passed argument for `null` and then returns 0. An alternative is an exception. If a `String` object is present, `trim()` trims whitespace at the front and back, and the string is converted to lowercase. The arrow notation of the switch-case statement performs a compact comparison on two strings, where the lowercase converted string `"Walking the Plank"` is hard-coded and the second string is referenced via a constant of another class. Small note: instead of initializing the constant `SEA_101_STATION_NAME` directly with the lowercase "sea 101", we could have evaluated the string dynamically:

```java
public static final String SEA_101_STATION_NAME="SEA 101".toLowerCase();
```

Class variables are our next topic.

Write Log Output with a Tracer Class

com/tutego/exercise/oop/Tracer.java

```java
public class Tracer {

  private static boolean tracingIsOn;
  public static void on() {
    tracingIsOn=true;
  }
```

```java
public static void off() {
  tracingIsOn=false;
}

public static void trace( String msg ) {
  if ( tracingIsOn )
    System.out.println( msg );
}

public static void trace( String format, Object... args ) {
  if ( tracingIsOn )
    System.out.printf( format+"%n", args );
}
}
```

The class `Tracer` has a private static variable `boolean tracingIsOn`, in which we keep track of whether tracing output is desired or not. The methods `on()` and `off()` set `tracingIsOn`. It is important that not only the methods are static but also the variable `tracingIsOn`. It would not work if the methods were connected to the class, but `tracingIsOn` were connected to an object. Static methods can only access their own class variables, unless they get access to an object, for example, via a parameter, or they build an object themselves. The actual `trace(...)` methods use this state to check whether they should output something to the screen.

The method named `trace(String format, Object... args)` delegates to `System.out.printf(...)` but appends an end-of-line character to the format string to make it behave like a `println(...)`. The advantage of this method is that it can be more performant because string concatenations are not done.

There are various logger libraries in Java for real enterprise use, also the Java SE brings something rudimentary with `java.util.logging`.

Quiz: Nothing Stolen

The program cannot be compiled because static and nonstatic properties are being mixed here. The core of the problem is accessing the instance variable `value` in the `print(...)` method. However, `value` is an instance variable, not a static variable.

The fact that the parameter variable is capitalized is just an irritation; if `println(...)` would fall back to `Value`, that would be fine, the instance variable would be out of the picture.

The call to the static method in the `main(...)` method via the object reference is unnecessary and only misleading. If the method would use its own instance variable, it would not need the argument either.

Give Radio an AM–FM Modulation

com/tutego/exercise/device/ewslfg/Modulation.java

```java
public enum Modulation {
  AM, FM
}
```

`Modulation` declares the two enumeration elements `AM` and `FM`. We capitalize them because they are constants, and constants are typically capitalized. Each constant references an object because enumeration elements are reference variables. That is, `AM` and `FM` reference objects of type `Modulation`.

The following excerpt from `Radio` is reduced to modulation:

com/tutego/exercise/device/ewslfg/Radio.java

```java
private Modulation modulation=Modulation.AM;
public void setModulation( Modulation modulation ) {
  this.modulation=Objects.requireNonNull( modulation );
}

public Modulation getModulation() {
  return modulation;
}
@Override public String toString() {
  return   "Radio["+"isOn="+isOn+", volume="+volume
        +", frequency="+frequency+", modulation="+modulation+']';
}
```

If we want to keep a reference to a modulation, we create a variable `modulation` for this purpose, which is of type `Modulation`. The instance variable `modulation` is pre-initialized with `Modulation`. `AM` to minimize the danger of a `NullPointerException` if a method is called on the modulation variable. The instance variable `modulation` is pre-initialized with `Modulation.AM` to minimize the danger of a `NullPointerException` if a method is called on the modulation variable. So, also `setModulation(Modulation)` checks via `Objects.requireNonNull(...)` that no null was passed via `Objects.requireNonNull(...)`—the method throws a `NullPointerException` if null was passed, and `requireNonNull(...)` returns the reference if it was not `null`, so we can take the parameter into the instance variable. This is a good programming style—all methods should check if no `null` was passed.

The `toString()` method is simple because since `Modulation` is an object that has `toString()` itself, the `toString()` method of the `Radio` object can directly access the `toString()` method of `Modulation`. With string concatenation, it is convenient that if the reference is `null` we don't have to test this separately, just the string `null` will appear in the string.

Set Valid Start and End Frequency for Modulation

com/tutego/exercise/device/ofmxo/Radio.java

```java
private Modulation modulation=Modulation.AM;

private static final double MIN_AM_FREQUENCY=148.5 * 1000      /* Hz */;
private static final double MAX_AM_FREQUENCY= 26.1 *1_000_000 /* Hz */;
private static final double MIN_FM_FREQUENCY= 87.5 *1_000_000 /* Hz */;
private static final double MAX_FM_FREQUENCY=108.0 *1_000_000 /* Hz */;
private double minFrequency=MIN_AM_FREQUENCY;
private double maxFrequency=MAX_AM_FREQUENCY;

public void setModulation( Modulation modulation ) {
  this.modulation=Objects.requireNonNull( modulation );
  minFrequency=modulation ==Modulation.AM ? MIN_AM_FREQUENCY
                                          : MIN_FM_FREQUENCY;
  maxFrequency=modulation ==Modulation.AM ? MAX_AM_FREQUENCY
                                          : MAX_FM_FREQUENCY;
}
```

We create four constants for the smallest and largest frequency for AM and FM, respectively. We preset the two instance variables `minFrequency` and `maxFrequency` given in the task with the frequency range of the AM modulation because this is the standard assignment of the instance variable `modulation`.

The method `setModulation(…)` has now different possibilities to check the assignment of the variable `modulation` and to set `minFrequency` and `maxFrequency` depending on the assignment afterward. One possibility would be a condition statement with `if-else`, another possibility offers the `switch-case`; the approach chosen here uses the condition operator. enum objects are so-called *singletons*, i.e., objects that exist only once, and reference comparison with == is allowed, which is unusual for regular objects—here `equals(…)` would have to be used.

Writing Radio Constructors

com/tutego/exercise/device/biwdxj/Radio.java

```java
public Radio() {
}

public Radio( double frequency ) {
  setFrequency( frequency );
}

public Radio( String station ) {
  this( stationNameToFrequency( station ) );
}
```

Our solution has three constructors. The parameterless constructor is empty but present; we do not perform any initialization here.

There are two parameterized constructors. The constructor that stores the frequency calls `setFrequency(double)` to have the frequency transferred to the internal instance variable. We are faced here with the decision of whether to directly initialize the instance variable with `this.frequency=frequency` or call the setter. The solution with the setter is generally better. There are two reasons: first, initializing states is an implementation detail. If we change something in the instance variable, we as developers would have to go to all places where there are read or write accesses. It is also important to consider that a setter can also perform validity checks. We would rather not repeat these in the constructor because code duplication is bad. Consequently, the constructor can defer saving to the instance variable and validation to the setter.

If a radio is initialized with a station, the string is first converted to a frequency, and then the constructor forward

```java
this( stationNameToFrequency( station ) );
```

so that the constructor `radio(double frequency)`, which takes a `double`, stores the frequency.

With `this(…)`, there might be only one constructor with the implementation and all other constructors forward to this one constructor. The advantage is that in the case of enhancements, only this particular constructor has to be changed. The disadvantage is however that there might come some default values or `null` into the object. However, initialization constructors are essential because they bring the object into a valid initial state so that each subsequent method call can start from a correct, valid object.

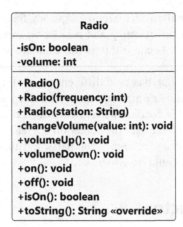

FIGURE 6.11   UML diagram of `Radio` with three constructors.

Implement Copy Constructor

com/tutego/exercise/device/ifqbap/Radio.java

```java
public Radio( Radio other ) {
  setFrequency( other.frequency );
  setModulation( other.getModulation() );
  if ( other.isOn() ) on(); else off();
  this.volume=other.volume;
}
```

The copy constructor has several special features. At its core, it is about reading the passed radio and then transferring the individual states to our own new radio.

We retrieve the states from the `radio` via the getter and `isOn()` methods and transfer them to our own instance variables using the setter and `on()`/`off()` methods.

However, there is no `setVolume(…)`/`getVolume(…)` for the instance variable `volume`. The special rules in Java's visibility allow accessing the private states from the passed `radio` as well, because we are a `radio` ourselves! We have to use this to read the `volume` from the passed `radio` and transfer it to the new `radio`. For the other states, we refrain from reading foreign private variables in the constructor and writing them to our private variables.

The copy constructor has several special features. At its core, it is about retrieving the radio state and then transferring them to our own new radio.

We retrieve the states from the `radio` via the getter and `isOn()` method and transfer them to our own instance variables using the setter and `on()`/`off()` methods.

However, there is no `setVolume(…)`/`getVolume(…)` for the instance variable `volume`. The special rules in Java's visibility allow accessing the private states from the passed `radio` as well, because we are a `Radio` ourselves! We have to use this to read the `volume` from the passed `radio` and transfer it to the new `radio`. For the other states, we refrain from reading foreign private variables in the constructor and writing them to our private variables.

Realize Factory Methods

com/tutego/exercise/device/TreasureChest.java

```java
public class TreasureChest {

  public final int goldDoubloonWeight;
  public final int gemstoneWeight;

  private TreasureChest( int goldDoubloonWeight, int gemstoneWeight ) {
    if ( goldDoubloonWeight<0 || gemstoneWeight<0 )
      throw new IllegalArgumentException( "Weight can't be negative" );
    this.goldDoubloonWeight=goldDoubloonWeight;
    this.gemstoneWeight    =gemstoneWeight;
  }

  public static TreasureChest newInstance() {
    return new TreasureChest( 0, 0 );
  }

  public static TreasureChest newInstanceWithGoldDoubloonWeight( int weight )
{
    return new TreasureChest( weight, 0 );
  }

  public static TreasureChest newInstanceWithGemstonesWeight( int weight ) {
    return new TreasureChest( 0, weight );
  }

  public static TreasureChest newInstanceWithGoldDoubloonAndGemstonesWeight(
      int goldDoubloonWeight, int gemstonesWeight ) {
    return new TreasureChest( goldDoubloonWeight, gemstonesWeight );
  }
}
```

The class declaration contains the two public variables. Since they are final, they cannot be modified after they have been written once. It is perfectly fine to make instance variables public; there is no need to always have getters if the variables can no longer be modified. Setters are primarily useful for ensuring that the value ranges are correct—in our case, this is done by the constructor, which accepts and validates the values.

We have a private constructor that cannot be called from the outside, but is only used by our own static factory methods. These four factory methods allow all permutations of the two instance variables.

1. Neither variable is set, then the values default to 0.
2. One of the two values is set, then the other is initialized to 0.
3. Both values are set.

Now, what is the advantage of these factory methods over constructors? A constructor is a good choice if there is an unambiguous way to initialize an instance. But in our case, there is the possibility to initialize goldDoubloonWeight or gemstoneWeight, and a constructor always has the predefined name of the class. It is not possible to write two different variants of the constructor that both take an integer and can distinguish whether goldDoubloonWeight or gemstoneWeight should be assigned. Of course, you could trick it and pass an enumeration as the second parameter for identification, for example, but it's not appealing. Factory methods have the charm of being named methods and making their function clear by the method name, even if the parameter lists of different methods are the same.

Connect Monitor Tube with TV

com/tutego/exercise/device/ihehzk/TVWithMonitorTube.java

```java
class MonitorTube {

  private final TV tv;

  public MonitorTube( TV tv ) {
    this.tv=tv;
  }

  public TV getTv() {
    return tv;
  }

  public void on() {
    System.out.println( "Tube is on." );
  }

  public void off() {
    System.out.println( "Tube is off." );
  }
}

class TV {
  private boolean isOn;
  private final MonitorTube tube=new MonitorTube( this );

  public void on() {
    isOn=true;
    System.out.println( "TV is on." );
    tube.on();
  }

  public void off() {
    isOn=false;
    System.out.println( "TV is off." );
    tube.off();
  }

  public String toString() {
    return String.format( "TV[on?=%s]", isOn );
  }
}
```

Let's start with the class MonitorTube. For a monitor tube to remember a TV set, we create a new variable of type TV—it will later contain the reference to a TV set. This reference is set via the constructor. Therefore, the variable can be final because there is no other place in the class where the variable is described. The constructor takes the reference, and there is also only a parameterized constructor, not a parameterless constructor because we would rather not be able to build a monitor tube without a TV. This is followed by a getter and the methods on() and off(), which report that the monitor tube is turned on or off.

The next class `TV` remembers in a private instance variable `isOn` whether the TV is on or off. We set this instance variable in the `on()` and `off()` methods. In the instance variable `tube` of type `MonitorTube`, the TV remembers the monitor tube. The initialization is:

```
private final MonitorTube tube=new MonitorTube( this );
```

At the constructor, `this` is passed, and so the reference to the current TV comes to the monitor tube. That is, the monitor tube thus receives the TV, and we had seen before that the monitor tube remembers the TV. So, we directly established a bidirectional relationship. If we only wanted a unidirectional relationship, we would have just built a `MonitorTube`, but not set a backreference from the `MonitorTube` to the `TV`.

The `on()` and `off()` methods now have two tasks: First, they set the internal flag, and then they delegate to the `MonitorTube` methods `on()` and `off()`.

Bidirectional relationships are convenient because you can always get to the other side. However, they bear the danger that two objects refer to the same opposite side, namely, if the first object forgets that it is no longer in a bidirectional relationship. Establishing a bidirectional relationship is less of a problem, but if the partners rebind, then both relationships must be resolved before a new relationship can be established. Methods can ensure that the other side is detached.

Quiz: Association, Composition, and Aggregation

A normal association is a link between two objects. This term is correct when one object refers to another object.

A composition and an aggregation are a special form of association that says something about a lifetime.

- In a *composition*, the lifetime of an associated object is bound to the lifetime of another object. Example: object A references an object B: if A "dies", i.e., is no longer referenced and can be removed by the garbage collector, B also "dies", at least if a reference does not still exist on B.
- *An aggregation* combines several objects, where the referenced objects have their own lifetime. If an object A associates to another object B and object A is removed, object B may still live. The term "aggregation" is not often used; people simply use the term "association", especially in UML diagrams. However, since the term "association" says nothing about the lifetimes of the referenced objects, one could explicitly emphasize this.

Add Radios with a 1:n Association to the Ship

com/tutego/exercise/device/luyyrl/Application.java

```java
class Ship {
  private final ArrayList<Radio> radios=new ArrayList<>();

  public void load( Radio radio ) {
    radios.add( Objects.requireNonNull( radio ) );
  }

  public int countDevicesSwitchedOn() {
    int result=0;
    for ( Radio radio : radios )
      if ( radio.isOn )
        result++;
```

```
    return result;
  }

  public String toString() {
    return "Ship["+radios+"]";
  }
}
```

In our class `Ship` we set the variable `radios` as described in the task.

The notation can also be shortened a bit with the so-called *diamond operator* to:

```
ArrayList<Radio> radios=new ArrayList<>();
```

Since the variable is private, the radios cannot be accessed from the outside, we have to go through helper methods which can then access the instance variable. `load(Radio radio)` allows adding radios. The method delegates to the `add(...)` method of the `ArrayList`.

The second `countDevicesSwitchedOn()` method returns the number of radios switched on. It is important to note that it is not about the total number of radios—that would be answered quickly—but really about the number of radios where the `isOn` state is set to `true`. So, we have to run the whole list and examine each radio individually. There are several solutions here:

- A quite practical variant is the extended `for` loop. We got to know this loop type in connection with arrays: to the right of the colon, there can be an `ArrayList`. This way, we can comfortably run the entire list from front to back. We get each radio and test if the instance variable is set, and if so, we increment our result counter.
- Another solution would have been to work with a counting loop, run from 0 to `radios.size()`, and use the `get(int)` method to pick out each radio at the position. The solution with the extended `for` loop is nicer.
- There is a third solution with the stream API, but it will take a while until we get there. But the question can then be answered with a one-liner.

If we wanted to give the ship other electrical appliances with our current knowledge, we would have to introduce different data structures with the special types, i.e., an `ArrayList` with ice machines or an `ArrayList` with TV sets. It should be clear that this gets confusing quickly, but object-oriented programming languages have a perfect solution for this: inheritance!

Introduce Abstraction into Electrical Devices via Inheritance

com/tutego/exercise/device/jkvzow/ElectronicDevices.java

```
class ElectronicDevice {

  private boolean isOn;

  public void on() {
    isOn=true;
  }

  public void off() {
    isOn=false;
  }
```

```
  boolean isOn() {
    return isOn;
  }

  public String toString() {
    return "ElectronicDevice[is "+(isOn ? "on" : "off")+"]";
  }
}

class IceMachine extends ElectronicDevice {
}

class Radio extends ElectronicDevice {
  int volume;
}
```

If we use inheritance, we implement an is-a-type-of relationship. It's essential that every subclass adheres to and supports the specifications and capabilities of its superclass. The decision of which instance variables and methods to elevate is confined to those related to the on/off state. If we look at the other instance variables and methods of `Radio`, we quickly realize that they don't belong in the `ElectronicDevice` superclass. Not every electronic device in the world has a frequency or volume. Once we have set instance variables in the superclass, they apply to all subclasses that will ever be written.

Using an IDE is a good way to move properties into a superclass so that no manual work is required at all. The refactoring is generally called *pull members up*.

The superclass `ElectronicDevice` gets an instance variable `isOn`, which is private, so it can only be read and written from `ElectronicDevice` via methods. The other three methods can set the state to true or false or query the state. But direct access from outside to the private variable is no longer possible; we have to go through the methods. Moreover, the superclass has an implementation of the `toString()` method. Here, the string cannot contain much more than the `isOn` state. Whether you go via the internal variable, or via the `isOn()` method, is a bit of a matter of taste. The subclasses keep their `toString()` method, and we will see later that the `toString()` methods can also be concatenated.

The superclass is joined by two subclasses `IceMachine` and `Radio`. Subclasses extend their superclasses, and superclasses know nothing about their subclasses.

Quiz: Three, Two, and One

The program can be executed, and after starting it, there is output on the screen:

```
12
```

An object of type `Three` is built, which causes the constructor `Three()` to be called. The constructor `Three()` calls the constructor of the class `Two`, the constructor `Two()` calls the constructor `One()`.

The nastiness is that in the class `Three` there is only a default constructor that the compiler created, and we added a method `void Three()` that has nothing in common with the constructor. The method is capitalized, which is a violation of the naming convention but is not forbidden. Each constructor automatically calls the constructor of the superclass.

However, there is no console output in the default constructor. We wrote the constructors `Two()` and `One()` ourselves with the console output, and since only the constructors run to the top, the output is first 1, then 2.

Quiz: Private and Protected Constructor

If a class has a private constructor, then no instance of the class can be built from the outside. However, it is possible to build an instance from inside the class, and we can do this by using a static method. Such a method, we also call *factory method*, if it gives this instance to the outside. The following example illustrates this:

```java
class Cloth {
  private Cloth() {
  }

  public static Cloth create() {
    return new Cloth();
  }
}
```

It is not possible to create instances from outside the class Cloth. The attempt is punished with a compiler error:

```java
class Skirt {
  Cloth skirt=new Cloth();
}
```

The error in the constructor call is: 'Cloth()' has private access in 'Cloth'.

Furthermore, it is not possible to create subclasses because each class automatically calls the constructor of the superclass. The class Cloth has only one constructor, and it is private. Consequently, it is not possible to create subclasses. A declaration like

```java
class Petticoat extends Cloth {
}
```

leads to the error There is no default constructor available in 'Cloth'.

This is the difference between a private constructor and a protected constructor because a protected constructor can be called by subclasses. However, since protected also means package-visible, other classes in the same package can also build instances of the class via the protected constructor.

Determine Number of Switched on Electrical Devices

com/tutego/exercise/device/mkwrrt/ElectronicDevice.java

```java
public static int numberOfElectronicDevicesSwitchedOn( ElectronicDevice...
devices ) {
  int result=0;
  for ( ElectronicDevice device : devices )
    if ( device.isOn )
      result++;

  return result;
}
```

The method is very similar to our object method numberOfElectronicDevicesSwitchedOn() that we wrote earlier. The only difference is that now we are not just asking for radios, but for any

ElectronicDevice objects that are switched on. That is, anything that is an ElectronicDevice can be introduced into the method via the vararg. This can be three radios, but also only one radio or one TV.

With a vararg, always keep in mind that it is an array, and these are objects, and object references can be null. Our method has no query on ElectronicDevice ==null and does not raise an exception itself. However, this exception is implicitly raised when the extended for loop accesses an array that is null. We can therefore skip explicitly querying for null because the result, a NullPointerException, would be the same.

Ship Should Hold Any Electronic Device

com/tutego/exercise/device/lofryn/Ship.java

```java
public class Ship {
  private final ArrayList<ElectronicDevice> devices=new ArrayList<>();

  public void load( ElectronicDevice device ) {
    Objects.requireNonNull( device );
    devices.add( device );
  }
}
```

To generalize, the ship only has the internal list and a method to add it. For the instance variable ArrayList<ElectronicDevice> devices, we change the type from previously Radio to ElectronicDevice, so we can store any electrical devices in the list. We also changed the variable name. We rewrite the add method a bit because we can now accept any ElectronicDevice objects. The parameter type changes from Radio to ElectronicDevice. So, we can accept anything that is an electronic device. This can be a radio, a TV, or an ice machine; anything that is a subclass of ElectronicDevice. This includes what we have in the program, or what will be added in the later development phase.

Objects.requireNonNull(...) protects against null references being added to the list.

Take Working Radios on the Ship

com/tutego/exercise/device/dxsyvb/Ship.java

```java
public class Ship {

  private final ArrayList<ElectronicDevice> devices=new ArrayList<>();

  public void load( ElectronicDevice device ) {
    Objects.requireNonNull( device );

    if ( device instanceof Radio radio ) {
      if ( radio.getVolume() ==0 )
        return;
      System.out.println( "Remember to pay license fee!" );
    }

    devices.add( device );
  }
}
```

The reference type of the variable `devices` is always `ElectronicDevice` (and neither `null`, which we have forbidden before), but at runtime, there can be quite different object types behind it. The `instanceof` operator helps to find out which object type we have in front of us at runtime. If we have a `Radio` or even something that extends `Radio` itself, then the `instanceof` operator will indicate that and declare the pattern variable `radio` of type `Radio` so that the volume can be retrieved in the next step.

Solve Equivalence Test with Pattern Variable

Before we get to the solution, let's remind ourselves why `instanceof` is necessary in the first place. The operator helps us exclude noncompatible object types. After all, the parameter type of the `equals(Object)` method is just `Object`, which means that any object can be passed to the method. However, only toasters should be compared with other toasters.

If we use the `instanceof` test, two different routes can be taken with it. In one variant, we can test whether the object passed was *not* a toaster, and terminate the method early:

com/tutego/exercise/oop/Toaster.java

```
@Override public boolean equals( Object o ) {
  if ( !(o instanceof Toaster other) ) return false;

  return    capacity == other.capacity
         && stainless == other.stainless && extraLarge == other.extraLarge;
}
```

There is an alternative notation to this variant: write the `instanceof` test and, exactly when the result is true, continue to check the object states in the body of the `if` block. But then the code moves further to the right in the block. What is attractive about the solution demonstrated is that if no toaster is passed into the `equals(Object)` method, the method returns. No `else` branch is needed; hence, the following code does not move to the right.

Consider the pattern variable `other` at `instanceof`; `other` is declared exactly when the passed object `o` is also a `Toaster`. The variable remains alive in the block and can be accessed in the following `return` statement.

We can program a second variant where we now include the condition in the previous `if` statement in the `return` statement:

com/tutego/exercise/oop/Toaster.java

```
@Override public boolean equals( Object o ) {
  return    o instanceof Toaster other
         && capacity == other.capacity
         && stainless == other.stainless && extraLarge == other.extraLarge;
}
```

With the logical AND operator, evaluation is from left to right, and execution ends when the result is fixed—we are talking about the short-circuit operator. So if the passed object `o` is a `toaster`, then the variable `other` is declared and is available for the two following tests of the object states.

Fire Alarm Does Not Go Off: Overriding Methods

com/tutego/exercise/device/hthiin/Firebox.java

```
public class Firebox extends ElectronicDevice {
```

```java
public Firebox() {
  on();
}
@Override void off() {
  System.out.println( "A firebox is always on, you can't switch it off" );
}
}
```

Firebox is another subclass of `ElectronicDevice`. The class inherits everything from the super-class, but overwrites the `off()` method. In the body, there is only a console output; the on/off flag is not modified. With the annotation `Override`, we mark that the method already exists in the superclass, but we overwrite it in the subclass with new behavior.

For the compiler—and the runtime environment—the annotation is not essential; both know when a method is overwritten. But with the annotation, the compiler can detect errors, such as typos or subsequent changes to, for example, the parameter list in the superclass, that the method in the subclass is no longer overwritten, but only overloaded.

We have often overridden a method, but perhaps we haven't noticed it yet: `toString()`. The method comes from the absolute superclass `java.lang.Object`.

Since a fire alarm should be on after it is created, we implement a constructor and call `on()`.

Calling the Methods of the Superclass

To save code, the proposed solution for TV is a bit more reduced and has only a unidirectional relationship with the `MonitorTube`.

com/tutego/exercise/device/rojnsv/TV.java

```java
class TV extends ElectronicDevice {

  private MonitorTube monitorTube=new MonitorTube();

  @Override void on() {
    super.on();
    monitorTube.on();
  }

  @Override void off() {
    super.off();
    monitorTube.off();
  }
}
```

When overwriting methods, the original implementation of the superclass is replaced by a new implementation. There is no contradiction in combining the two—on the one hand, realizing a new implementation for a method and on the other hand still calling the original implementation. Java makes this possible with the keyword `super`. The keyword `super` exists in two versions: once for calling the constructor of the superclass and once for calling an overridden method because `super` brings us into the namespace of a supertype. If we were to call a method without `super`, we would run into a recursion.

On the one hand, the TV should store the state of whether it is on in the supertype, and the methods of the superclass `on()` and `off()` do that. The TV must call these methods to get to the state of the superclass. On the other hand, the `on()`/`off()` methods on the TV need to turn the monitor tube on and off, and that is handled by delegation. Delegation is when one object passes the call to another object. When the TV is turned on or off, the monitor tube is also turned on or off.

Holiday! Switch Off All Devices

com/tutego/exercise/device/mkwrrt/Ship.java

```java
public void holiday() {
  for ( ElectronicDevice device : devices )
    device.off();
}
```

To allow us to run over all the electrical devices, we again use the extended `for` loop. On each of the `ElectronicDevice` objects, we call the `off()` method. The method is dynamically bound, and the runtime environment decides where the method call actually will go, such as to radio, TV, and so on. The chosen implementation of `Firebox` also ensures that the alarm is not disabled; instead, an appropriate message is an output.

The Big Move

```java
void printLoadingList() {
  for ( ElectronicDevice device : devices ) {
    System.out.println( switch ( device ) {
      case Radio radio when radio.getWatt() > 0 -> AsciiArt.RADIO;
      case TV tv when tv.getWatt() >= 10_000 -> AsciiArt.BIG_TV;
      case TV tv -> AsciiArt.TV;
      default -> AsciiArt.SOCKET;
    } );
  }
}
```

com/tutego/exercise/device/xbmgom/Ship.java

The `for` loop iterates over all devices in the `devices` list, and the *pattern matching for switch* helps to distinguish the different device types with little code. Since the mere device type `Radio` alone is not enough to generate suitable output, the condition after the keyword `when` checks whether the wattage is positive. Similarly, the `when` keyword proves useful in identifying televisions since it allows us to distinguish between a large and a small television.

Quiz: Bumbo Is a Great Drink

The program compiles and does not lead to any exception at runtime. The output is:

```
2 ounces rum, 1 ounce water, 2 sugar cubes, cinnamon, nutmeg.
```

One Java property is special about this program: so-called *covariant return types*. The superclass declares the method `printIngredients()`, which is overridden in the subclass. If you override methods in Java, you must choose the same parameter list, but there is some flexibility in the return type and exceptions. Namely, the subclass can return a subtype of the return type of the overridden method. `getInstance()` in `Drink` returns `Drink`, and `getInstance()` in `Bumbo` returns a `YummyDrink`, a subtype of `Drink`. This makes the compiler happy. In principle, we could have written more concrete in `Bumbo`:

```java
public Bumbo getInstance() { // instead of YummyDrink getInstance()
  return this;
}
```

Reference types are of no interest to the runtime environment; the overridden methods are bound dynamically, and since there is a Bumbo in memory with new Bumbo(), printIngredients() will also give us the recipe of the drink.

Quiz: Vodka with Taste

The exercise tests understanding of type conversion, overriding, and dynamic binding. The subclass has the same method as the superclass, so the subclass overwrites the seasoned() method. Intentionally, the annotation @Override is missing here, but it is clear to the compiler that the method is overridden.

The output is blackcurrant because the compiler has an object of type vodka in memory and all methods are dynamically bound. With the explicit type conversion to AlcoholicDrink, it is not possible to suspend the dynamic binding; the reference type known to the compiler is irrelevant for the method call. The runtime environment knows exactly what kind of object it has in front of it, and the type conversion is not necessary for that.

Quiz: Rum-Paradise

The program compiles and can be run without throwing an exception. The outputs are:

```
7
2
```

At its core, the program demonstrates two features of Java: first, how initializers work, and then the difference between dynamic binding when methods are overridden and that instance variables cannot be overridden.

Let's start with the classes themselves. Both have an instance variable, a constructor, and a method. Underneath Rum is the subclass AlcoholicDrink, and since it has the same method older(), the method is overridden. Both classes contain their own instance variable aged, but the instance variable aged in the subclass has nothing to do with the instance variable aged in the superclass—in Java, the peculiarity is called *hiding*. The hiding of instance variables is not to be confused with *shadowing*, which occurs when a local variable is named as an instance variable; we do not have that in our example. shadowing variable)

To understand the output, we need to know how constructors and initialized instance variables are related. Initialized instance variables do not exist in bytecode, nor do initialize class variables. They have to be implemented via a different construction. The assignment of instance variables is used in each constructor, and the assignment of static variables is set in a static initialization block static {} of the class. From the code

```java
class Rum extends AlcoholicDrink {
  int aged=3;
  Rum() { aged += 4; }
}
```

becomes the following:

```java
class Rum extends AlcoholicDrink {
  int aged;
  Rum() {
    aged=3;
```

```
     aged += 4;
  }
}
```

So the constructor says:

```
Rum() {
  aged=7;
}
```

If we create the variable lakeGay in main(...), then it is of object type Rum and reference type AlcoholicDrink. If we call the older() method, then the overridden method is called at the Rum type because there is a Rum object in memory, and overridden methods are bound dynamically. The older() method queries the variable aged and returns it. We saw earlier that aged was set to 7 by default. But why is the return not 8? This is because of the post-increment operator ++ that comes after the variable name. That is, the assignment of aged is saved for the return, then incremented, and then the save is returned. We do not inquire that the number afterward is 8.

The instance variable aged exists in the classes AlcoholicDrink and Rum. As a reminder, class and instance variables are not dynamically bound. Only *object* methods are bound dynamically, but never class and instance variables or static methods!

When we refer to the instance variable aged, the compiler responds to the reference type AlcoholicDrink, and their aged defaults to 2. How can this be explained? We have not built an object of type AlcoholicDrink, why does the constructor run? The constructor of AlcoholicDrink is called indirectly during instantiating Rum. When a Rum object is built, the constructor of Rum is called, which in turn automatically calls the constructor of the superclass. The constructor of AlcoholicDrink increments the variable by 1, and consequently age in AlcoholicDrink becomes 2. This is the output we see.

Quiz: Consumer Devices as an Abstract Superclass?

There is no need to make instances of the ElectronicDevice class, and in our implementation, we only use it as a superclass. Therefore, it is no problem to make the class ElectronicDevice abstract. It also suggests that this class is a modeling class that stands as a data type for a group of electrical devices and specifies a commonality.

TimerTask as an Example for an Abstract Class

com/tutego/exercise/oop/FreeDiskSpaceTimer.java

```
public class FreeDiskSpaceTimer {
  public static void main( String[] args ) {
    final int REPETITION_PERIOD=2000 /* ms */;
    new Timer().schedule( new FreeDiskSpaceTimerTask(), 0, REPETITION_PERIOD
);
  }
}
class FreeDiskSpaceTimerTask extends TimerTask {
  private static final long MIN_CAPACITY=100_000_000_000L;
  private final File root=File.listRoots()[ 0 ];

  @Override public void run() {
    long freeDiskSpace=root.getFreeSpace();
```

```
   if ( freeDiskSpace<MIN_CAPACITY )
     System.out.printf(
         "Device %s has less than %,d byte available, currently %,d byte%n",
         root, MIN_CAPACITY, freeDiskSpace );
   }
}
```

We split the task into two classes. The first class contains the main(...) method and starts the timer, the second class extends the TimerTask class for our task, the task.

Every single task is a subclass of TimerTask. The abstract class prescribes an abstract method run() that our task must override. As described in the assignment, we use the one-liner to determine the number of free bytes on the first drive that File.listRoots() returns, and then perform a test. If the number of free bytes is less than the minimum capacity, we print a message on the console. If we have more free space, everything is fine, and we have no screen output.

To start our task, we must first create a Timer object. A Timer gives us a schedule(...) method that we can pass an instance of our concrete task to, along with the delay time and repetition frequency. We want to start immediately, so there is no delay time, and the repetition frequency is 2 seconds, which is 2,000 ms, the time unit of the parameter.

NOTE

1 The two modulation methods, AM and FM, differ in how one uses a carrier frequency to encode a signal to be transmitted. Wikipedia provides an overview at https://en.wikipedia.org/wiki/Modulation

Records, Interfaces, Enumerations, and Sealed Classes

7

RECORDS

Records are useful in Java because they provide a simple and compact way to define and use data objects with a fixed number of attributes.

Quiz: Which Statements Are True for Records? ★

Given the following Java Record:

```
record Candy( String name, int calories ) { }
```

Which of the following statements is true?

1. The name and age of a `candy` cannot be changed after the object is created.
2. The attributes of a `Candy` object are accessed via getter methods.
3. `Candy` cannot have static methods.
4. The `equals()` and `hashCode()` methods must be implemented manually.
5. The `toString()` method of `Candy` yields a string resembling JSON (JavaScript Object Notation) format.

Develop Record for Complex Numbers ★

Complex numbers are an important mathematical concept used in various fields such as engineering, physics, and computer science. A complex number consists of a real part and an imaginary part. It is written in the form a+bi, where a is the real part and b is the imaginary part. Mathematical operations are realized as follows:

- Addition and Subtraction: The operation is performed element-wise, meaning the real part/imaginary part of one number is added/subtracted with the real part/imaginary part of the other number.
- Multiplication: The operation follows the rule: $(a+bi) \times (c+di) = (ac - bd) + (ad+bc)i$.
- Absolute value of a complex number: The absolute value of $z = a + bi$ is defined as $|z| = \text{sqrt}(a^2 + b^2)$.

DOI: 10.1201/9781003454502-8

Task:

- Write a new Java record Complex with the record components real and imaginary.
- Create a constant I representing the imaginary unit, which is the square root of -1.
- Implement the methods add(Complex   other), subtract(Complex   other), multiply(Complex other), and abs().
- Override the toString()   method, rounding the real and imaginary parts to three decimal places, so that the output becomes for example (-3.000+2.000i) or (2.000 - 3.000i).

Quiz: Records with Static Variables ★

Given the following Java Record:

```
record Candy( String name, int calories ) {
  public static String id=UUID.randomUUID().toString();
}
```

Does the record compile?
    Is the following a valid alternative notation?

```
record Candy( String name, int calories ) {
  public static String id;
  Candy {
    id=UUID.randomUUID().toString();
  }
}
```

Record Patterns ★

Daredevil pirates not only have a keen sense of prey but also a fondness for exotic pets. So far, one application represents pets in two records:

```
record MischiefMonkey( String name, boolean isMutinous ) { }
record FeistyParrot( String name, String favoritePhrase, boolean isMutinous )
{ }
```

The modeling has proven to be rigid as new animal types are added and properties change. Therefore, the data from the records should be converted into java.util.Properties objects. Properties is a special associative store that associates one string with another string. The method setProperty(String key, String value) sets a new key-value pair into the Properties object.
Task:

- Write a method Properties convertToProperties(Object) to convert pets of type MischiefMonkey and FeistyParrot into Properties objects.
- Pets that are mutinous (state isMutinous) should be ignored and result in an empty Properties object with no entries.
- The method should be able to be called with null or unknown types and return an empty Properties object in those cases.

Examples (output shows the `toString()` representation of `Properties`):

- `new MischiefMonkey( "Jack", true ) →` {}
- `new FeistyParrot( "Captain Squawk", "Avast, ye scallywags!",false )` `→` {favoritePhrase=Avast, ye scallywags!, name=Captain Squawk}
- `new MischiefMonkey( "Barbossa", false ) →` {name=Barbossa}
- `new FeistyParrot( "Polly", "Pieces of eight!",true ) →` {}
- `new   FeistyParrot(   "Marauder",   "Walk   the   plank!",false   )   →` {favoritePhrase=Walk the plank!, name=Marauder}

INTERFACES

Abstract classes are still classes with all their capabilities: instance variables, constructors, methods, and different visibilities. Often a simpler form of specification is sufficient, and for this Java provides interfaces. They do not have instance variables, but can have constants, abstract methods, static methods, and `default` methods—an instance variable is a way of storing something that belongs to a class, not to the interface.

Compare Consumption of Electrical Devices ★

Every electrical device has a power output, which is measured in watts.
Task Part 1:

1. Declare in `ElectronicDevice` a private `int` instance variable `watt`, and generate with the development environment Setter/Getter.
2. Add   a   `toString()`   method   that   returns   something   like   the   following: `"ElectronicDevice[watt=12kW]"`.   Some   subclasses   had   already   overridden `toString()`; they should then include a `super.toString()` in their `toString()` methods.

Task Part 2:

1. Write a new class `ElectronicDeviceWattComparator` that implements the interface `java.util.Comparator<ElectronicDevice>`.
2. Let the `compare(...)` method define an ordering of electrical devices, where an electrical device is "smaller" if it consumes less power.
3. Put a `println(...)` in your own `compare(...)` method for a better understanding, so that you can see which objects are compared.

Example:

```
ElectronicDevice ea1=new Radio(); ea1.setWatt( 200 );
ElectronicDevice ea2=new Radio(); ea2.setWatt( 20 );
Comparator<ElectronicDevice> c=new ElectronicDeviceWattComparator();
System.out.println( c.compare(ea1, ea2) );
System.out.println( c.compare(ea2, ea1) );
```

Objective of the exercise: `ElectronicDeviceWattComparator` as an implementation of the Comparator interface, as shown in the UML diagram:

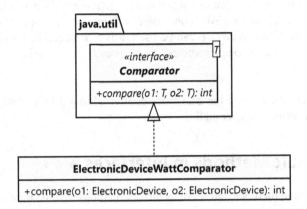

FIGURE 7.1   UML diagram.

Find Electronic Devices with the Highest Power Consumption ★

The `java.util.Collections` class has a static method that returns the largest element of a collection (the generics in the angle brackets have been removed for simplicity):

```
static T max( Collection coll, Comparator comp )
```

The following must therefore be passed to the `max(...)` method

1. A Collection implementation like `ArrayList` and
2. A Comparator implementation. Here we can use our `ElectronicDeviceWattComparator`.

Task:

- Put a method `findMostPowerConsumingElectronicDevice()` in the ship that returns the device with the highest consumption.

Example:

- The following program returns the output 12000.

```
Radio grannysRadio=new Radio();
grannysRadio.volumeUp();
grannysRadio.setWatt( 12_000 );

TV grandpasTv=new TV();
grandpasTv.setWatt( 1000 );

Ship ship=new Ship();
ship.load( grannysRadio );
ship.load( grandpasTv );
System.out.println( ship.findMostPowerConsumingElectronicDevice().
getWatt() );
```

Use Comparator Interface for Sorting ★

If you want to sort objects of a list, you can use the sort(...) method on List implementations. It is important to tell the sort(...) method when one object is "smaller" than another. For this purpose, our ElectronicDeviceWattComparator can be used; it is a prerequisite for objects that you want to sort—the signature void sort(Comparator<...> c) already reveals this.
Task:

- Call sort(...) in load(...) of the ship object after adding it to its data structure, to always have an internal sorted list after adding.

Static and Default Methods in Interfaces ★★★

Interfaces can contain static methods and serve as factory methods, that is, they can provide instances of classes that implement that interface.
Task:

1. Create an interface Distance.
2. Set two static methods Distance   ofMeter(int   value) and Distance ofKilometer(int value) in Distance, which return a new object of type Distance.
3. Set in Distance an abstract method int meter(). What must be implemented?
4. Set a default method int kilometer() in the interface Distance.

Example in use:

```
Distance oneKm=Distance.ofKilometer( 1 );
System.out.printf( "1 km=%d km, %d m%n", oneKm.kilometer(), oneKm.meter() );

Distance moreMeter=Distance.ofMeter( 12345 );
System.out.printf( "12345 m=%d km, %d m", moreMeter.kilometer(), moreMeter.
meter() );
```

Delete Selected Elements with Predicate ★★

If we want to make ships energy efficient, we need to remove all devices with excessive power consumption.
   The List method removeIf(Predicate<...>filter) deletes all elements that satisfy a predicate. The ArrayList class is an implementation of the List interface, so the method is available on an ArrayList.
   For example, if we want to delete from a List<String> all empty strings, we can call removeIf(new IsStringEmpty()) on the list, where IsStringEmpty is declared as follows:

```
class IsStringEmpty implements Predicate<String> {
  @Override public boolean test( String t ) {
    return t.trim().isEmpty();
  }
}
```

Task:

- Set in the ship a new method `removePowerConsumingElectronicDevices()` that deletes all devices with power consumption greater than a self-selected constant `MAXIMUM _ POWER _ CONSUMPTION`.

ENUMERATION TYPES (ENUM)

Enumeration types (enum) represent closed sets and are powerful in Java; they not only allow additional object and class variables, new private constructors, but they can also implement interfaces, override methods, and they have some built-in methods. The upcoming exercises address these nice features.

Enumeration for Candy ★

Captain CiaoCiao wants to appeal to a younger crowd of buyers and is experimenting with candy instead of rum in his lab.

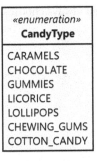

FIGURE 7.2   UML diagram of enumeration type (without method).

Task:

- Declare an enumeration `CandyType` with constants for
  - Caramels.
  - Chocolate.
  - Gummies.
  - Licorice.
  - Lollipops.
  - Chewing gums.
  - Cotton candy.
- Respect the usual naming convention.
- Users should be able to enter a candy from the console. The appropriate `enum` object should be retrieved for the input, case-insensitivity should not matter. Add a new static method `Optional<CandyType> fromName(String  input)` in the enumeration type `CandyType` for the conversion from a `String` to an enumeration element of type `CandyType`. The method must not throw exceptions due to incorrect input; unknown names will result in an `Optional.empty()`.

Deliver Random Candies ★

Captain CiaoCiao launches his food tour and always chooses random candies.

Task:

- Give the enumeration type `CandyType` a method `random()` that returns a random candy.
  ```
  System.out.println( CandyType.random() ); // e.g., CHOCOLATE
  System.out.println( CandyType.random() ); // e.g., LOLLIPOPS
  ```

Tagging Candy with Addictive Value ★★

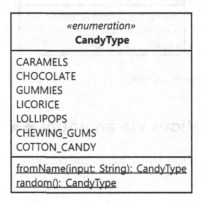

FIGURE 7.3 UML diagram of the enumeration type with static methods.

We know that sweets are addictive, some more, some less.
Task:

- Associate an addictive value (`int`) with each enumerated element from `CandyType`:
  - Caramels: 9.
  - Chocolate: 5.
  - Gummies: 4.

- Licorice: 3.
- Lollipops: 2.
- Chewing gums: 3.
- Cotton candy: 1.

   To store the addiction value, use a constructor in enum. The addiction value should be provided by a new nonstatic method `addictiveQuality()`.
- Since Captain CiaoCiao wants to achieve a dependency toward candy with a higher addiction factor, a new `CandyType` method `next()` shall return the candy with the next higher addiction. Lollipops have two potential successors, here the selection shall randomly go to Chewing Gums and Licorice. Caramels have no `successor`, and it stays with Caramels.

Examples:

- `CandyType.COTTON _ CANDY.next()` is LOLLIPOPS.
- `CandyType.LOLLIPOPS.next()` is, e.g., LICORICE.
- `CandyType.LOLLIPOPS.next()` is, e.g., CHEWING_GUMS.
- `CandyType.CARAMELS.next()` is CARAMELS.

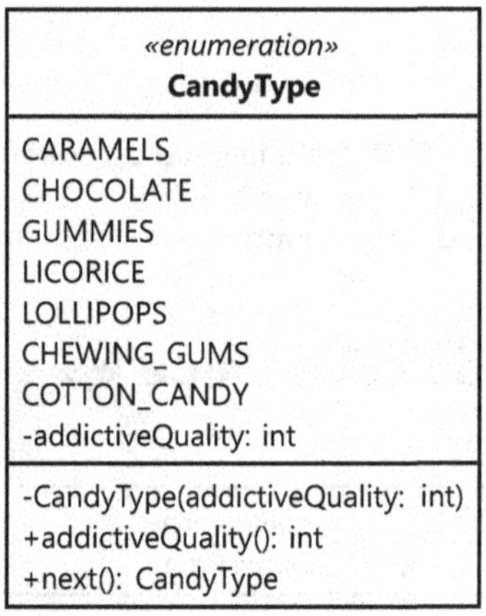

```
          «enumeration»
          CandyType
─────────────────────────────
  CARAMELS
  CHOCOLATE
  GUMMIES
  LICORICE
  LOLLIPOPS
  CHEWING_GUMS
  COTTON_CANDY
  -addictiveQuality: int
─────────────────────────────
  -CandyType(addictiveQuality: int)
  +addictiveQuality(): int
  +next(): CandyType
```

FIGURE 7.4 UML diagram of enumeration type.

Interface Implementations via an enum ★★

An enum type can implement interfaces but cannot extend classes.

   Given an interface `Distance`:

```
interface Distance {
  double distance( double x1, double y1, double x2, double y2 );
  double distance( double x1, double y1, double z1, double x2, double y2,
double z2 );
}
```

Task:

- Take the interface `Distance` into your project.
- Declare an enumeration type `Distances` that implements `Distance` with exactly one enumeration element EUCLIDEAN:

```
enum Distances implements Distance {
  EUCLIDEAN
}
```

If you now need a `Distance` implementation for the Euclidean distance, you can get it using `Distances.EUCLIDEAN`.

- Add the implementation that the Euclidean distance of two points is calculated; remember, for a 2D point:
```
Math.sqrt( (x1 - x2) * (x1 - x2)+(y1 - y2) * (y1 - y2) ).
```
- Extend the enumeration type `Distances` with another enumeration element `MANHATTAN` so that there are two constants `EUCLIDEAN` and `MANHATTAN`.

The Manhattan distance is formed by the sum of the absolute differences of the single coordinates, so for a 2D point `Math.abs(x1 - x2)+Math.abs(y1 - y2)`.

Quiz: Aviso and Brig ★

Given the following declaration of an enumeration type. Does the program compile? If it compiles, and you run it, is there a result? If there is a result, what is the output?

```
enum ShipType {
  AVISO( "Aviso" ), BRIG( "Brig" );
  private final String type;

  public ShipType( String type ) { this.type=type; }

  public String toString( String name ) {
    return this.type+" "+name;
  }

  public static void main( String[] args ) {

    System.out.println( AVISO.toString( "Golden Hind" ) );
  }
}
```

SUGGESTED SOLUTIONS

Quiz: Which Statements Are True for Records?

Reminder:

```
record Candy( String name, int calories ) { }
```

- Since records are immutable, name and calories cannot be changed later. Especially since String itself is immutable and int is a primitive type. However, care must be taken when Records reference mutable objects, such as a `StringBuilder`. In this case, although the record variable cannot be reassigned, the string in the `StringBuilder` can be changed.
- The term setter/getter must always be seen in the context of the JavaBean standard. According to this standard, getters have the prefix `get`. This does not apply to records where access is not via getters, but in this case, via the `name()` or `calories()` methods, for example.

- Records can have additional static variables and methods.
- Records have the advantage that they implement `equals()`, `hashCode()`, and `toString()`. We do not have to implement these methods, but we can override them.
- The `toString()` method of `Candy` does not return a JSON-like string. The format is as usual in Java, e.g., `Candy[name=Choco, calories=600]`.

Quiz: Records with Static Variables

```java
public record Complex( double real, double imaginary ) {

  public static final Complex I=new Complex( 0, 1 );

  public Complex add( Complex other ) {
    return new Complex( this.real+other.real, this.imaginary+other.imaginary );
  }

  public Complex subtract( Complex other ) {
    return new Complex( this.real - other.real, this.imaginary - other.imaginary );
  }

  public Complex multiply( Complex other ) {
    double realPart=this.real * other.real - this.imaginary * other.imaginary;
    double imaginaryPart=this.real * other.imaginary+this.imaginary * other.real;
    return new Complex( realPart, imaginaryPart );
  }

  public double abs() {
    return Math.sqrt( this.real * this.real+this.imaginary * this.imaginary );
  }

  @Override
  public String toString() {
    return String.format( "(%.3f %c %.3fi)",
                          real,
                          (imaginary >= 0 ? '+' : '-'),
                          Math.abs( imaginary ) );
  }
}
```

com/tutego/exercise/oop/Complex.java

The record `Complex` contains the components real for the real part and imaginary for the imaginary part.

The static constant `I` represents the imaginary unit i and is declared `final` to prevent the constant from being changed externally. Custom static variables are not automatically `final`, unlike the internal states of records.

The toString() method is overridden, and depending on whether the imaginary part is negative or positive, a plus or minus sign is placed between the real and imaginary parts. While it is possible to set a sign using format strings, adding a space between the sign and the number directly is not straightforward.

Quiz: Records with Static Variables

Records can contain static variables, and therefore both variants compile. They are equivalent in the result that the variable id contains a Universally Unique Identifier (UUID) string. In the second case, the initialization is written only in the compact constructor. Another notation would be to use the canonical constructor like this:

```java
record Candy( String name, int calories ) {
  public static String id;

  Candy( String name, int calories ) {
    this.name=name;
    this.calories=calories;
    id=UUID.randomUUID().toString();
  }
}
```

Record Patterns

```java
static Properties convertToProperties( Object pet ) {
  Properties result=new Properties();
  switch ( pet ) {
    case MischiefMonkey( String name, boolean isMutinous ) when !isMutinous
-> {
      result.setProperty( "name", name );
    }
    case FeistyParrot( String name, String favoritePhrase, boolean isMutinous
)
    when !isMutinous -> {
      result.setProperty( "name", name );
      result.setProperty( "favoritePhrase", favoritePhrase );
    }
    case null, default -> { }
  }
  return result;
}
```

com/tutego/exercise/oop/PetPropertyDemo.java

The solution consists of three steps.

1. A new Properties object is created for the return. This object is left empty if the pet is rebellious or an unknown type, or if the passed argument is null.
2. The switch statement analyzes the object based on its type. Here one could use the *pattern matching for switch*. However, since all record components are needed for further processing, the extended *record pattern* is helpful. This makes it possible to transfer the record states directly to new local variables. The additional condition with when excludes mutinous pets. If the pet does not mutinate, the local variables of the extracted components are used to populate the Properties object with the corresponding information. The branch with null, default handles unknown types or a call of convertToProperties(null).
3. At the end, the result object is returned.

Compare Consumption of Electrical Devices

com/tutego/exercise/device/bhdavq/ElectronicDevice.java

```java
public class ElectronicDevice {

  private int watt;

  public int getWatt() {
    return watt;
  }

  public void setWatt( int watt ) {
    this.watt=watt;
  }

  @Override public String toString() {
    return "ElectronicDevice[watt="+watt / 1000+"kW]";
  }
}
```

The `ElectronicDevice` class has only wattage, everything else is removed because it is not necessary for the assignment. The `toString()` method divides the wattage by 1000 for conversion to kilowatts.

Let's look at the simplified declaration of the `Comparator` interface again:

```java
public interface Comparator<T> {
  int compare(T o1, T o2);
}
```

The `Comparator` is a generic interface with a type parameter T. If our class implements the `Comparator` interface, we would need to form a parameterized type with a type argument. The type argument represents the types that `Comparator` wants to compare, in our case `ElectronicDevice`. When we implement `Comparator`, we implement the `int compare(T o1, T o2)` method; the type parameter T becomes the type argument `ElectronicDevice`.

There are different ways to get an implementation of the `Comparator` interface. The first variant is shown in the solution. A second variant would be via enum, the third variant via lambda expressions. We will stick with the simple solution and come back to the `Comparator` implementations in more detail later with the lambda expressions.

com/tutego/exercise/device/bhdavq/ElectronicDeviceWattComparator.java

```java
import java.util.Comparator;

public class ElectronicDeviceWattComparator
    implements Comparator<ElectronicDevice> {

  @Override

  public int compare( ElectronicDevice ea1,
                      ElectronicDevice ea2 ) {
    System.out.println( ea1+" is compared with "+ea2 );
    return Integer.compare( ea1.getWatt(), ea2.getWatt() );
  }
}
```

We put @Override on the method to clarify it for the reader that a method is overridden here. For the compiler, the annotation is not significant because the method has to be implemented in any case, and the compiler reports an error if the implementation is missing.

The implementation itself first outputs on the command line the toString() representations of the first and second electrical devices. Later, when the compare(…) method is called, we can easily keep track of which electrical devices were fed to the method.

At its core, every Comparator looks identical. It must extract the relevant instance variables and then compare them. In this case, the Comparator accesses the wattages of two electrical appliances, which are represented as integers. Instead of manually comparing the two integers by checking if the wattage of the first appliance is greater than, equal to, or less than that of the second, we can use a method provided by the Java library. The Integer class offers a static method called compare(int, int) that performs this comparison for us. It returns a negative integer, positive integer, or 0 depending on whether the first integer is less than, greater than, or equal to the second integer. Similar methods are available for other wrapper classes.

The compare(…) method of our ElectronicDeviceWattComparator class and the Integer.compare(…) method are so-called *three-way comparison functions* because they get two values and tell what the relationship between the values is via three different returns.

Find Electronic Devices with the Highest Power Consumption

com/tutego/exercise/device/bhdavq/Ship.java

```
public ElectronicDevice findMostPowerConsumingElectronicDevice() {
  if ( devices.isEmpty() )
    throw new IllegalStateException(
        "Ship has no devices, there can't be a maximum in an empty
collection" );
  return Collections.max( devices, new ElectronicDeviceWattComparator() );
}
```

There are different methods in the Java library that you can pass a comparator to. Overall, these are all methods that need to somehow put elements of collections into order. This can be in determining maximum or minimum, or in sorting. The task specifies that the method Collection.max(…) can find out from a collection of elements the one that is largest according to the Comparator.

The max(…) method must be passed in two things: first the collection with the elements, then the Comparator. If we called our findMostPowerConsumingElectronicDevice() method very often or if we needed the ElectronicDeviceWattComparator more often for other operations, we could think about creating it as an object and keeping it, e.g., in a static variable. A Comparator usually never has a state, so it can be well shared. But if our Comparator instance is only needed a few times, it is redundant to keep a reference in memory to an object that is rarely needed.

The max(…) method returns the largest element, which is also the return of findMostPowerConsumingElectronicDevice(). But with one difference: if the collection is empty, min(…)/max(…) will return a NoSearchElementException, which we do not want. Therefore, we check beforehand if the collection is empty, and throw an exception in that case.

When we run the program, we will nicely see via the console outputs that compare(…) is automatically called by the max(…) method. This is a common occurrence: We do not call the overridden methods of interfaces, but the library or framework does.

Use Comparator Interface for Sorting

com/tutego/exercise/device/idulay/Ship.java

```
private final static ElectronicDeviceWattComparator
    ELECTRONIC_DEVICE_WATT_COMPARATOR=new ElectronicDeviceWattComparator();

public void load( ElectronicDevice device ) {
  devices.add( device );
  devices.sort( ELECTRONIC_DEVICE_WATT_COMPARATOR );
}
```

The Comparator instance is immutable, so we can keep the reference in a class variable; this saves us from having to rebuild it every time we add it. The sort(...) method is passed its own ELECTRONIC_DEVICE_WATT_COMPARATOR after the addition.

Static and Default Methods in Interfaces

com/tutego/exercise/oop/Distance.java

```
class DistanceImplementation implements Distance {

  private final int value;
  DistanceImplementation( int value ) {
    this.value=value;
  }

  @Override public int meter() {
    return value;
  }
}

public interface Distance {
  static Distance ofMeter( int value ) {
    return new DistanceImplementation( value );
  }

  static Distance ofKilometer( int value ) {
    return new DistanceImplementation( value * 1000 );
  }

  int meter();
  default int kilometer() {
    return meter() / 1000;
  }
}
```

If an interface provides a static factory method, then of course you can't build an instance from the interface itself. Instances can only be built from classes. Hence, we have to provide an implementation for the interface, this is called DistanceImplementation in the proposed solution. The class provides a parameterized constructor and stores the value in meters in a private variable. The implementation is also responsible for overriding the meter() method; it passes the internal state to the outside.

The distance interface has four methods. First are the two static factory methods that build instances of DistanceImplementation. In the case of meters, the parameter of ofMeter() can be put directly as an argument into the constructor of `DistanceImplementation`; in the case of `ofKilometer(int)`, the value is taken times 1,000, and then used as a constructor argument.

The method `meter()` is the only abstract method. Therefore, the class `DistanceImplementation` must also implement only this one method. The fourth method `kilometer()` is a default method and accesses the abstract method `meter()` by requesting the meters, dividing them by 1000 and returning them as kilometers.

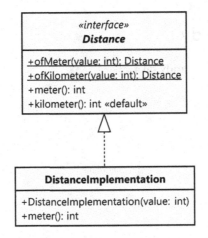

FIGURE 7.5   UML diagram of `distance` and implementation.

Delete Selected Elements with Predicate

com/tutego/exercise/device/bhdavq/Ship.java

```java
private final static int MAXIMUM_POWER_CONSUMPTION=1000;

public void removePowerConsumingElectronicDevices() {
  class IsPowerConsumingElectronicDevice
      implements Predicate<ElectronicDevice> {
    @Override public boolean test( ElectronicDevice electronicDevice ) {
      return electronicDevice.getWatt()>MAXIMUM_POWER_CONSUMPTION;
    }
  }
  devices.removeIf( new IsPowerConsumingElectronicDevice() );
}
```

In the first step, we declare a constant with the maximum accepted consumption. The variable is private because only we are interested in it, it is final because it should not be changed, it is static because constants like this do not belong to an object. The data type is `int` because the wattage within the electrical appliances is also an `int`.

Inside the method, we again use the possibility of a local class. In principle, the class declaration can be done outside because this class does not use local variables. However, as a nested class, it is quite comfortable because the class declaration is only necessary for the context of the `removePowerConsumingElectronicDevices()` method. If there is a case where the predicate should also be relevant for other methods, we should pull the nested local class out of the method.

The class `IsPowerConsumingElectronicDevice` implements a predicate for electrical devices, performs a test on a concrete electrical device, and returns a truth value about this electrical device. Our predicate accesses the wattage and queries whether it is greater than the constant `MAXIMUM_POWER_CONSUMPTION`. If it is, the electrical device has a high consumption. It is up to us whether we write the test with a "real less than" or "less than or equal to".

In the next step, we build an instance of `IsPowerConsumingElectronicDevice` and feed it to the `removeIf(...)` method of the list `devices`. The method runs an internal loop over all the electrical devices, passes each electrical device to our predicate, and if our predicate says that the electrical device has too much consumption, `removeIf(...)` deletes it from the list. The nice thing about these methods is that we don't have to worry about deleting and traversing the data structure ourselves; that functionality is internally in `removeIf(...)`.

Enumeration for Candy

com/tutego/exercise/lang/AskForCandy.java

```java
enum CandyType {
  CARAMELS,
  CHOCOLATE,
  GUMMIES,
  LICORICE,
  LOLLIPOPS,
  CHEWING_GUMS,
  COTTON_CANDY
}

static Optional<CandyType> fromName( String input ) {
  try {
    input = input.trim().toUpperCase().replace( ' ', '_' );
    return Optional.of( CandyType.valueOf( input ) );
  }
  catch ( IllegalArgumentException e ) {
    return Optional.empty();
  }
}
```

The new enumeration type `CandyType` consists of several constants, which are usually completely capitalized in Java. Since there are no spaces in identifier names, we put an underscore, just as is usual for constants.

The `fromName(String)` method is later passed the user input and returns the corresponding `CandyType`. Since the input might have unwanted whitespace in the front and back, we truncate it. Since the input can be case-insensitive, we first convert it to uppercase and replace the space with an underscore—which corresponds to the name of the constant in the best case. The compiler generates a class from each enumeration type that has a static `valueOf(String)` method. It helps us to return the corresponding enumeration type for a string. A problem exists if an assignment is not possible: then `valueOf(...)` generates an exception; we catch it and return `Optional.empty()`. If `valueOf(...)` returns a result, we wrap it in an `Optional`.

The usage may look like this:

com/tutego/exercise/lang/AskForCandy.java, CandyType

```java
System.out.println( "Name a candy" );
String input = new Scanner( System.in ).nextLine();
fromName( input ).ifPresentOrElse( System.out::println,
                                   () -> System.out.println("Unknown") );
```

Deliver Random Candies

com/tutego/exercise/lang/RandomCandy.java

```java
enum CandyType {
  CARAMELS,
  CHOCOLATE,
  GUMMIES,
  LICORICE,
  LOLLIPOPS,
  CHEWING_GUMS,
  COTTON_CANDY.

  public static Optional<CandyType> fromName( String input ) {
    try {
      input=input.trim().toUpperCase().replace( ' ', '_' );
      return Optional.of( valueOf( input ) );
    }
    catch ( IllegalArgumentException e ) {
      return Optional.empty();
    }
  }

  public static CandyType random() {
    return values()[ (int) (Math.random() * values().length) ];
  }

//    private static CandyType[] VALUES=values();
//    public static CandyType random() {
//       return VALUES[ (int) (Math.random() * VALUES.length) ];
//    }
}
```

If we add methods or other variables to the enumeration type, we have to put a semicolon after the last enumeration element.

We can copy the method `fromName`(...) directly into the enumeration type, we don't have to change anything at all. However, we could omit the qualification with `CandyType` for `valueOf`(...) because `valueOf`(...) is now part of its own data type.

Besides `valueOf`(...) there is a second method that is automatically generated by the compiler. The method `values`() returns an array with all enumeration elements. Here we can take out a random element, and thus the method `random`() is implemented.

The own `random`() method can be made more efficient. Because this way, `values`() is called twice, and this generates some runtime costs because a new array is always returned. We could optimize the code by having our own private static variable reference the constants in the array. This way, the array can be accessed directly later without having to keep creating it at runtime.

Tagging Candy with Addictive Value

The `next`() method can be implemented in different ways. Three different variants are presented. The first variant is the simplest one.

This-Query in `next()`

com/tutego/exercise/lang/AddictiveQualityCandy.java

```java
enum CandyType {
  CARAMELS     ( 9 ),
  CHOCOLATE    ( 5 ),
  GUMMIES      ( 4 ),
  LICORICE     ( 3 ),
  LOLLIPOPS    ( 2 ),
  CHEWING_GUMS ( 3 ),
  COTTON_CANDY ( 1 );

  private final int addictiveQuality;

  CandyType( int addictiveQuality ) {
    this.addictiveQuality=addictiveQuality;
  }

  public int addictiveQuality() {
    return addictiveQuality;
  }

  public CandyType next() {
    return switch ( this ) {
      case GUMMIES -> CHOCOLATE;
      case LOLLIPOPS -> Math.random()>0.5 ? LICORICE : CHEWING_GUMS;
      case COTTON_CANDY -> LOLLIPOPS;
      case LICORICE, CHEWING_GUMS -> GUMMIES;
      case CARAMELS, CHOCOLATE -> CARAMELS;
    };
  }
}
```

In the first step, we put our addictive quality values after the enumeration elements in round parentheses. We pass that integer to our constructor, which is implicitly private because the Java compiler rewrites it. The constructor takes the integer and stores it in a private variable, which is accessible via the public method `addictiveQuality()`. Since there is no corresponding setter and the enumeration element is not a JavaBean, the `get` prefix is omitted.

The `next()` method is an object method on each of the enumeration elements, so the `this` reference is available. Consequently, `this` points to the current enumeration element, which we can examine with a modern `switch` statement. Depending on the type, we return the successor drug via the `return` statement. For LOLLIPOPS, we have a special case: it is arbitrary whether LICORICE or CHEWING_GUMS is returned.

At the end, refraining from using a `default` and explicitly specifying case CARAMELS, CHOCOLATE -> CARAMELS offers the benefit that the `switch` expression will no longer be fully covered when a new constant is added. This leads to a compiler error, thereby necessitating us to explicitly choose the next appealing trait for the new enumeration element.

Array Solution

As developers, we write source code and notice certain structural patterns, it indicates a possible simplification. Especially if we have mappings, as in the task. `next()` is a function, that is, values "come in" and values "come out". The types in our case:

```
next: CandyType ↦ CandyType
```

The function argument is enumeration elements (via `this`), but since they have associated ordinal numbers, positions in the enumeration type, the mapping can also be understood from an integer to a `CandyType`:

```
next: int ↦ CandyType
```

Mappings of this type can be well implemented with associative data structures, with the pleasant feature here that the ordinal numbers of the enumeration elements start at 0 and that the numbers are ascending without gaps. Then an array can be used, and this is the second proposed solution:

com/tutego/exercise/lang/AddictiveQualityCandy.java

```java
private static CandyType[] NEXT={

  // CARAMELS, CHOCOLATE, GUMMIES,
LICORICE, LOLLIPOPS, CHEWING_GUMS, COTTON_CANDY
  CARAMELS,    CARAMELS, CHOCOLATE, GUMMIES, null,      GUMMIES,      LOLLIPOPS
};

public CandyType next() {
  if ( this == LOLLIPOPS )
    return Math.random()>0.5 ? LICORICE : CHEWING_GUMS;
  return NEXT[ ordinal() ];
}
```

The program contains an array `NEXT`, which contains each of the following candies. The `next()` method retrieves the ordinal number and then jumps to the array. If new enumeration items are added, we need to adjust the array.

The only problem remains `LOLLIPOPS`, which the program checks with special treatment. In the array, there is `null` at this position because there is never access to this element.

Lambda Solution for Advanced Users

Still not nice is this mixture between an array on one side and the special handling inside `next()` on the other. Therefore, we want to finish with a very advanced third variant, which is based on a whole set of Java possibilities:

com/tutego/exercise/lang/AddictiveQualityCandy.java

```java
interface CandyTypeSupplier extends Supplier<CandyType> {}

private static CandyTypeSupplier[] NEXT={
  ()->CARAMELS, ()->CARAMELS, ()->CHOCOLATE, ()->GUMMIES,
  ()->Math.random()>0.5 ? LICORICE : CHEWING_GUMS, ()->GUMMIES, ()->LOLLIPOPS
};

public CandyType next() {
  return NEXT[ ordinal() ].get();
}
```

At the core, we have an array, but this now contains producers for `CandyType` objects rather than `CandyType` objects. For producers, there is an interface in Java: `Supplier`. `Supplier` is a generic type, and since generic types and array don't fit together properly, we first create a special type `CandyTypeSupplier`, which is a `Supplier` for `CandyType`.

The array NEXT is of type CandyTypeSupplier[]. The array is initialized with a set of Supplier lambda expressions. These Supplier objects return the following CandyType in the simple case; in the special case LOLLIPOPS the condition operator is found, which randomly returns LICORICE or CHEWING _ GUMS.

If the array contains the Supplier elements, next():

1. Query the ordinal number of an enumeration element.
2. Go to the array with the ordinal number and get the Supplier.
3. Ask the Supplier to produce the result.

Variant with Overridden Abstract Methods

There remains one more possibility, which will be outlined only briefly. The next() method can be declared abstract and overridden by the individual enumeration elements so that it responds with the next sweet. More about this possibility of overriding methods in the next task.

Interface Implementations via an enum

com/tutego/exercise/lang/DistanceImplementations.java

```java
enum Distances implements Distance {
  EUCLIDEAN;

  @Override
  public double distance( double x1, double y1, double x2, double y2 ) {
    return Math.sqrt( (x1 - x2) * (x1 - x2)+(y1 - y2) * (y1 - y2) );
  }

  @Override
  public double distance( double x1, double y1, double z1,
                          double x2, double y2, double z2 ) {
    return Math.sqrt(    (x1 - x2) * (x1 - x2)
                      +(y1 - y2) * (y1 - y2)
                      +(z1 - z2) * (z1 - z2) );
  }
}
```

We start with the enumeration type Distances and put a constant EUCLIDEAN in it. Now Distances must implement the Distance interface. In the first step, Distances has only one constant EUCLIDEAN. If Distances implements the interface, then the implementation can be placed directly in the body of the enumeration type, then the implementation applies to all enumeration elements. Since we have only one EUCLIDEAN element, the distance(...) implementation can implement that distance metric. It does not need to query whether the algorithm might apply to some other constant.

com/tutego/exercise/lang/DistanceImplementations.java

```java
enum Distances implements Distance {
  EUCLIDEAN {
    @Override
    public double distance( double x1, double y1, double x2, double y2 ) {
      return Math.sqrt( (x1 - x2) * (x1 - x2)+(y1 - y2) * (y1 - y2) );
    }

    @Override
    public double distance( double x1, double y1, double z1,
```

```
                      double x2, double y2, double z2 ) {
      return Math.sqrt(    (x1 - x2) * (x1 - x2)+(y1 - y2) * (y1 - y2)
                    +(z1 - z2) * (z1 - z2) );
    }
  },
  MANHATTAN {
    @Override
    public double distance( double x1, double y1, double x2, double y2 ) {
      return Math.abs( x1 - x2 )+Math.abs( y1 - y2 );
    }

    @Override
    public double distance( double x1, double y1, double z1,
                            double x2, double y2, double z2 ) {
      return Math.abs(x1 - x2)+Math.abs(y1 - y2)+Math.abs(z1 - z2);
    }
  }
}
```

In the second solution as well, the enumeration type `Distances` implements the interface, containing two constants: `EUCLIDEAN` and `MANHATTAN`.

When implementing the two methods from the `Distance` interface, the solution takes a slightly different approach. Instead of having a common implementation for all constants, now the implementation is merged with the enumeration element. The syntax is similar to the anonymous inner classes. Following the name of the constants, a body enclosed in curly brackets contains the two overridden methods, with no need for a semicolon after `MANHATTAN { ... }`.

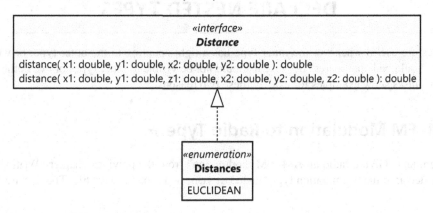

FIGURE 7.6   UML diagram of the enumeration type.

Quiz: Aviso and Brig

The program does not compile and therefore cannot be executed. The reason for the compiler error is solely due to the visible constructor `ShipType`. Enumeration types are allowed to have constructors, but they are always private. Unless we write a visibility modifier, `private` is the default; we could also add `private` ourselves, but that is unnecessary. In no case can the constructor be public because no new enumeration items can be created from the outside.

An enumeration type can declare a `main(...)` method, and such programs can be executed. The compiler converts an enumeration type into a class anyway, and an `enum` can have static methods. Consequently, for the runtime environment, an enumeration type is nothing special, but just a class that has a few constants and is derived from a superclass `Enum`.

If we were to remove the visibility at the constructor and run the program, the output would be:
`Aviso Golden Hind`.

Nested Types

8

In the previous examples, we always had exactly one type of declaration in each file, the so-called *compilation unit*. However, Java also allows for nested types, where a type declaration can be placed inside another type declaration, making the relationship between them even closer. The following exercises demonstrate the usefulness of nested types, but there are also some potential issues that need to be considered. To gain a deeper understanding of nested types, several quizzes will be provided.

Prerequisites

- Know static nested types.
- Know inner types (nonstatic nested types).
- Know local (inner) types.
- Know anonymous inner class.

DECLARE NESTED TYPES

Nested types are useful whenever the inner type has a tight coupling to the outer type, or when a type declaration should be kept "secret" because it should not be visible to other types or even other methods. The next two tasks show examples for exactly these two reasons.

Set AM–FM Modulation to Radio Type ★

In the assignment "Giving radio an AM–FM modulation" from the previous chapter "Writing your own classes" we declared the enumeration type `Modulation`, in a separate Java file. The declaration looked like this:

```
public enum Modulation { AM, FM }
```

The sound waves with the tones are modulated, resulting in radio waves, which the radio receives and translates back into sound waves. Since a radio always requires modulation, the type `Modulation` can be placed in the type `Radio` and thus this tight coupling can be well represented with nested types. For example, this makes it easy to separate the modulation of sound waves of a radio from the modulation of a video signal; such a second enumeration could be placed in a class `TV`.

Task:

- Put the enumeration type `Modulation` in the class `Radio`.
- When we call `setModulation(…)` on a radio, how is AM/FM qualified and passed?

DOI: 10.1201/9781003454502-9

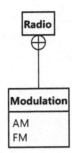

FIGURE 8.1   UML diagram with nested type.

Write Three Kinds of Watt-Comparator Implementations ★

In the previous chapter, "Writing your own classes", we implemented the interface `Comparator` in the exercise "Comparing consumption of electrical appliances". As a reminder:

com/tutego/exercise/device/bhdavq/ElectronicDeviceWattComparator.java

```java
import java.util.Comparator;

public class ElectronicDeviceWattComparator
    implements Comparator<ElectronicDevice> {

  @Override
  public int compare( ElectronicDevice ea1,
                      ElectronicDevice ea2 ) {
    System.out.println( ea1+" is compared with "+ea2 );
    return Integer.compare( ea1.getWatt(), ea2.getWatt() );
  }
}
```

The implementation of the interface is in its own compilation unit, but the interface can also be implemented more locally using nested types.
Task:

- Write the `ElectronicDeviceWattComparator` once as a
  - static nested class,
  - local class,
  - anonymous inner class.

NESTED TYPES QUIZ

The following are some quizzes that test understanding of nested types.

Quiz: Pirate Could Have Waved ★

What do we need to write at _____to call the `wave()` method from the `main(...)` method?

```java
public class Pirate {
```

```
static class Body {
  class Arm {
    public void wave() { }
  }
}

public static void main( String[] args ) {
  // _____.wave()
}
}
```

Quiz: Name in a Bottle ★★

Does the following program compile? If so, what does it output?

```
class Distillery {
  private String name="Captain CiaoCiao";

  class Bottle {
    private Bottle() { }
    String brand() { return name; }
  }

  Bottle createBottle() { return new Bottle(); }
}

public class CaptainsDistillery {
  public static void main( String[] args ) {
    System.out.println( new Distillery().createBottle().brand() );
  }
}
```

Quiz: Get Me Another Bottle of Rum ★

Does the following program compile? If so, what is the output when we run the program?

```
public class Bottle {
  public void drink() { }

  public class Rum {
    public static void drink() {
      System.out.println( "At a gulp" );
    }
  }

  public static void main( String[] args ) {
    new Bottle().new Rum().drink();
  }
}
```

SUGGESTED SOLUTIONS

Set AM–FM Modulation to Radio Type

com/tutego/exercise/device/fzrcph/Radio.java

```java
package com.tutego.exercise.device.fzrcph;

public class Radio {

  public enum Modulation {
    AM, FM
  }
  private Modulation modulation=Modulation.AM;

  public void setModulation( Modulation modulation ) {
    this.modulation=modulation;
  }

  // remaining fields and methods omitted
}
```

Modulation is a nested type (strictly speaking a static nested class because the compiler translates an enum into a class declaration) of Radio and must now be addressed differently. Let's look at three possibilities; the radio and the three example programs are all in the same package.

Full qualification

> **com/tutego/exercise/device/fzrcph/Application1.java**

```java
package com.tutego.exercise.device.fzrcph;

public class Application1 {
  public static void main( String[] args ) {
    Radio radio=new Radio();
    radio.setModulation( Radio.Modulation.AM );
  }
}
```

Enum import

> **com/tutego/exercise/device/fzrcph/Application2.java**

```java
package com.tutego.exercise.device.fzrcph;
import com.tutego.exercise.device.fzrcph.Radio.*;

public class Application2 {
  public static void main( String[] args ) {
    Radio radio=new Radio();
    radio.setModulation( Modulation.AM );
  }
}
```

Static import
   com/tutego/exercise/device/fzrcph/Application3.java

```java
package com.tutego.exercise.device.fzrcph;

import static com.tutego.exercise.device.fzrcph.Radio.Modulation.*;

public class Application3 {
  public static void main( String[] args ) {
    Radio radio=new Radio();
    radio.setModulation( AM );
  }
}
```

Write Three Kinds of Watt-Comparator Implementations

com/tutego/exercise/device/cgwmpe/Application.java

```java
public class Application {
  static class ElectronicDeviceWattComparator
      implements Comparator<ElectronicDevice> {
    @Override public int compare( ElectronicDevice ea1,
                                  ElectronicDevice ea2 ) {
      return Double.compare( ea1.getWatt(), ea2.getWatt() );
    }
  }

  public static void main( String[] args ) {

    class ElectronicDeviceWattComparator
        implements Comparator<ElectronicDevice> {
      @Override public int compare( ElectronicDevice ea1,
                                    ElectronicDevice ea2 ) {
        return Double.compare( ea1.getWatt(), ea2.getWatt() );
      }
    }

    Comparator<ElectronicDevice> wattComparator=new Comparator<>() {
      @Override public int compare( ElectronicDevice ea1,
                                    ElectronicDevice ea2 ) {
        return Double.compare( ea1.getWatt(), ea2.getWatt() );
      }
    };
  }
}
```

Application is the outer class. ElectronicDeviceWattComparator is introduced as a static nested class. In the main(...) method, the local class then follows, and via the inner anonymous class we create a copy electronicDeviceWattComparator directly.

Quiz: Pirate Could Have Waved

You have to write:

```
new Pirate.Body().new Arm().wave();
```

The special feature of inner classes is that they always have a reference to an outer object. When building instances of inner classes, we have to do it via a reference to an object of the outer class, followed by the keyword new.

Body is a static class. To build an object of type Body we do not need an instance of the outer class Pirate. We use the ClassName.StaticProperty style when accessing static properties. When we write Pirate.Body, we use it to refer to the nested static class, and new Pirate.Body() creates an instance. This reference is necessary so that we can build an object of type Arm because Arm is the actual inner class. With this reference, we can call the wave() method.

Quiz: Name in a Bottle

The program compiles, and the output is:

```
Captain CiaoCiao
```

The class Bottle is an inner class, and consequently can only be created if there is an instance of the outer class Distillery. To create the inner class, a factory method is used. Thus, first an instance of the outer class Distillery must be created, then the factory method must be called, so that a Bottle object is created. The special fact, however, is that the constructor of Bottle is private. Normally, it would be impossible to construct an instance from the outside via a private constructor, unless the factory method resides inside that very class. But Java somewhat leverages this visibility for inner classes. The outer class Distillery can also call the private constructor of Bottle and build an object. From this Bottle object, we can now retrieve and return the name via the brand() method. Again, we can see that the private visibility has been removed in the other direction as well. Because name is a private instance variable of the outer class Distillery to which other classes have no access. Distillery and Bottle form a union in terms of visibility, and the private designation is, so to speak, annulled.

Quiz: Get Me another Bottle of Rum

The program cannot be compiled. The reason is in the declaration of the static drink() method in the class Rum. There is an important rule: nonstatic inner classes must not have static properties, i.e., neither static methods nor static variables. If we delete the static keyword, the program will run normally and at a gulp will appear on the screen.

The reason nonstatic inner classes cannot have static properties is that the inner class cannot be accessed at all without an instance of the outer class. That is, the notation Classname.staticproperty does not work for inner classes. Instances of these inner classes have however always a reference to the instance of the outer class because the inner classes can access instance variables of the outer class. Static properties are always completely independent of any objects, so they are also independent of outer surrounding objects.

Exception Handling

9

Unforeseen errors can occur at any time. Our programs must be prepared for them and be able to handle this situation. The next exercises will be about catching exceptions, handling them, and even reporting problems via exceptions.

Requirements

- Understand the need for exceptions.
- Distinguish between checked and unchecked exceptions.
- Catch exceptions with `try-catch`.
- Know exception forwarding with throws.
- Be able to throw exceptions with throw.
- Be able to write your own exception classes.
- Be able to close resources with `try-with-resources`.

Data types used in this chapter:

- `java.lang.Throwable`
- `java.lang.Exception`
- `java.lang.RuntimeException`
- `java.lang.Error`
- `java.io.IOException`
- `java.lang.AutoCloseable`

CATCHING EXCEPTIONS

Checked exceptions must be caught or passed up to the caller. For checked exceptions, the compiler forces us to do this, and for unchecked exceptions, this is not mandatory; however, if we do not handle a `RuntimeException`, this will cause the executing thread to abort. Therefore, it is recommended to always catch and at least log even unchecked exceptions.

Get the Longest Line of a File ★

Successful pirates must have a good memory, and Captain CiaoCiao wants to test if everyone can think like a whiz. He reads a list of names to everyone for a test. At the end of the list, everyone must be able to recite the longest name. But since Captain CiaoCiao is too busy reading aloud, he wants software to output the longest name at the end.

DOI: 10.1201/9781003454502-10

Task:

1. The file http://tutego.de/download/family-names.txt contains family names. Save the file locally on your file system.
2. Create a new class `LongestLineInFile` with a `main(..)` method.
3. Put the `Files.readAllLines(...)` into the `main(...)` method.
4. Which exception(s) must be caught?
5. What is the longest name (according to the `string length()`) in the file?
6. Bonus: what are the two longest names in the file?

You can read a file in Java like this:

```
String filename=...
List<String> lines=Files.readAllLines( Paths.get( filename ) );
```

Identify Exceptions, Laughing All the Time ★

Developers must remember which language constructs, constructors, and methods can throw exceptions. While IDEs provide hints for checked exceptions, they may not provide warnings for every situation where an exception could potentially occur, such as with array access, where an `ArrayIndexOutOfBoundsException` can be thrown.
Task:

• What exceptions do we need to catch if we want to compile the following block? Use *only* the Javadoc to find out.
  ```
  Clip clip=AudioSystem.getClip();
  clip.open( AudioSystem.getAudioInputStream( new File("") ) );
  clip.start();
  TimeUnit.MICROSECONDS.sleep( clip.getMicrosecondLength()+50 );
  clip.close();
  ```
• Can/should exceptions be grouped together?
• Optional task: find some laughter files on the Internet (at https:// soundbible.com/tags-laugh. html, for example, there are free WAV files). Save the WAV files locally. Play random laughs one after the other in an endless loop.

Convert String Array to Int Array and Be Lenient on Nonnumbers ★

The `Integer.parseInt(String)` method converts a `string` to an integer of type `int` and throws a `NumberFormatException` if no such conversion is possible, such as for `Integer.parseInt("0x10")` or `Integer.parseInt(null)`. The Java library does not provide a method for converting a string array of numbers to an `int` array.
Task:

• Write a new method `static int[] parseInts(String... numbers)` that converts all given strings to integers.
• The number of strings passed determines the size of the return array.

- If a string in the array cannot be converted at a position, a 0 comes at the position. `null` as an argument is allowed and results in 0.
- Calling `parseInts()` with no arguments is fine, but `parseInts(null)` must result in an exception.

Example:

```
String[] strings={ "1", "234", "333" };
int[] ints1=parseInts( strings ); // [1, 234, 333]
int[] ints2=parseInts( "1", "234", "333" ); // [1, 234, 333]
int[] ints3=parseInts( "1", "11234", "3", null, "99" ); // [1, 0, 3, 0, 99]
int[] ints4=parseInts( "Person", "Woman", "Man", "Camera, TV" ); // [0, 0, 0,
0]
```

Quiz: And Finally ★

What is the output of the following Java program?

```java
public class TryCatchFinally {
  public static void main( String[] args ) {
    try {
      System.out.println( 1 / 0 );
      System.out.println( "I'm gettin' too old to jump out of cars." );
    }
    catch ( Exception e ) {
      System.out.print( "That's why everybody talks about you." );
    }
    finally {
      System.out.println( "Frankly, my dear, I don't give a damn." );
    }
  }
}
```

Quiz: A Lonely Try ★

Is there a `try` block without `catch`?

Quiz: Well Caught ★

Inheritance plays an important role in exception classes. Each exception class is derived from a superclass, for example, `IOException` from `Exception`, `Exception` itself from `Throwable`. This class hierarchy comes into play when exceptions are caught. In principle, it is possible to use a single `catch` block to react to all exceptions that occur in a piece of program code:

```java
try {
  // Do something
} catch ( Exception e ) { // or ( Throwable e )
  // Log
}
```

The exception handler could catch all exceptions in the catch block, that is, use a `catch (Exception e)` or `catch (Throwable e)`. Is this good or bad?

Quiz: Too Much of a Good Thing ★

What is the response of the following Java program?

```java
public class TooMuchMemory {
  public static void main( String args[] ) {
    try {
      byte[] bytes=new byte[ Integer.MAX_VALUE ];
    }
    catch ( Throwable e ) {
      System.out.println( "He had the detonators." );
      e.printStackTrace();
    }
  }
}
```

Quiz: Try-Catch in Inheritance ★★

Suppose class `Pudding` wants to implement interface `Eatable` and implement `calories()`:

```java
interface Eatable {
  void calories() throws IOException;
}
class Pudding implements Eatable {
  @Override
  public void calories() ??? {
  }
}
```

What kind of `throws` clause must `calories()` have in `Pudding` instead of the three question marks?

THROWING CUSTOM EXCEPTIONS

Exceptions originate in:

- Incorrect use of certain language constructs, such as integer division by 0, dereferencing via a `null` reference, impossible type matching for objects, incorrect array access, etc.
- Explicitly generated exceptions by the keyword `throw`.

Behind `throw` there is a reference to an exception object. This object is usually constructed with `new`. The types come from libraries, like `IOException`, but they can also be our own exception classes, which have to be derived from `Throwable` but are typically subclasses of `Exception`.

Quiz: Throw and Throws ★

What is the difference between the keywords `throw` and `throws`? Where are the keywords placed?

Quiz: The Division Fails ★

Can the following program be translated? If so, and if we run it, what is the result?

```java
class Application {
 public static void main( String[] args ) {
   try { throw 1 / 0; }
   catch ( int e ) { e.printStackTrace(); }
 }
}
```

WRITING YOUR OWN EXCEPTION CLASSES

Java SE provides numerous exception types, but they are usually technology-dependent, such as when there is a network timeout or the SQL command is wrong. This is fine for low-level functionality, but the software is built in layers, and the outermost layer is more about the consequence of these low-level events: there was an IOException → configuration could not be loaded; there was an SQLException → customer data could not be updated, etc. These exceptions are modeled by new semantic exception classes.

Show Impossible Watt with Own Exception ★

Electrical devices without power consumption do not exist, just like negative wattage values.
Task:

- Create your own exception class IllegalWattException. Derive the class from RuntimeException.
- The exception should be thrown whenever setWatt(watt) has a wattage less than or equal to zero.
- Test the exception occurrence by catching it.

Quiz: Potatoes or Other Vegetables ★

Can the following program be successfully compiled?

```java
class VegetableException extends Throwable { }

class PotatoException extends VegetableException { }

class PotatoVegetable {
 public static void main( String[] args ) {
   try { throw new PotatoException(); }
   finally { }
   catch ( VegetableException e ) { }
   catch ( PotatoException e ) { }
 }
}
```

TRY-WITH-RESOURCES

An important guideline is: if you open something, you close it afterward. It is easy to forget this, and then there are unclosed resources that can lead to problems. These include data loss and memory issues. To make it as easy as possible for developers to close resources, there is a special interface called `AutoCloseable` and a language construct that helps make closing short and simple. This reduces the number of lines of code and avoids bugs, for example, when exceptions are thrown again during the closing process itself.

Write Current Date to File ★

A `java.io.PrintWriter` is a simple class for writing text documents and can also write directly into files.
Task:

- Study the Javadoc of `PrintWriter`.
- Find out how to connect a `PrintWriter` to an output file. The character encoding should be of the platform.
- Close the `PrintWriter` correctly with try-with-resources.
- The Java program should write the string representation of `LocalDateTime.now()` to the text file.

Read Notes and Write Them to a New ABC File ★★

Renowned composer Amadeus van Trout discusses his latest works over the phone. Captain CiaoCiao is a big fan of the composer and secretly obtains an audio recording, which is delivered as a transcribed text file. It contains all the notes one below the other, such as:

```
C
D
C
```

The assignment is divided into two parts.
Task part A, reading from a file:

- `java.util.Scanner` is a simple class for reading and processing text resources. Study the constructors in the Javadoc.
- In the Scanner constructor, various sources can be specified, including `Path`. Open a `Scanner`, and pass a file in the constructor via `Paths.get("file.txt")`. Close the `Scanner` correctly with try-with-resources.
- The `hasNextLine()` and `nextLine()` methods are of most interest. Read a text file line by line, and output all lines to the console. For example, if the input file contains the lines
  ```
  C,
  d
  d'
  ```
  the output on the screen is
  ```
  C, d d'
  ```

- Extend the program to include only the lines with content. For example, if the file contains a blank line or a line with only white space, i.e., spaces or tab characters, it will not be included. Example:

```
C,
d
```

    leads to

```
C, d
```

- Only valid notes are allowed, these are:

```
C, D, E, F, G, A, B, C D E F G A B c d e f g a b c' d' e' f' g' a' b'
```

    Keep in mind that the comma on the uppercase letters is not a separator, but part of the note indication, as is the apostrophe on the lowercase letters of the last octave.

Captain CiaoCiao wants to listen to the new composition and see it on a sheet of music. Here the notation *ABC* is suitable; a file with notes from C, to b' looks like this:

```
M:C
L:1/4
K:C
C, D, E, F, G, A, B, C D E F G A B c d e f g a b c' d' e' f' g' a' b'
```

The first three lines are a header and contain metadata for ABC. At https://www.abcjs.net/abcjs-editor.html, you can display the ABC file and even play it.

FIGURE 9.1   Note display from https://www.abcjs.net/abcjs-editor.html

    The basic idea of the algorithm is the following: we go through the file line by line using the class Scanner and check if the content of the line, the note, occurs in a data structure that we use for validation. If the note is valid, we write it to the desired output format.

    The program for reading in the notes is to be supplemented by a writing part.

    Task part B, write to file:

- Open a second file for writing with PrintWriter; in the constructor, you can pass a file name directly. Attention: choose a different file name than the source file because otherwise the file will be overwritten!
- Continue to read the file from the first part of the task, but write the output to the new file instead of to the console, so that a valid ABC file is created. The PrintWriter provides the print(String) and println(String) methods known from System.out.
- Note: both resources can (and should) be in a common try with resources.

Quiz: Excluded ★

Given the following program code in the main(...) method:

```
class ResourceA implements AutoCloseable {
```

```
  @Override public void close() {
    System.out.println( "close() ResourceA" );
  }
}

class ResourceB implements AutoCloseable {
  private final ResourceA resourceA;

  public ResourceB( ResourceA resourceA ) {
    this.resourceA=resourceA;
  }

  @Override public void close() {
    resourceA.close();
    System.out.println( "close() ResourceB" );
  }
}

// version 1
try ( ResourceA resourceA=new ResourceA();
      ResourceB resourceB=new ResourceB( resourceA ) ) {
}

// version 2
try ( ResourceB resourceB=new ResourceB( new ResourceA() ) ) { }
}
```

1. What output follows when the program is executed?
2. Resources are often nested, and there are two variants for `try`-with resources. How do the variants differ, and what are their advantages and disadvantages?

SUGGESTED SOLUTIONS

Get the Longest Line of a File

com/tutego/exercise/util/LongestLineInFile.java

```
String filename="src\\main\\resources\\com\\tutego\\exercises\\util\\
family-names.txt";
try {
  Collection<String> lines=Files.readAllLines( Paths.get( filename ) );
  String first="", second="";
  for ( String line : lines ) {
    if ( line.length()>first.length() ) {
      second=first;
      first=line;
    }
    else if ( line.length()>second.length() )
      second=line;
  }
  System.out.println( first+","+second );
}
```

```
catch ( IOException e ) {
  System.err.println( "Error reading file "
                    +new File( filename ).getAbsolutePath() );
  e.printStackTrace();
}
```

Anything in Java that has to do with a data store can throw exceptions. The Java standard library uses checked exceptions by default, for input/output operations we find IOException. Frameworks and open-source libraries are more likely to utilize unchecked exceptions because it is more convenient to just let the exceptions go up until there is a handler.

A look at the Javadoc of Files shows that an IOException is thrown:

```
public static List<String> readAllLines(Path path) throws IOException
```

Read all lines from a file. Bytes from the file are decoded into characters using the UTF-8 charset.

Throws: IOException − if an I/O error occurs reading from the file or a malformed or unmappable byte sequence is read.

Whether checked or unchecked exceptions, we should react to exceptions. Java offers two ways to do this:

- We could either write a throws to the method, which then passes the exception to the caller of the method, or
- We handle the error with a try-catch block.

Since IOException is a checked exception, we must handle the exception. Our solution uses a try-catch block. If an exception occurs, the catch block is processed. This is followed by the output on the standard error channel, and the printStackTrace() method prints a call stack on the command line as well. printStackTrace() originates from Throwable, the base class of all exception classes. It is a matter of taste whether you want this form of output; you won't find such a thing in production software, here you would use a logger to report exceptions.

The chosen solution works as follows: we note the longest and second-longest line in the variables first and second. The extended for loop runs overall lines, reads and examines them. Now each line is considered. If the length of line is longer than the length of the first stored string first, then we have found a new candidate for the longest line, so that the previously longest line is now the second-longest line. However, if first was longer than line, nothing is updated, but line may still have been longer than second, so we test again with the second stored line.

At the end of the for loop, we output the first and second lines.

One alternative solution is to use a Comparator to sort the list based on the length of the lines. However, sorting the entire list may be unnecessary if we only need to find the two longest lines. If performance is not a concern, sorting may be the most concise solution. Furthermore, sorting has the added benefit of easily accommodating extensions to the task, such as finding the first ten longest lines instead of just the first two.

Identify Exceptions, Laughing All the Time

Exceptions can be thrown by faulty program constructs, such as a division by 0 or dereferencing a null reference. There may be checked exceptions or unchecked exceptions for this purpose. Methods and constructors can throw these exceptions. To understand which exceptions we need to throw, we need to look at all methods and constructors:

TABLE 9.1 Constructor and method exceptions

METHOD/CONSTRUCTOR	CHECKED EXCEPTION(S)	UNCHECKED EXCEPTION(S)
getClip()	LineUnavailableException	SecurityException, IllegalArgumentException
File(…)		NullPointerException
getAudioInputStream(…)	UnsupportedAudioFileException, IOException	NullPointerException[a]
open(…)	LineUnavailableException, IOException	IllegalArgumentException, IllegalStateException, SecurityException
sleep(…)	InterruptedException	
close()		SecurityException
getAudioInputStream(…)	UnsupportedAudioFileException, IOException	NullPointerException
open(…)	LineUnavailableException, IOException	IllegalArgumentException, IllegalStateException, SecurityException
sleep(..)	InterruptedException	
close()	SecurityException	

We can easily see that the constructor or the methods can throw numerous exceptions. The checked exceptions are always listed behind the throws in the Java documentation, but the unchecked exceptions are listed in the Java documentation itself and not behind the throws because it is unusual that unchecked exceptions appear there. With the unchecked exceptions, it is not always known what can be thrown; the table lists what the Javadoc documents for unchecked exceptions.

Those who want to handle the exceptions should consider grouping exceptions together or what the inheritance hierarchy looks like to catch an entire category of exceptions.

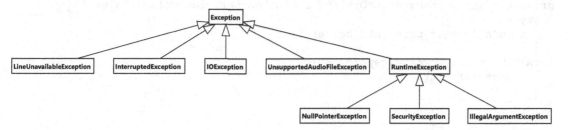

FIGURE 9.2 UML diagram of the inheritance relationship.

The following program catches all exceptions and prints messages, except for InterruptedException because these are interrupts from sleep() and do not need to be handled. In the case of RuntimeException they are programming errors on the software developer's side, that's why we output the stack trace on the logger channel.

com/tutego/exercise/lang/exception/LaughingMyArseOff.java

```java
static void play( String filename ) {
  try {
    Clip clip=AudioSystem.getClip();
    clip.open( AudioSystem.getAudioInputStream( new File( filename ) ) );
    clip.start();
    TimeUnit.MICROSECONDS.sleep( clip.getMicrosecondLength()+50 );
    clip.close();
  }
```

```
catch ( LineUnavailableException e ) {
  System.err.println( "Line cannot be opened because it is unavailable" );
}
catch ( IOException e ) {
  System.err.println( "An I/O exception of some sort has occurred" );
}
catch ( UnsupportedAudioFileException e ) {
  System.err.printf(
    "File %s did not contain valid data of a recognized file type and
format%n",
    filename );
}
catch ( InterruptedException e ) {
  // No-op
}
catch ( RuntimeException e ) {
  Logger.getLogger( LaughingMyArseOff.class.getSimpleName() )
      .log( Level.SEVERE, e.getMessage(), e );
}
}
```

There is no selection of different laughs, but the own method play(String) can well be put into a loop of its own.

Convert String Array to Int Array and Be Lenient on Nonnumbers

com/tutego/exercise/lang/exception/StringsToInteger.java

```
private static int parseIntOrElse( String number, int defaultValue ) {
  try {
    return Integer.parseInt( number );
  }
  catch ( NumberFormatException e ) {
    return defaultValue;
  }
}

public static int[] parseInts( String... numbers ) {
  int[] result=new int[ numbers.length ];

  for ( int i=0; i<numbers.length; i++ )
    result[ i ]=parseIntOrElse( numbers[ i ], 0 );

  return result;
}
```

Our current method parseInts(...) gets an array of strings that need to be converted to integers one by one. When converting to integers via Integer.parseInt(String), there is an exception if the string cannot be converted to a number. We want to outsource this conversion from a String to an integer to a separate method parseIntOrElse(String, int). The method gets a String and a default value if the String cannot be converted to an integer. The method catches the exception that occurs if the conversion fails and then returns the default value, otherwise returns the converted value. A NumberFormatException also exists in the case of Integer.parseInt(null), for which we consequently automatically get the default value.

If the method parseInts(String..) was called with the argument null, numbers.length leads to a NullPointerException, which is intentional. If the argument is not equal to null, we create a new array of integers that is the same size as the passed string array. The for loop iterates over the String array and passes each value into the parseIntOrElse(...) method, passing 0 as the default value. So, we always get back an integer result, either the converted one or 0. Finally, we return the array.

Advanced Java developers can replace the loop. Because there is a useful Arrays method setAll(...) implemented like this:

OpenJDK's implementation of setAll(…)

```java
public static void setAll(int[] array, IntUnaryOperator generator) {
  Objects.requireNonNull(generator);
  for (int i=0; i<array.length; i++)
    array[i]=generator.applyAsInt(i);
}
```

The special feature of this method is that it is not us running over the array with our own loop, but the setAll(...) method does that for us. The caller only has to pass the array and a special object of type IntUnaryOperator, which is a function that maps the index (int) to an object that is stored as an element in the array.

We can replace our loop with this:

com/tutego/exercise/lang/exception/StringsToInteger.java

```java
public static int[] parseInts( String... numbers ) {
  int[] result=new int[ numbers.length ];
  Arrays.setAll( result, index ->parseIntOrElse( numbers[ index ], 0 ) );
  return result;
}
```

The notation here is formulated with a lambda expression, something we will look at later.

Quiz: And Finally

The program compiles, and when we run it, it throws an ArithmeticException at runtime due to division by 0. As a result, there is no output in the try block. The exception is caught in the catch block because an ArithmeticException is a subclass of Exception, and that leads to the first output:

```
That's why everybody talks about you.
```

Furthermore, since a finally block follows, whose code is always executed—no matter whether an exception occurred or not—the screen displays:

```
Frankly, my dear, I don't give a damn.
```

Quiz: A Lonely Try

Yes, it is quite legitimate that there is only one try-finally block:

```java
try {
} finally {
}
```

Such blocks can be used when post-processing is needed regardless of a possible exception, but possible exceptions should be passed to a higher level.

A `try` block without `catch` and without `finally` is not correct. However, there is a `try`-with-resources without `catch` or `finally` that automatically closes resources and is not necessarily associated with event handling.

Quiz: Well Caught

General catching of every exception is not recommended. This notation often catches and handles exceptions that do not belong to the same error category at all, such as programming errors that throw a `NullPointerException`.

The base type `Throwable` is a bit worse because under `Throwable` there is also `Error`, so that `catch (Throwable e)` catches, for example, a `StackOverflowError` as well. If you catch an exception, you want to handle it. However, an `Error` usually indicates a problem with the JVM that cannot be handled.

Quiz: Too Much of a Good Thing

The program compiles and executes, but attempting to create a huge `byte` array results in an `OutOfMemoryError`.

A special feature of Java is that even these hard errors thrown by the virtual machine as `Error` exceptions can be caught because `Error` objects are also subtypes of `Throwable`.

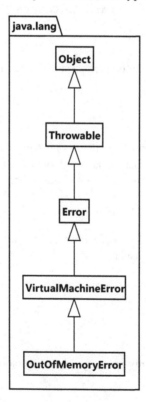

FIGURE 9.3   UML diagram: `OutOfMemoryError` is a special `Throwable`.

So, our program successfully catches `OutOfMemoryError` and gives a console output as if nothing happened:

```
He had the detonators.
java.lang.OutOfMemoryError: Requested array size exceeds VM limit
 at TooMuchMemory.main(T.java:66)
```

Catching `Error` objects is highly critical because an error indicates a problematic state within the JVM. Simply continuing can lead to unforeseen errors. The Javadoc writes at `java.lang.Error`:

An `Error` is a subclass of `Throwable` that indicates serious problems that a reasonable application should not try to catch. Most such errors are abnormal conditions.

If you can't handle `Error`, a program shouldn't catch the type either and better let the JVM exit. However, there may be cases where you want to catch an `Error`. For example, a program might try to load native libraries and, if that fails, choose a different path.

Quiz: Try-Catch in Inheritance

When classes are implementing methods of interfaces, the method in the class may look slightly different from the method in the interface in some places:

- The method name must be identical to the one in the interface, but subtypes are allowed in the return type. Since we only have `void` here and the methods do not return anything, we also do not have an example for these so-called *covariant return types*.
- Modifiers can be added, for example, `final` or `synchronized`. Subclasses can, in fact, increase visibility in principle, but since all abstract methods in interfaces are implicitly `public`, this is already maximally visible.

Certain adjustments are also possible for the `throws` clause. It can be extended in two directions:

- The method may choose not to throw exceptions at all, so the `throws` clause may be left out.
- The method can throw subtypes of exceptions thrown by the superclass. Talking informally, if the superclass method throws a general exception, and we have handling for that general exception type, then that handling can also handle a more specific type.

Quiz: Throw and Throws

Both of these keywords appear in the context of exceptions. The keyword `throws` is used for checked exceptions at the method signature (in principle, unchecked exceptions can also be specified, but this is unnecessary). `throws` expresses that the method *can* throw checked exceptions. Here, several exceptions can stand comma-separated. The caller of the method must then handle all of these exceptions.

The keyword `throw` on the other hand is used in the inside of methods, to throw exceptions, which then terminates the program flow in the method. In principle, there can be various places with `throw` in the method.

Quiz: The Division Fails

You cannot compile the program, there are compiler errors at three places.

```
class Application {
 public static void main( String[] args ) {
    try {
      throw 1 / 0;
    }
    catch ( int e ) {
      e.printStackTrace();
    }
  }
}
```

- In Java, only exceptions of type throwable can be thrown. However, 1/0 is of type int. The division 1/0 *does* throw an ArithmeticException; however, the expression 1/0 is, not a Throwable, but simply of type int.
- The next error is at the catch branch. Here must be something of type Throwable—you cannot use a primitive data type.
- The third error is with printStackTrace() because method calls on primitive data types are not allowed.

In Java, all exceptions must be derived from the Throwable type. This is different from the other programming languages. Similarly, you can execute the program in JavaScript because in JavaScript, you can report arbitrary things as exceptions.

Show Impossible Watt with Own Exception

com/tutego/exercise/device/nswigu/IllegalWattException.java

```
public class IllegalWattException extends RuntimeException {

  public IllegalWattException() {
  }

  public IllegalWattException( String format, Object... args ) {
    super( String.format( format, args ) );
  }
}
```

IllegalWattException extends a superclass RuntimeException that provides us with several constructors. We provide two constructors ourselves that delegate to the superclass constructors. The parameterless constructor automatically delegates upward, the second parameterized constructor builds a string for the error message and thus goes to the superclass noting this error message. The message is available later via the getMessage() method. The actual message is noted in the superclass Throwable.

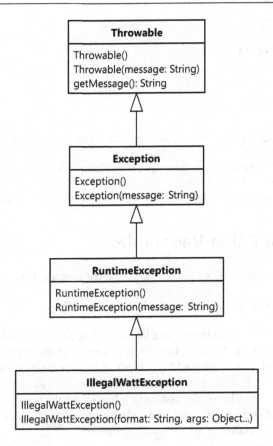

FIGURE 9.4   UML diagram of the inheritance relationship.

The parameterized constructor of `IllegalWattException` has a special feature that is not common for exception classes: The constructor `IllegalWattException(String format, Object... args)` takes a format string and also the format arguments and builds a `String` with the desired formatting using `String.format(...)` and passes the error message to the superclass for storage.

The `ElectronicDevice` is a class that checks in the setter if the power is nonnegative or 0. If so, the constructor of `IllegalWattException` is built with a full error message, and the exception is thrown.

com/tutego/exercise/device/nswigu/ElectronicDevice.java

```java
public void setWatt( int watt ) {
  if ( watt <= 0 )
    throw new IllegalWattException( "Watt cannot be 0 or negative but was
%f",
                                     watt );
  this.watt=watt;
}
```

The test code calls the setter method with wrong values, so there is an exception written to the console.

com/tutego/exercise/device/nswigu/Application.java

```java
ElectronicDevice gameGirl=new ElectronicDevice();
try {
```

```
  gameGirl.setWatt( 0 );
}
catch ( IllegalWattException e ) {
  e.printStackTrace();
}
```

The console output is:

```
com.tutego.exercise.device.nswigu.IllegalWattException: Watt cannot be 0 or
negative but was 0.000000
    at com.tutego.exercise.device.nswigu.ElectronicDevice.
setWatt(ElectronicDevice.java:10)
    at com.tutego.exercise.device.nswigu.Application.main(Application.java:8)
```

Quiz: Potatoes or Other Vegetables

The program cannot be compiled. There is the following error message from the compiler:

```
Exception 'PotatoException' has already been caught.
```

For exception classes, you can build an inheritance hierarchy, like for other classes. In our example, the first own exception class is VegetableException. From it, there is a subclass PotatoException. When we throw a PotatoException in the main(...) method, this checked exception is caught in a catch block. However, the first catch block does not catch the precise type PotatoException, but the base type VegetableException. That is, the first catch block with the general VegetableException already catches PotatoException, and the subsequent catch block with the more specific PotatoException is inaccessible at all.

Write Current Date to File

com/tutego/exercise/io/WriteDateToFile.java

```
String fileName="current-date.txt";
try ( PrintWriter writer=new PrintWriter( fileName ) ) {
  writer.print( LocalDateTime.now() );
}
catch ( FileNotFoundException e ) {
  System.err.println( "Can't create file "+fileName );
}
```

The constructor of PrintWriter takes a String for the file name. In principle, we can also specify a character encoding for PrintWriter, but this was not required in the task—the encoding of the platform is used automatically. However, if we specify an encoding as, for example, string, we have to handle another exception. So only a FileNotFoundException is to be handled, which is thrown by the constructor. The created object is stored temporarily in a variable writer, and this is precisely the resource that is automatically closed at the end.

In the body of the try-with-resources block, a LocalDateTime object is built with the static now() method and then passed to the overloaded print(...) method. The print(...) method invokes the toString() method on the LocalDateTime and writes the String to the IO stream. We could have written the conversion explicitly with writer.write(LocalDateTime.now().toString()), but it is undoubtedly the task of the print*(...) methods to generate textual representations.

Read Notes and Write Them to a New ABC File

com/tutego/exercise/io/ReadTextAndWriteABC.java

```
private static final String VALID_MUSICAL_NOTES =
    "C, D, E, F, G, A, B, C D E F G A B c d e f g a b c' d' e' f' g' a' b'";

public static void readTextAndWriteAsABC( String source, String target ) {
  try ( Scanner in        =new Scanner( Paths.get( source ) );
        PrintWriter out=new PrintWriter( target ) ) {

    out.println( "M:C" );
    out.println( "L:1/4" );
    out.println( "K:C" );

    String[] sortedMusicalNotes=VALID_MUSICAL_NOTES.split( " " );
    Arrays.sort( sortedMusicalNotes );

    while ( in.hasNextLine() ) {
      String line=in.nextLine();
      if ( Arrays.binarySearch( sortedMusicalNotes, line ) >= 0 ) {
        out.print( line );
        out.print( ' ' );
      }
    }
    out.println();
  }
  catch ( IOException e ) {
    System.err.println( "Cannot convert text file due to an input/output
error" );
    e.printStackTrace();
  }
}
```

The actual processing is as follows: from the two parameters source and target, we construct a Scanner for reading and a PrintWriter for writing. Both are resources that must be closed in try-with-resources. A semicolon separates the two resources. At the end of the try block, all resources are closed again independently, regardless of whether there was an exception or not. This is done in reverse order. First, the PrintWriter is closed, followed by the Scanner. The constructors of the two classes are slightly different. We have to be careful that the constructor of Scanner is not called with a String because otherwise we will split the String with the filename, and that would be wrong. To allow Scanner to separate a file from strings, we convert the filename to a Path object and pass it into the constructor of Scanner.

The body of the try block writes the three lines with the prologue of the file. Afterward, we keep going through the input file with hasNextLine() until there are no more lines to process. We then read the line and must check if the note is valid. From the assignment, we know all the notes. Of course, we could use a large switch-case statement to ask if the line contains a valid note, but the programming overhead would be high. Instead, we want to put the notes into a String array. In the constant VALID_MUSICAL_NOTES we have all valid notes, a split(" ") returns an array with valid notes. Unfortunately, it is not possible to use a compact expression to check whether an element is in the array, so we need a workaround. First, we sort the array with the notes, and then we can use Arrays.binarySearch(...). This is on average faster than linear search methods, for example, using Arrays.asList(...).

contains(...). In principle, we could pre-sort the notes in the `String`, then sorting per method call could be omitted. The pre-sorted `String` would then look like this:

```
"A A, B B, C C, D D, E E, F F, G G, a a' b b' c c' d d' e e' f f' g g'"
```

`Arrays.binarySearch(...)` returns an index greater than or equal to zero if the note is present. We don't need to check for empty rows, they are not part of the array. We write a valid note in the file, followed by a space.

Errors can occur in various places—because the file was not present because no file could be opened for writing because errors occur during reading, or errors occur during writing. All these errors are caught by a common `catch` block.

Quiz: Excluded

When we run the program, it gives the following output for version 1:

```
close()  ResourceA
close()  ResourceB
close()  ResourceA
```

And the following output for version 2:

```
close()  ResourceA
close()  ResourceB
```

Both resources are `AutoCloseable`, so the types in the `try` can be used with resources. The `close()` method of the first resource, `ResourceA`, prints a message on the screen. The second resource, `ResourceB`, wraps the first one. When `close()` is called on `ResourceB`, `close()` is first called from the wrapped `ResourceA` and then outputs a screen message. This is common behavior for input/output streams in Java.

In versions 1 and 2, the output differs for the following reason: in the first version, the `try`-with-resources involves two resources that are closed again in reverse order. After `ResourceA` was opened first, followed by `ResourceB`, `ResourceB` is the first to be closed again, and after that `ResourceA`. A call to `close()` on `ResourceB` will close `ResourceA` first, and from that, we have the first screen output. Then it goes back to the `close()` method of `ResourceB`, and we have the second screen output. After `ResourceB` is closed, `ResourceA` also calls the `close()` method. With this construction, we can see that from `ResourceA` the `close()` method is called twice, which may cause a problem. There are special resources that you are not allowed to close twice. So, an exception may be thrown on a second `close()` call because closing twice is not allowed. However, most resources in Java can handle being closed multiple times just fine and ignore it. However, it is important to study the API documentation to determine whether a closed resource may be closed again without an exception.

Variant 2 prevents `ResourceA` from being closed twice. This means that this variant has an advantage. However, there is also a disadvantage: `ResourceA` is not closed if the constructor `ResourceB` throws an exception. The object of type `ResourceA` created by `new` is not internally referenced by a variable and does not participate in the closing process of `try`-with-resources.

Both variants have their drawbacks. In Java, variant 1 is often preferred because it provides a clearer execution of different resources, and most resources in Java can handle being closed twice. Variant 2 is also acceptable since wrapped constructors typically do not throw exceptions, except for cases where the resource is `null`, but only for later operations.

Lambda Expressions and Functional Programming

10

Lambda expressions are the foundation of functional programming and serve as mappings. Functional programming is centered around functions, with a focus on pure expressions that don't have side effects. In Java, it's not possible to pass functions (methods) directly to other functions or return them, so the workaround is to encapsulate these methods in a class and pass them as objects. Lambda expressions provide a convenient way to quickly implement a class with a specific interface. They serve as implementations of functional interfaces—interfaces with only one abstract method—and are an alternative and efficient shortcut to classes that implement interfaces. As a result, expressing program code and passing it to other methods becomes more straightforward.

The following tasks deal with the different notations of lambda expressions and some important functional interfaces that occur repeatedly in various places in Java libraries.

Prerequisites

- Be able to read generics.
- Understand functional interfaces and relation to lambda expressions.
- Know the annotation `@FunctionalInterface`.
- Be able to distinguish and use variants of lambda expressions.
- Be able to use method and constructor references.
- Know the basic content and structure of the `java.util.function` package.
- Know how to use internal and external iteration.

Data types used in this chapter:

- `java.util.List`
- `java.util.function.Consumer`
- `java.util.function.Predicate`
- `java.util.function.Supplier`
- `java.util.function.Function`
- `java.util.function.BinaryOperator`
- `java.util.function.ToIntFunction`
- `java.util.Comparator`
- `java.lang.Comparable`

LAMBDA EXPRESSIONS

Due to the compact notation of lambda expressions, the modeling of mappings becomes more important. Of course, an implementation of interfaces has been possible since Java 1.0, but the code size has been too large with regular classes, and modeling libraries that accept and supply "functions" has not generated much interest. The first prototypes appeared around 2006, but it took until Java 8 (March 2014) for lambda expressions to enter the language.[1]

Quiz: Recognize Valid Functional Interfaces ★

Which of the following declarations are correct functional interfaces that a lambda expression can implement?

```
@FunctionalInterface
interface Distance {
  abstract public int distance( int a, int b );
}


@FunctionalInterface
interface MoreDistance extends Distance {
  double distance( double a, double b );
}


@FunctionalInterface
interface MoreDistance2 extends Distance {
  default double distance( double a, double b ) {
    return distance( (int) a, (int) b );
  }
}


@FunctionalInterface
interface DistanceImpl {
  default int distance( int a, int b ) { return a+b; }
}


@FunctionalInterface
interface DistanceEquals {
  int distance( int a, int b );
  boolean equals( Object other );
}
```

Quiz: From Interface Implementation to Lambda Expression ★

Given an interface declaration `Distance` and an implementation `ManhattanDistance` of the functional interface.

```
@FunctionalInterface
interface Distance {
  int distance( int a, int b );
}
```

```
class Schmegeggy {
  static void printDistance( Distance distance, int a, int b ) {
    System.out.println( distance.distance( a, b ) );
  }
  public static void main( String[] args ) {
    class ManhattanDistance implements Distance {
      @Override public int distance( int a, int b ) {
        return a+b;
      }
    }

    printDistance( new ManhattanDistance(), 12, 33 );
  }
}
```

During a code revision, the interface implementation should be dropped and replaced by a lambda expression. Which lambda expressions are equivalent and valid?

```
1. printDistance( ( a, b ) -> a+b, 12, 33 );
2. printDistance( ( a, b ) -> { return a+b; }, 12, 33 );
3. printDistance( (int a, int b) -> a+b, 12, 33 );
4. printDistance( (int a, b) -> a+b, 12, 33 );
5. printDistance( a, b -> { return a+b; }, 12, 33 );
6. printDistance( ( a, b ) -> return a+b, 12, 33 );
7. printDistance( ( a, b ) -> {int a; return b+b;}, 12, 33 );
8. printDistance( (Integer a, Integer b) -> a+b, 12, 33 );
```

Write Lambda Expressions for Functional Interfaces ★

There are many interfaces in the Java library, especially functional interfaces, which are interfaces with only one abstract method. These can be well implemented with lambda expressions.
Task:

- Assign a valid lambda expression to each of the following variables. The variable types are functional interfaces.
  ```
  /* interface Runnable        { void run(); }
  interface ActionListener { void actionPerformed(ActionEvent e); }
  interface Supplier<T>     { T get(); }
  interface Consumer<T>     { void accept(T t); }
  interface Comparator<T>   { int compare(T o1, T o2); } */
  Runnable                 runnable    =...
  ActionListener           listener    =...
  Supplier<String>         supplier    =...
  Consumer<Point>          consumer    =...
  Comparator<Rectangle>    comparator  =...
  ```
- The lambda expressions only have to be compilable, the implementation does not have to make sense.
- The declarations of the functional interfaces are in the comment for better understanding, but do not serve any other purpose.
- Experiment with different compact notations.

Quiz: Write Lambda Expressions Like This? ★

We have a class with a nested type declaration. Compiler errors exist in the main(…) method. Can you identify the specific location of these errors?

```
public class Ackamarackus {
  @FunctionalInterface
  interface Flummadiddle {
    void razzmatazz();
  }

  public static void main( String[] args ) {
    Flummadiddle a=()->System.out.println();
    Flummadiddle b=()->{ System.out.println(); };
    Flummadiddle c=()->{ System.out.println() };
    Flummadiddle d=()->{ System.out.println(); return; };
    Flummadiddle e=->{ System.out.println(); };
    Flummadiddle f=_->{ System.out.println(); };
    Flummadiddle g=__->{ System.out.println(); };
    Flummadiddle h=void->System.out.println();
    Flummadiddle i=(void)->System.out.println();
    Flummadiddle j=System.out::println;
  }
}
```

Developing Lambda Expressions ★

We have observed that there are many functional interfaces in the java.util.function package. However, many of the interfaces contain multiple methods, default methods, and static methods. Task:

• From the Javadoc, find the abstract method of the following types, and implement it using a lambda expression that does not have to make sense:
DoubleSupplier ds=…
LongToDoubleFunction ltdf=…
UnaryOperator<String> up=…

Quiz: Contents of the Package java.util.function ★

Browse the Javadoc of the package java.util.function. Can the interfaces be divided into groups?

Quiz: Know Functional Interfaces for Mappings ★

Given the following mappings; what are the known functional interfaces for these mappings?

MAPPING	FUNCTIONAL INTERFACE
() → void	
() → T	
() → boolean	
() → int	
() → long	
() → double	
(T) → void	
(T) → T	
(T) → R	
(T) → boolean	
(T) → int	
(T) → long	
(T) → double	
(T, T) → T	
(T, U) → void	
(T, U) → R	
(T, U) → boolean	
(T, U) → int	
(T, U) → long	
(T, U) → double	
(T, T) → int	
(T, T) → long	
(T, T) → double	
(int) → void	
(int) → R	
(int) → boolean	
(int) → int	
(int) → long	
(int) → double	
(int,int) → int	
(long) → void	
(long) → R	
(long) → boolean	
(long) → int	
(long) → long	
(long) → double	
(long,long) → long	
(double) → void	
(double) → R	
(double) → boolean	
(double) → int	
(double) → long	
(double) → double	
(double,double) → double	

METHOD AND CONSTRUCTOR REFERENCES

Method references and constructor references are among the most unusual notations of Java. Many developers are unfamiliar with the very compact notation, and this is why practicing is so important. Firstly, it's essential to be able to read foreign code without problems of understanding. Secondly, it's indispensable to be able to comprehend why an intelligent IDE suggests us to rewrite a lambda expression in some cases, and thirdly to be able to use this reference notation completely on your own.

Rewriting Lambda Expressions ★★

How do you write the following lambda expressions as method or constructor references?

TYPE	LAMBDA EXPRESSION	METHOD/CONSTRUCTOR REFERENCE
Static method	`(args) -> TypeName.method(args)`	
Nonstatic method (in instance)	`(args) -> instance.method(args)`	
Nonstatic method (no instance)	`(instance, args) -> instance.method(args)`	
Constructor	`(args) -> new TypeName(args)`	
Array Constructor	`(int size) -> new TypeName[size]`	

The task is deliberately kept abstract; in the following chapters, we will see practical examples.

SELECTED FUNCTIONAL INTERFACES

The types `Predicate`, `UnaryOperator`, and `Consumer` are functional interfaces that often occur as parameter types, for example, in the Collection API, when it is a requirement to delete or transform elements according to a certain condition.

Delete Entries, Remove Comments, Convert to CSV ★

The assignment focuses on three methods that exists on every `List`:

- `default boolean removeIf(Predicate<? super E> filter)` (Collection)
- `default void replaceAll(UnaryOperator<E> operator)` (List)
- `default void forEach(Consumer<? super T> action)` (Iterable)

The three methods perform an *internal iteration*, so it is not us who have to iterate through the list. We just need to specify the operation that will be performed on each element.

Bonny Brain and the crew are planning a city tour. Each city is given two pieces of information: name and population:

```
record City( String name, int population ) { }
```

The destinations of the city trip are in an `ArrayList`.

```
List<City> cityTour=new ArrayList<>();
City g=new City( "Gotham (cathedral)", 8_000_000 );
City m=new City( "Metropolis (pleasure garden)", 1_600_000 );
City h=new City( "Hogsmeade (shopping street)", 1_124 );
Collections.addAll( cityTour, g, m, h );
```

Task:

- Use `removeIf(...)` so that in the end only the larger cities with more than 10,000 inhabitants remain.
- The city names contain comments in round brackets. If comments are included, they are always at the end of the string. Delete the comments and use the `replaceAll(...)` method to replace the `City` objects.
- Use `forEach(...)`, so that at the end the data of the cities appear on the screen in CSV format (comma-separated output).

Example:

- From the given list above, the output is:
  ```
  Gotham,8000000
  Metropolis,1600000
  ```

SUGGESTED SOLUTIONS

Quiz: Recognize Valid Functional Interfaces

Distance

The `distance` interface is a proper functional interface, and the `abstract` keyword is unnecessary because if a method is not a `default` method, it is automatically an abstract method with no implementation. The visibility modifier `public` is also unnecessary because the abstract methods of an interface are automatically public. By the way, the visibility modifier should be first, but in our case, you should remove both keywords.

MoreDistance

At first glance, the `MoreDistance` interface looks the same as `Distance`; however, we would need to take a look at inheritance, which gives `MoreDistance` two abstract methods, namely, its own and the inherited one from the base type. In the end, there are two abstract methods in the interface; this is invalid for functional interfaces.

MoreDistance2

The interface is functional interface because it contains exactly one abstract method, from the extended interface `Distance`. Whether an interface itself contains an abstract method or inherits one from the superclass is irrelevant. If an interface has exactly one abstract method, it can still have any number of `default` methods or static methods; it remains a functional interface.

DistanceImpl

The interface contains a `default` implementation, which is fine as such; however, this does not count as a functional interface. A functional interface must declare exactly one abstract method. This method must not already have implementation as a default method.

DistanceEquals

This is a functional interface even though it has two methods. But this is because the method `equals(...)` is a special method from `java.lang.Object`, which is always present on every object anyway. You put the `equals(...)` method in an interface now and then, so that an individual Javadoc can describe the meaning of the method.

Quiz: From Interface Implementation to Lambda Expression

1st, 2nd, and 3rd
All three compiles and are equivalent.
   All other notations will result in a compiler error for different reasons.
   4.
Either both types are determined or no type.
   5.
Multiple lambda parameters must always be parenthesized.
   6.
Either you use a block with {} and write `return`, or the shorter notation does not contain `return`.
   7.
The variable a must not be declared again, and b + b is not equivalent to a + b.
   8.
There is no autoboxing concerning the types in the parameter list. `int` and `Integer` are entirely different types.

Write Lambda Expressions for Functional Interfaces

com/tutego/exercise/lambda/LambdaTargetType.java

```
Runnable                runnable  =() -> {};
ActionListener          listener  =event -> {};
Supplier<String>        supplier  =() -> "";
Consumer<Point>         consumer  =point -> {};
Comparator<Rectangle> comparator=(r1, r2) ->0;
```

The implementations are as simple as possible and do not implement any logic because that always depends on the semantics.

Quiz: Write Lambda Expressions Like This?

The following assignments lead to a compiler error:

c

The semicolon at the end of `System.out.println()` is missing, and there must be complete statements in the `{}` block.

e

Lambda parameters are missing on the left, in our case `()`.

f and **g**

The method in the functional interface has no parameter list; therefore, only `()` must be left of the arrow.

h and **i**

For methods, `void` stands for no return, but `void` *cannot* be left for a missing parameter list for lambda expressions.

Developing Lambda Expressions

com/tutego/exercise/lambda/LambdaTargetType2.java

```
DoubleSupplier        ds   =() -> Math.random();
LongToDoubleFunction  ltdf =value -> value * Math.random();
UnaryOperator<String> up   =s -> s.trim();
```

Quiz: Contents of the Package java.util.function

Firstly, we recognize different suffixes:

- `Consumer`: something is consumed and used up, but it is not returned.
- `Predicate`: a test is made, a value goes in, and a `boolean` comes out. Basically, a specialization of `Function` with a special return type.
- `Supplier`: something is produced, so it is returned, but no input is expected.
- `Function`: something is transformed by a function, that is, a value comes in, and a value comes out.
- `UnaryOperator`: a special `function` where the input type and output type are always the same. In a `Function`, the input type and output type can be entirely different.

Then different prefixes can be identified. These are `Double`, `Int`, and `Long`. These are special functional interfaces, which exist instead of a generic type only for these three special primitive data types. For these primitive data types, there are also combinations, e.g., `IntToDoubleFunction`.

Quiz: Know Functional Interfaces for Mappings

MAPPING	FUNCTIONAL INTERFACE
() → void	Runnable
() → T	Supplier
() → boolean	BooleanSupplier
() → int	IntSupplier
() → long	LongSupplier
() → double	DoubleSupplier
(T) → void	Consumer<T>
(T) → T	UnaryOperator<T>
(T) → R	Function<T,R>
(T) → boolean	Predicate<T>
(T) → int	ToIntFunction<T>
(T) → long	ToLongFunction<T>
(T) → double	ToDoubleFunction<T>
(T, T) → T	BinaryOperator<T>
(T, U) → void	BiConsumer<T,U>
(T, U) → R	BiFunction<T,U,R>
(T, U) → boolean	BiPredicate<T,U>
(T, U) → int	ToIntBiFunction<T,U>
(T, U) → long	ToLongBiFunction<T,U>
(T, U) → double	ToDoubleBiFunction<T,U>
(T, T) → int	ToIntBiFunction<T,T>
(T, T) → long	ToLongBiFunction<T,T>
(T, T) → double	ToDoubleBiFunction<T,T>
(int) → void	IntConsumer
(int) → R	IntFunction<R>
(int) → boolean	IntPredicate
(int) → int	IntUnaryOperator
(int) → long	IntToLongFunction
(int) → double	IntToDoubleFunction
(int,int) → int	IntBinaryOperator
(long) → void	LongConsumer
(long) → R	LongFunction<R>
(long) → boolean	LongPredicate
(long) → int	LongToIntFunction
(long) → long	LongUnaryOperator
(long) → double	LongToDoubleFunction
(long,long) → long	LongBinaryOperator
(double) → void	DoubleConsumer
(double) → R	DoubleFunction<R>
(double) → boolean	DoublePredicate
(double) → int	DoubleToIntFunction
(double) → long	DoubleToLongFunction
(double) → double	DoubleUnaryOperator
(double,double) → double	DoubleBinaryOperator

Rewriting Lambda Expressions

TYPE	LAMBDA EXPRESSION	METHOD/CONSTRUCTOR REFERENCE
Static method	`(args) -> TypeName.method(args)`	`TypeName::method`
Nonstatic method (in instance)	`(args) -> instance.method(args)`	`instance::method`
Nonstatic method (no instance)	`(instance, args) -> instance.method(args)`	`TypeName::method`
Constructor	`(args) -> new TypeName(args)`	`TypeName::new`
Array constructor	`(int size) -> new TypeName[size]`	`TypeName[]::new`

Delete Entries, Remove Comments, and Convert to CSV

com/tutego/exercise/util/CityTourList.java

```java
public static void main( String[] args ) {

  List<City> cityTour=new ArrayList<>();
  City g=new City( "Gotham (cathedral)", 8_000_000 );
  City m=new City( "Metropolis (pleasure garden)", 1_600_000 );
  City h=new City( "Hogsmeade (Shopping Street)", 1_124 );
  Collections.addAll( cityTour, g, m, h );

  cityTour.removeIf( city -> city.population() <= 10_000 );
  cityTour.replaceAll(
      city -> new City( city.name().replaceAll( "\\s*\\(.*\\)$","" ),
                        city.population() )
  );
  cityTour.forEach( CityTourList::printAsCsv );
}

private static void printAsCsv( City city ) {
  System.out.printf( "%s,%s%n", city.name(), city.population() );
}
```

After creating a copy of the list in the first step, we call three methods on the list.

In the first method, `removeIf(Predicate)`, we must specify a predicate that determines if the size of the city is as needed. If not, it must be removed. The `Predicate` tests the `City` object and returns `true` or `false`.

The next method, `replaceAll(UnaryOperator)`, expects a function—a `UnaryOperator<T>` is a subtype of `Function<T, T>`. This function is applied to every element and replaces every element in the list. Since `City` objects cannot be modified (the instance variables are `final`), we create a new `City` object and transfer the values, using the `String` method `replaceAll(...)` to help us remove anything in round brackets. The `List` method `replaceAll(...)` will replace each `City` in the list with a new `City` that we build in the implementation from the `UnaryOperator`.

The third method, forEach(Consumer), expects a consumer. Now, instead of using a lambda expression directly, as we did with the other two methods, forEach(...) references its method print-AsCsv(...) via a method reference. It has the same parameter list as a Consumer: it expects something, namely, a City, and returns nothing. Inside the method, we put the two components together, separated by a semicolon, and output them.

NOTE

---

1 For those interested in history, see http://www.javac.info/ for old drafts.

Special Types from the Java Class Library

11

The class library includes thousands of types, with a huge number added via the Java Enterprise Frameworks and open-source libraries. Fortunately, you don't need to know all of these types to write software successfully. Much of Java SE is also very low level and intended more for framework developers.

Some common types are particularly closely related to the language, so even the compiler knows them. We need to understand these so that we can make the most of the language's capabilities. This chapter is therefore about the absolute superclass `Object`, which methods are relevant for us, ordering principles, the use of primitive types, and wrapper types (autoboxing).

Prerequisites

- Know the difference between == (identity) and `equals(...)` (equivalence).
- Be able to implement `equals(...)` and `hashCode()`.
- Implement `Comparator` and `Comparable` for ordering criteria.
- Understand the working of autoboxing.

Data types used in this chapter:

- `java.lang.Object`
- `java.lang.Comparable`
- `java.util.Comparator`
- `java.lang.Double`
- `java.lang.Integer`

ABSOLUTE SUPERCLASS JAVA.LANG.OBJECT

From `Object`, there are three methods that subclasses usually override: `toString()`, `equals(Object)` and `hashCode()`. While identity is tested with == and !=, equivalence is handled by the `equals(Object)` method. `equals(Object)` and `hashCode()` are always implemented together so that both match each other; for example, if the hash code of two objects is not equal, `equals(...)` must also return `false` and if `equals(...)` returns `true`, the two hash codes must also be equal. There are certain rules to follow when implementing this, which is why the next two tasks focus on `equals(Object)` and `hashCode()`.

DOI: 10.1201/9781003454502-12

Generate `equals(Object)` and `hashCode()` ★

Every modern Java development environment can generate various methods, for example, `toString()`, but also `equals(Object)` and `hashCode()`.

The development environments have slightly different menu items and dialogs. `equals(Object)`/ `hashCode()` can be created for the three known IDEs as follows:

IntelliJ
In this IDE, we press the shortcut `Alt+Ins`. A list of items that can be generated follows, and *equals() and hashCode()* is listed below it. If we activate the entry, a dialog opens first where we can select different templates. IntelliJ can generate the methods in different ways. We stay with the default setting and switch to the next dialog with *Next*. We now select the instance variables that will be used for the `equals(...)` method; by default, these are all of them. We press *Next*. The next step is the same dialog but now we select the instance variables for the `hashCode(...)` method; by default, all are preselected again. We press *Next* and reach the next dialog, where we may still determine whether the name may be `null` or not. Since we assume it could be `null`, we do not select the field, but go directly to *Finish*.

Eclipse
In Eclipse we put the cursor in the body of the class, activate the context menu, navigate to the menu item *Source*, and go to *Generate hashCode() and equals()*. Unlike in IntelliJ, in Eclipse the instance variables are displayed only once and used for both the `equals(Object)` and `hashCode()` methods at the same time. Code generation starts with a click on *Generate*.

NetBeans
Go to the menu item under *Source* (or activate the context menu in the editor), then select *Insert Code*; alternatively activate via keyboard `Alt+Ins`. A small dialog follows, where you can select *equals() and hashCode()....* Also, other things like a setter, getter, constructor, and `toString()` can be generated this way.

Task:

- Copy the following class into the project:
  ```java
  public class Person {
    public long id;
    public int age;
    public double income;
    public boolean isDrugLord;
    public String name;
  }
  ```
- Create the methods `equals(Object)` and `hashCode()` for the class `Person` with the IDE.
- Study the generated methods cautiously.

Existing `equals(Object)` Implementations ★★

What does the Javadoc have to say, or what do the `equals(Object)` implementations look like for the following classes?

- `java.awt.Rectangle` (module `java.desktop`)
- `java.lang.String` (module `java.base`)
- `java.lang.StringBuilder` (module `java.base`)
- `java.net.URL` (module `java.base`)

The code for the individual modules can be viewed online from OpenJDK at https://github.com/openjdk/jdk/tree/master/src/; the classes can be found at *share/classes*.

INTERFACES COMPARATOR AND COMPARABLE

A comparison with `equals(...)` tells whether two objects are equal, but says nothing about the order, which object is larger or smaller. For this, there are two interfaces in Java:

- `Comparable` is implemented by the types that have a natural order, that is, for which there are usually common ordering criteria. If there are two date values, it is clear which was before and which was after, or if both dates are the same.
- There is an implementation of the interface `Comparator` for each ordering criterion. We can sort people by name, but we can also sort by age: that would be two implementations of `Comparator`.

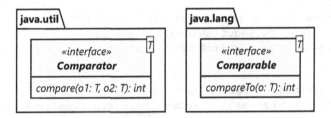

FIGURE 11.1   UML diagram of `Comparator` and `Comparable`.

Quiz: Natural Order Or Not? ★

If we execute the following in a `main(...)` method, what happens? The type `Point` is from the `java.awt` package.

```
String[] strings={ "A", "B", "C" };
Arrays.sort( strings );

Point[] points={
 new Point( 9, 3 ),
 new Point( 3, 4 ),
 new Point( 4, 3 ),
 new Point( 1, 2 ),
};

Arrays.sort( points );
```

Handle Superheroes

Bonny Brain has been interested in superheroes since she was a child. And there are so many exciting things to know. For Bonny Brain to get answers to her questions, we first need to define the dataset.

Task: Copy the following class declaration into your Java project:[1]

com/tutego/exercise/util/Heroes.java

```java
import java.util.List;
import java.util.Objects;
import java.util.stream.Stream;

public class Heroes {

  private Heroes() { }

  public record Hero( String name, Heroes.Hero.Sex sex, int yearFirstAppearance ) {
    public enum Sex { MALE, FEMALE }
    public Hero {
      Objects.requireNonNull( name ); Objects.requireNonNull( sex );
    }
  }

  public static class Universe {
    private final String      name;
    private final List<Hero> heroes;

    public Universe( String name, List<Hero> heroes ) {
      this.name  =Objects.requireNonNull( name );
      this.heroes=Objects.requireNonNull( heroes );
    }

    public String name() { return name; }
    public Stream<Hero> heroes() { return heroes.stream(); }
  }

  // https://github.com/fivethirtyeight/data/tree/master/comic-characters
  private static final Hero DEADPOOL=new Hero( "Deadpool (Wade Wilson)",
Hero.Sex.MALE, 1991 );
  private static final Hero LANA_LANG=new Hero( "Lana Lang", Hero.Sex.FEMALE,
1950 );
  private static final Hero THOR=new Hero( "Thor (Thor Odinson)", Hero.Sex.
MALE, 1950 );
  private static final Hero IRON_MAN=new Hero( "Iron Man (Anthony 'Tony'
Stark)", Hero.Sex.MALE, 1963 );
  private static final Hero SPIDERMAN=new Hero( "Spider-Man (Peter Parker)",
Hero.Sex.MALE, 1962 );
  private static final Hero WONDER_WOMAN=new Hero( "Wonder Woman (Diana
Prince)", Hero.Sex.FEMALE, 1941 );
  private static final Hero CAPTAIN_AMERICA=new Hero( "Captain America
(Steven Rogers)", Hero.Sex.MALE, 1941 );
  private static final Hero SUPERMAN=new Hero( "Superman (Clark Kent)", Hero.
Sex.MALE, 1938 );
  private static final Hero BATMAN=new Hero( "Batman (Bruce Wayne)", Hero.
Sex.MALE, 1939 );

  public static final List<Hero> DC =
      List.of( SUPERMAN, LANA_LANG, WONDER_WOMAN, BATMAN );
```

```java
public static final List<Hero> MARVEL =
    List.of( DEADPOOL, CAPTAIN_AMERICA, THOR, IRON_MAN, SPIDERMAN );

public static final List<Hero> ALL =
    Stream.concat( DC.stream(), MARVEL.stream() ).toList();

public static final List<Universe> UNIVERSES =
    List.of( new Universe( "DC", DC ), new Universe( "Marvel", MARVEL ) );
}
```

If you have added the class to your project, you are done with the exercise! The class declaration is a preparation for the next tasks. About the content of the class: `Heroes` declares the two nested classes `Hero` and `Universe` and also collections with heroes. Which Java API is used to initialize the variables and which private variables exist are not relevant for the solution. We will come back to the class `Heroes` in the section about the Java Stream API. Those interested are welcome to rewrite the classes in records.

Compare Superheroes ★★

Not all heroes are the same! Some appear earlier or are bald. We can use `Comparator` objects to individually determine the order between heroes.

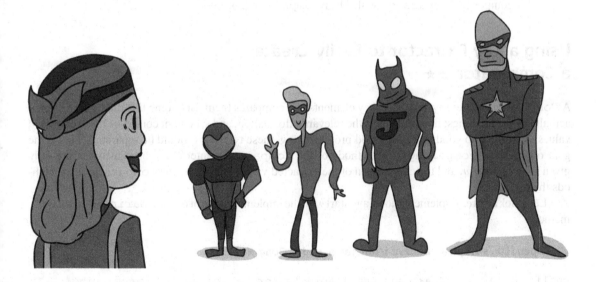

Task:

- First, build a mutable list of all heroes:
  `List<Hero> allHeroes=new ArrayList<>( Heroes.ALL );`
- Write a `comparator` so that heroes are ordered by year of release. Use for implementation:
  1. A local class.
  2. An anonymous class.
  3. A lambda expression.

- The `List` interface has a `sort(...)` method. Sort the list `allHeroes` with the new `Comparator`.
- Extend the one `Comparator` so that if the year of publication is the same, it is also compared by name. Evaluate the approach that the `Comparator` tests several criteria at the same time.

Concatenate Hero Comparators ★

Sorting is often done not only by one criterion, but by many. A typical example is the phone book. First, the entries are sorted by the last name and then, in the case of a group of people with the same last names, by the first name.

Often several criteria are involved in the ordering. We do not have to do the chaining of the `Comparator` instances ourselves, but we can use the default method `thenComparing(...)`.
Task:

- Study the API documentation (or implementation) for the `Comparator` method `thenComparing(Comparator<? super T> other)`.
- Some heroes have the same release year.
  1. Write a `Comparator` implementation that *only* compares heroes by name.
  2. Write a second `Comparator` that compares the heroes *only* by their year of publication.
  3. Sort all heroes in the first criterion by year of publication, then by name. Implement the composite `Comparator` with `thenComparing(...)`.

Using a Key Extractor to Easily Create a Comparator ★★

A `Comparator` generally "extracts" key elements and compares them. But doing this the `Comparator` actually does two things: first, it extracts the relevant information, and second, it compares these extracted values. According to good object-oriented programming, these two steps should be separated. This is the goal of the static `comparing*(...)` methods of the `Comparator` interface. These methods are only given a *key-extractor*, and the comparison of the extracted values is done by the `comparing*(...)` methods themselves.

Let's look at three implementations, and start with the implementation of the `comparing(Function)` method:

OpenJDK's Implementation from `java.util.Comparator`.

```
public static <T, U extends Comparable<? super U>> Comparator<T> comparing(
        Function<? super T, ? extends U> keyExtractor)
{
    Objects.requireNonNull(keyExtractor);
    return (Comparator<T> & Serializable)
        (c1, c2) -> keyExtractor.apply(c1).compareTo(keyExtractor.apply(c2));
}
```

Initially, the mandatory `null` test takes place. Then, `keyExtractor.apply(...)` gets the value from the first object and the second object. Since both objects have a natural order (they are `Comparable`), `compareTo(...)` returns this order. `comparing(Function)` returns a `Comparator`, here as a lambda expression.

The key extractor is a function that returns a value, and exactly this value is compared internally. comparing(Function) can be used if the objects have a natural order. Now, there are different factory methods for Comparator instances that, in addition to comparing Comparable objects, extract selected primitive data types and compare them. Let's look at the second method comparingInt(ToIntFunction) when two integers are extracted via a ToIntFunction:

OpenJDK's Implementation from java.util.Comparator.

```
public static <T> Comparator<T> comparingInt(ToIntFunction<? super T>
keyExtractor) {
    Objects.requireNonNull(keyExtractor);
    return (Comparator<T> & Serializable)
        (c1, c2) -> Integer.compare(keyExtractor.applyAsInt(c1), keyExtractor.
applyAsInt(c2));
}
```

The key extractor extracts an integer value from the objects to be compared and then defers to Integer. compare(...) to compare these two integers.

Let's take a look at the last function. It combines a key extractor with a Comparator. This is handy when the objects have no natural order, but a foreign Comparator has to determine the order.

OpenJDK's Implementation from java.util.Comparator

```
public static <T, U> Comparator<T> comparing(
        Function<? super T, ? extends U> keyExtractor,
        Comparator<? super U> keyComparator)
{
    Objects.requireNonNull(keyExtractor);
    Objects.requireNonNull(keyComparator);
    return (Comparator<T> & Serializable)
        (c1, c2) -> keyComparator.compare(keyExtractor.apply(c1),
                                    keyExtractor.apply(c2));
}
```

First, the key extractor will extract the values for the two objects c1 and c2. Thereafter, the values will go into the compare(...) method of the passed Comparator instance. The lambda expression returns a new Comparator.

If you compare this with your own Comparator implementations, you will generally do the same, namely, extract the values from two objects and compare them. This is precisely what factory functions do! We just have to specify how a key has to be extracted, and then this key extractor is applied to the two values to be compared.

Vary the previous task as follows:

1. Use the static method Comparator.comparingInt(ToIntFunction<? super T> keyExtractor) and a lambda expression to create a Comparator to sort the list by years.
2. For comparison of names, also use a Comparator method that uses a key extractor.
3. Sort by name and then by age, again using thenComparing(...). Then change the concatenation method, and use thenComparingInt(...) instead of thenComparing(...).
4. Write a Comparator<Hero>, based on CASE_INSENSITIVE_ORDER from String, for the hero name regardless of case. Call the comparator method comparing(Function, Comparator).

Sort Points by Distance to Center ★

Captain CiaoCiao runs his *Absolutus Zero-Zero Vodka Distillery* at the North Pole. On an imaginary rectangular map, the distillery is located exactly at the zero point. A `java.awt.Point` is represented by x/y coordinates, which is quite appropriate for storing the location information. Now the question is whether certain locations are closer or further from the distillery.

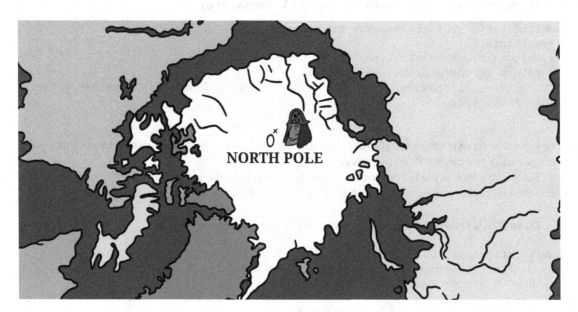

Task:

- Write a comparison comparator `PointDistanceToZeroComparator` for `Point` objects. The distance to the zero points is to be used for the comparison. If the distance of a point *p1* from the zero point is smaller than the distance of a point *p2*, let *p1* < *p2* hold.
- Build an array of `Point` objects and sort them using the `Arrays` method `sort(T[] a, Comparator<? super T> c)`.

Example:

```
Point[] points={ new Point( 9, 3 ), new Point( 3, 4 ), new Point( 4, 3 ), new
Point( 1, 2 ) };
Arrays.sort( points, new PointDistanceToZeroComparator() );
System.out.println( Arrays.toString( points ) );
```

The output is:

```
[java.awt.Point[x=1,y=2], java.awt.Point[x=3,y=4], java.awt.Point[x=4,y=3],
java.awt.Point[x=9,y=3]]
```

The class `java.awt.Point` provides various class and object methods for calculating the distance. See the API documentation for more information.

Find Stores Nearby ★★

For the liquors of the Absolutus Zero-Zero Vodka distillery, Bonny Brain builds the distribution channels and plans stores in different locations.

Task:

1. Create a new record `Store`.
2. Give the `Store` two instance variables `Point location` and `String name`.
3. Collect several `Store` objects in a list.
4. Write a method `List<Store> findStoresAround(Collection<Store> stores, Point center)` that returns a list, sorted by distances from the `center`; at the head of the list are those closest to the distillery.

AUTOBOXING

Autoboxing is a capability of the compiler to pack primitive types into wrapper objects (called *boxing*) and then unbox them when needed (called *unboxing*). With autoboxing there are some oddities that you should be aware of. Otherwise, you will get an unexpected `NullPointerException` or performance problems.

Quiz: Handling Null Reference in Unboxing ★

Unboxing extracts the primitive value from a wrapper object. Since object references can be `null`, questions arise:

1. Can a `null` be converted to 0 in such a way: `int i =null`?

2. What will happen?

```
Character c=null;
switch ( c ) { }
```

3. Does it make sense to write the following?
```
Map<String, Integer> map=Map.of( "number-of-ships", 102 );
int ships=map.get( "number_of_ships" );
```
    Research for the answer the return of the method get(...) of the interface java.util.Map.

Quiz: Unboxing Surprise ★★

What are the screen outputs if the following lines were in the main(...) method?

```
Integer i11=1;
Integer i12=1;
System.out.println( i11 == i12 );
System.out.println( i11 <= i12 );
System.out.println( i11 >= i12 );

Integer i21=1000;
Integer i22=1000;
System.out.println( i21 == i22 );
System.out.println( i21 <= i22 );
System.out.println( i21 >= i22 );
```

The task is tricky.
    Autoboxing calls the valueOf(...) method. The Javadoc gives a crucial hint.

SUGGESTED SOLUTIONS

Generate `equals(Object)` and `hashCode()`

Generated `equals(Object)` Method from IntelliJ

Let's take a look at equals(Object) first:

Generated Method equals(Object) **from IntelliJ**

```
public boolean equals( Object o ) {
  if ( this ==o )
    return true;
  if ( o ==null || getClass() !=o.getClass() )
    return false;

  Person person=(Person) o;

  if ( id !=person.id )
    return false;
```

```
  if ( age != person.age )
    return false;
  if ( Double.compare( person.income, income ) != 0 )
    return false;
  if ( isDrugLord != person.isDrugLord )
    return false;
  return name != null ? name.equals( person.name ) : person.name == null;
}
```

First, we test if the incoming object is identical to our object, then we have a short path, and the answer is `true` because, of course, we are equivalent to ourselves. If the incoming object reference is `null` or if our own `Class` object is not identical to the passed `Class` object, then we do not want to continue the comparison, and we can exit with `false`. By the way, the `Class` comparison is not the only option; we can also test the type relationships with `instanceof`, which also includes subtypes in the comparison.

After the initial queries, we continue with the object state tests. We know that the object is a `Person`, so we introduce a new variable of type `Person`. Next, we need to compare our states with those of the `person`. For integers and truth values, we can compare directly. The approach here is to compare the values and if they are not equal, exit the `equals(...)` method with `false` because there is no point in checking any further.

It remains interesting to compare the floating-point number and the reference. With floating-point numbers, we have the problem that there is a NaN (Not-a-Number). And a NaN is not equal to a NaN! This special case is covered by the `compare(...)` method of `Double`. Although the `compare(...)` method checks much more, namely, the order of two floating-point numbers, we do not need this property, we only compare if the result is not equal to `0`; the method returns `0` if two floating-point numbers are equal, otherwise something negative or positive.

The previous instance variables were primitive; last we look at the equality test on reference types. Here, we delegate to the `equals(Object)` method of the referenced object. However, we have to consider a special case, namely, that `name` can be `null`. In the dialog, we could select whether an instance variable can be `null` or not; since we selected `null` as a possibility, a special query is added. A nice alternative would be:

```
return Objects.equals( name, person.name );
```

Generated equals(Object) Method from Eclipse

Let's move on to Eclipse:

Generated Method `equals(Object)` from Eclipse

```
public boolean equals( Object obj ) {
  if ( this == obj )
    return true;
  if ( obj == null )
    return false;
  if ( getClass() != obj.getClass() )
    return false;
  Person other=(Person) obj;
  if ( age != other.age )
    return false;
  if ( id != other.id )
    return false;
  if ( Double.doubleToLongBits( income ) !=
       Double.doubleToLongBits( other.income ) )
    return false;
  if ( isDrugLord != other.isDrugLord )
    return false;
```

```
if ( name == null ) {
  if ( other.name != null )
    return false;
}
else if ( !name.equals( other.name ) )
  return false;
return true;
}
```

In Eclipse, the query is essentially the same, but the code is slightly longer. This is partly because the checks on null and the Class objects take place in two individual case distinctions and have not been combined. The checks on the name on null are also somewhat more extensive. The only real difference is when comparing floating-point numbers. Here Eclipse takes a slightly different approach. A double is the same size as a long with 64 bits. The double method doubleToLongBits(double) queries the bit pattern as long. Then, if we have two integers, we can compare them like any other integer. This solves the problem with the NaN.

Generated Method hashCode() from IntelliJ

Let's take a look at hashCode().

generated hashCode() method of IntelliJ

```
public int hashCode() {
  int result;
  long temp;
  result=(int) (id ^ (id >>> 32));
  result=31 * result+age;
  temp=Double.doubleToLongBits( income );
  result=31 * result+(int) (temp ^ (temp >>> 32));
  result=31 * result+(isDrugLord ? 1 : 0);
  result=31 * result+(name != null ? name.hashCode() : 0);
  return result;
}
```

The job of the method is to bring the values of the various instance variables together algorithmically to produce an int. In the best case, the hash code changes when any instance variable changes. So, the desire is to get an entirely different hash code for a changed bit of some instance variable.

When setting up the calculation, the IntelliJ and Eclipse development environments use a special pattern. After the initialization of result, the calculation continues with result=31 * result+hash-Code, where hashCode is the hash code to be added in each step.[2] How the hash code is composed now for int, long, double, and a reference type shows exactly the code. Since the hash code is an int, age, which is also an int, is added directly. In the case of a truth value, IntelliJ uses either 1 or 0. In the case of a long integer, first the upper 32 bits, then the lower 32 bits are combined using an XOR operation. The same happens in principle with a double floating-point number, here the bit pattern is used, similar to what the equals(...) method uses for comparison.

Generated Method hashCode() from Eclipse

Eclipse takes a similar approach:

generated hashCode() method of Eclipse

```
public int hashCode() {
  final int prime=31;
  int result=1;
```

```
    result=prime * result+age;
    result=prime * result+(int) (id ^ (id >>> 32));
    long temp;
    temp=Double.doubleToLongBits( income );
    result=prime * result+(int) (temp ^ (temp >>> 32));
    result=prime * result+(isDrugLord ? 1231 : 1237);
    result=prime * result+((name == null) ? 0 : name.hashCode());
    return result;
}
```

There are two minor differences between Eclipse and IntelliJ.

- First, the magic value 31 is pulled out as a variable. This is handy if we want to change the number later. If we have numerous instance variables, we may need to adjust the prime. Otherwise, multiplication may result in large numbers running out of the value range, so the first instance variables are not considered at all. We have to reduce the prime number in such a case.
- The second difference is the use of a different number for truth values: Eclipse uses $1231 = 0b10011001111$ and $1237 = 0b100110101$.

Overriding the `hashCode()` method manually, some developers fall back to the static `Objects` method hash(Object... values):

```
public int hashCode() {
  return Objects.hash( age, income, isDrugLord, name );
}
```

This is short and elegant, but you should rather refrain from this. Firstly, the method has to do boxing for primitive values, and secondly an array always must be created for the vararg and later swept away by the automatic garbage collection. For an immutable object, however, this makes it easy to calculate the hash code once and then cache it.

Existing equals(Object) Implementations

java.awt.Rectangle (module java.desktop)

From the Javadoc you can read what `equals(...)` does: "The result is true if and only if the argument is not null and is a Rectangle object that has the same upper-left corner, width, and height as this Rectangle." This is even more evident when looking at the source code of the implementation:

OpenJDK's Implementation of the equals(...) Method from java.awt.Rectangle.

```
public boolean equals(Object obj) {
    if (obj instanceof Rectangle) {
        Rectangle r=(Rectangle)obj;
        return ((x == r.x) &&
                (y == r.y) &&
                (width == r.width) &&
                (height == r.height));
    }
    return super.equals(obj);
}
```

The method `equals(Object obj)` from the superclass `Object` has the parameter type `Object` for `obj`, which the overriding class must, of course, adopt. The idea: in general, you may also ask an apple whether it is equivalent to a pear, but the answer must always be `false`. This is how the class `Rectangle` does it. The `instanceof` test first checks whether the object type is also `Rectangle`, which includes subclasses. Only then does it proceed with the actual checks, and the x and y position, as well as height and width of its own object, are compared with the other rectangle. If it is not a `Rectangle`, then the superclass should deal with the comparison. In the implementation of `equals(...)`, we typically see checks for `null` or `this`. However, in this case, those checks have been moved to the superclass.

`java.lang.String` (module `java.base`)

The `String` class has an `equals(...)` method, and the Java API documentation describes how to implement it:

It compares this string to the specified object. The result is `true` if and only if the argument is not `null` and is a `String` object that represents the same sequence of characters as this object.

We don't need to look further into the implementation.

`java.lang.StringBuilder` (module `java.base`)

The Java documentation does not show an overridden `equals(...)` method for `StringBuilder`, and the entry under *Methods declared in class java.lang.Object* shows that an `equals(...)` method comes from `Object`. The class documentation also states:

`StringBuilder` implements `Comparable` but does not override `equals`. Thus, the natural ordering of `StringBuilder` is inconsistent with equals. Care should be exercised if `StringBuilder` objects are used as keys in a `SortedMap` or elements in a `SortedSet`. See `Comparable`, `SortedMap` or `SortedSet` for more information.

The consequence is that we get into trouble when we put a `StringBuilder` into a data structure because the vast majority of data structures use the `equals(...)` method.

`java.net.URL` (module `java.base`)

Of all the `equals(...)` methods in the Java library, the one for the `URL` class might be the weirdest. The Java documentation explains why.

Two URL objects are equal if they have the same protocol, reference equivalent hosts, have the same port number on the host, and the same file and fragment of the file. Two hosts are considered equivalent if both hostnames can be resolved into the same IP addresses; else if either hostname can't be resolved, the hostnames must be equal without regard to case; or both hostnames equal to `null`. Since hosts' comparison requires name resolution, this operation is a blocking operation. Note: The defined behavior for `equals` is known to be inconsistent with virtual hosting in HTTP.

This has far-reaching consequences. Firstly, the `equals(...)` method can take a very long time to execute, namely, when network access has to be made. Even in the best case, when everything is in an internal cache, the performance is still worse than when a few instance variables are compared. Furthermore, network access is always required, which means that if the computer is disconnected from the network, the `equals(...)` method cannot respond. Another problem is that the `equals(...)` method can suddenly give a different answer. What may not have been the same before can suddenly be the same.

For this reason, it is unusual for URL objects to be held in data structures such as lists or sets because the standard implementations almost always fall back on the `equals(...)` method. The Java library provides a second class URI that implements `equals(...)` as a simple comparison of instance variables, i.e., Schema, Fragment, Path, Query, etc.

Quiz: Natural Order Or Not?

This is followed by an

```
Exception in thread "main" java.lang.ClassCastException: class java.awt.Point
cannot be cast to class java.lang.Comparable (java.awt.Point is in module
java.desktop of loader 'bootstrap'; java.lang.Comparable is in module java.
base of loader 'bootstrap')
```

The reason: The method sort(Object[]) from java.util.Arrays assumes that the objects have a natural order and therefore implement the Comparable interface. However, Point does not do that.

If we want to compare unknown objects with each other, we have to give the sort(...) method a special object that respects the sort criterion. This is the task of a Comparator object.

Compare Superheroes

com/tutego/exercise/util/HeroComparators.java

```java
// local class
class YearFirstAppearanceComparator implements Comparator<Heroes.Hero> {
  @Override public int compare( Heroes.Hero h1, Heroes.Hero h2 ) {
    return Integer.compare( h1.yearFirstAppearance(), h2.yearFirstAppearance() );
  }
}

// inner anonymous class
Comparator<Heroes.Hero> innerClassComparator=new Comparator<>() {
  @Override public int compare( Heroes.Hero h1, Heroes.Hero h2 ) {
    return Integer.compare( h1.yearFirstAppearance(), h2.yearFirstAppearance() );
  }
};

// Lambda expression
Comparator<Heroes.Hero> lambdaComparator =
    (h1, h2) -> Integer.compare( h1.yearFirstAppearance(),
h2.yearFirstAppearance() );

// Comparator with 2 criteria
Comparator<Heroes.Hero> combinedComparator=(h1, h2 ) -> {
  int yearComparison=Integer.compare( h1.yearFirstAppearance(),
h2.yearFirstAppearance() );
  return (yearComparison != 0) ? yearComparison : h1.name().compareTo(
h2.name() );
};

List<Heroes.Hero> allHeroes=new ArrayList<>( Heroes.ALL );
allHeroes.sort( new YearFirstAppearanceComparator() );
allHeroes.sort( innerClassComparator );
allHeroes.sort( lambdaComparator );
allHeroes.sort( combinedComparator );
```

The `Comparator` implementations rely on `Integer.compare(..)` to compare the two integers, which is implemented like this:

OpenJDK's implementation of `Integer.compare(int, int)` method.

```java
public static int compare(int x, int y) {
  return (x<y) ? -1 : ((x == y) ? 0 : 1);
}
```

For `Comparator` instances to do more than a comparison, there are two approaches. First, they can completely realize the logic itself, as in the proposed solution, or two existing `Comparator` objects can be concatenated, which is the topic of the next task.

The merging of the logic is shown in the proposed solution: first, the year is compared, and if the years are equal, `compare(...)` returns 0, then the second criterion must be considered, the name. `name` is a `String` and implements `Comparable` for a natural order, so `compareTo(...)` must then make the decision.

Concatenate Hero Comparators

com/tutego/exercise/util/HeroCombinedComparators.java

```java
Comparator<Heroes.Hero> nameComparator =
    (h1, h2) -> h1.name().compareTo( h2.name() );

Comparator<Heroes.Hero> yearComparator =
    (h1, h2) -> Integer.compare( h1.yearFirstAppearance(),
h2.yearFirstAppearance() );

Comparator<Heroes.Hero> combinedComparator=yearComparator.thenComparing(
nameComparator );

List<Heroes.Hero> allHeroes=new ArrayList<>( Heroes.ALL );
allHeroes.sort( combinedComparator );
System.out.println( allHeroes );
```

To better understand how it works, a look at the `thenComparing(...)` implementation from the OpenJDK:

OpenJDK's Implementation from `java.util.Comparator`.

```java
default Comparator<T> thenComparing(Comparator<? super T> other) {
   Objects.requireNonNull(other);
   return (Comparator<T> & Serializable) (c1, c2) -> {
      int res=compare(c1, c2);
      return (res != 0) ? res : other.compare(c1, c2);
   };
}
```

The focus is on the `return` statement with the lambda expression, which thus returns a `Comparator`. The implementation first calls its own `compare(...)` method because its own `Comparator` goes first and checks first. If the comparison is not 0, then our `compare(...)` method can return the result directly. However, if the result was equal to 0, then our own `compare(...)` method says that the two objects are equal, and then we have to proceed to the second `Comparator` from the parameter passed to the `thenComparing(Comparator)` method. This second `Comparator` must then decide what to do next.

Using a Key Extractor to Easily Create a Comparator

Building new `Comparator` objects using static methods and the key extractor is a bit unfamiliar at the beginning. You also have to get used to chaining `Comparator` objects. The assignment introduces the implementation extensively so that the solution results from it:

com/tutego/exercise/util/HeroKeyExtractorComparators.java

```
Comparator<Heroes.Hero> nameComparator =
    Comparator.comparing( h -> h.name() );

Comparator<Heroes.Hero> yearComparator =
    Comparator.comparingInt( h -> h.yearFirstAppearance() );

Comparator<Heroes.Hero> combinedComparator1 =
    yearComparator.thenComparing( nameComparator );

Comparator<Heroes.Hero> combinedComparator2 =
    nameComparator.thenComparingInt( h -> h.yearFirstAppearance() );

Comparator<Heroes.Hero> insensitiveNameComparator =
    Comparator.comparing( h -> h.name(), String.CASE_INSENSITIVE_ORDER );
```

Sort Points by Distance to Center

com/tutego/exercise/util/PointComparatorDemo.java

```
class PointDistanceToZeroComparator implements Comparator<Point> {
  @Override
  public int compare( Point p1, Point p2 ) {
    double distanceToZeroPoint1=p1.distanceSq( 0, 0 );
    double distanceToZeroPoint2=p2.distanceSq( 0, 0 );
    return Double.compare( distanceToZeroPoint1, distanceToZeroPoint2 );
  }
}
```

The `sort(...)` method expects a `Comparator` from us. The `Comparator` is a functional interface with a single abstract method `compare(...)`.

Since `Comparator` is a generic data type, we need to specify a type argument, and that is our `Point`. To implement the `Comparator` interface, we write a class `PointDistanceToZeroComparator`. It implements `compare(Point p1, Point p2)`. In the body of the method, we first calculate the distance of the first point to the zero points and then the second distance to the zero points. Strictly speaking, we don't calculate the distance, but the distance squared, but that's perfectly fine for the comparison and even a bit faster because the root isn't necessary.

Once we have obtained the two distances, we can simply return the appropriate value (negative, positive, or 0) for the `compare(...)` method. We can achieve this by using the `Double.compare(...)` method, which provides a three-way comparison.

We can pass the `Comparator` as a second argument to `sort(...)` like this:

```
Arrays.sort( points, new PointDistanceToZeroComparator() );
```

Find Stores Nearby

com/tutego/exercise/oop/StoreFinder.java

```java
class Store {
  String name;
  Point  location;

  Store( String name, int x, int y ) {
    this.name=name;
    this.location=new Point( x, y );
  }

  @Override
  public String toString() {
    return "Store[name=%s, location=%s]".formatted( name, location );
  }
}

public class StoreFinder {

  static List<Store> findStoresAround( Collection<Store> stores, Point center ) {
    List<Store> result=new ArrayList<>( stores );

    class StoreDistanceComparator implements Comparator<Store> {
      @Override
      public int compare( Store s1, Store s2 ) {
        double dist1ToCenter=s1.location.distance( center );
        double dist2ToCenter=s2.location.distance( center );
        return Double.compare( dist1ToCenter, dist2ToCenter );
      }
    }

    result.sort( new StoreDistanceComparator() );
    return result;
  }

  public static void main( String[] args ) {
    Store s1=new Store( "ALDI", 10, 10 );
    Store s2=new Store( "LIDL", 90, 80 );
    Store s3=new Store( "REWE", 51, 51 );
    List<Store> list=Arrays.asList( s1, s2, s3 );
    System.out.println( list );
    List<Store> around=findStoresAround( list, new Point( 50, 50 ) );
    System.out.println( around );
  }
}
```

First, we model the Store class with the two instance variables name and location. For practical reasons, we give the class a parameterized constructor that takes the name, as well as the x-y coordinate, and transfers it to the internal states. The toString() method returns a representation with the name and location.

The next class StoreFinder has the desired findStoresAround(…) method and a main(…) method with a small demonstration.

The actual findStoresAround(…) method uses a special trick to make the implementation a bit more compact. Firstly, the general solution: we work with a List and a Comparator, so we can use the Comparator object to sort the list. The Comparator only has to use the distance between the points as an ordering criterion. Here we can make it easy for ourselves because the java.awt.Point class has a distance(…) method, with which we can easily calculate the distance of points.

In the first step of findStoresAround(…), we put the Store objects from the Collection into an ArrayList. This is a requirement for sorting because a Collection cannot be sorted, only a list can. Furthermore, the assignment does not explicitly say that we are allowed to modify the Collection as well. Therefore, we want to be conservative here and not modify the incoming Collection, which may not be possible if the Collection is immutable.

Now we take advantage of the special feature of the Java language that you can declare classes inside methods. We call such a feature *local inner classes*. The advantage of local inner classes is that they can access (explicitly or implicitly final) variables from the environment. Our Comparator needs this because if it is to judge which of the two Store objects is closer to the center, a comparison must take place from the first Store to the center and then from the second Store to the center. If you want to avoid working with the local inner classes, you would have to give the Comparator implementation a parameterized constructor so that you can get the center into the Comparator implementation from the outside.

The inside of the compare(…) method calculates the distance of the two stores to the center. This results in two floating-point numbers, which we again translate into something negative, positive, or 0 using the familiar Double.compare(…) method. If we have the Comparator, we can use it to sort our list and return the list.

Quiz: Handling Null Reference in Unboxing

The first statement does not compile. What you can compile, however, is the following code:

```
Integer int1=null;
int     int2=int1;
int     i    =(Integer) null;
```

While running the code, a NullPointerException occurs due to unboxing. In Java, the compiler will invoke the relevant methods to extract the primitive value from the wrapper object. For instance, when working with an Integer object, the compiler will add a bytecode instruction to call the intValue() method automatically.

A NullPointerException also exists in the switch example. The Java compiler will automatically unbox and call charValue()—this will not succeed at runtime. switch has no special treatment on a wrapper, which can be null.

A Map is an associative store that connects key-value pairs. The get(…) method has the property that it returns null if there is no associated value to the key. Our example is just such a case. Under a wrong key, we query the associative store, there is no associated value, so the return is null. The compiler will automatically unbox and call the intValue() method, resulting in a NullPointerException at runtime. The solution to this is to explicitly include a check for null in the code whenever null expresses a missing return. So safer would be:

```
Integer maybeShips=map.get( "number_of_ships" );
if ( maybeShips !=null ) {
  int ships=maybeShips;
}
```

To summarize: There is no automatic conversion from null to 0 or false.

Quiz: Unboxing Surprise

The output of the program is noted in the comment.

```
Integer i11=1;
Integer i12=1;
System.out.println( i11 == i12 );   // true
System.out.println( i11 <= i12 );   // true
System.out.println( i11 >= i12 );   // true

Integer i21=1000;
Integer i22=1000;
System.out.println( i21 == i22 );   // false
System.out.println( i21 <= i22 );   // true
System.out.println( i21 >= i22 );   // true
```

It is surprising at first glance that in one case, the == operator produces true and then suddenly false. There are three things to know:

1. The relational operators <, >, <=, and >= force the values to be taken from the wrapper objects and the comparison to be made. However, the == comparison operator does not perform unboxing but merely compares two references and consequently makes an identity comparison. That is, the code does not compare the numbers 1 and 1 or 1000 and 1000, but compares the references of the two Integer objects, respectively. The question is: why are the two Integer objects identical for 1 and not for 1000? We will come to that now …

2. The compiler does not build wrapper objects with new but goes to the factory method valueOf(…).

3. The Integer class internally uses a cache for all Integer objects in the value range from −128 to +127. The valueOf(…) method consequently returns already existing Integer objects for exactly the integers from the mentioned value range. Everything outside the value range is always built and returned as a new object. Thus, calling valueOf(1000) results in two different Integer objects, which are of course not identical.

NOTES

1 Source: https://github.com/fivethirtyeight/data/tree/master/comic-characters.
2 31 is a prime number, which gives a good spread of bits. The fact that ultimately 31 is used so often in the Java library for the hash codes is also due to the authors' gut feeling, as documented by https://bugs.java.com/bugdatabase/view_bug.do?bug_id=4045622.

Appendix A
Most Frequent Types and Methods in the Java Universe

A.1 PACKAGES WITH THE MOST COMMON TYPES

java.io
BufferedReader, ByteArrayInputStream, ByteArrayOutputStream, Data-OutputStream, FileInputStream, FileOutputStream, File, IOException, InputStream, ObjectInputStream, ObjectOutputStream, OutputStream, PrintStream, PrintWriter, StringReader, StringWriter, Writer

java.lang
Appendable, AssertionError, Boolean, Byte, CharSequence, Character, ClassLoader, Class, Double, Enum, Exception, Float, IllegalArgumentException, IllegalStateException, IndexOutOfBoundsException, Integer, Iterable, Long, Math, NullPointerException, Number, Object, RuntimeException, Short, StringBuffer, StringBuilder, String, System, ThreadLocal, Thread, Throwable, UnsupportedOperationException

java.lang.annotation
Annotation

java.lang.ref
SoftReference

java.lang.reflect
Array, Constructor, Field, InvocationTargetException, Method, ParameterizedType

java.math
BigInteger

java.net
URI, URL

java.nio
ByteBuffer

java.security
AccessController

java.sql
PreparedStatement

java.text
MessageFormat

java.util
AbstractList, ArrayList, Arrays, BitSet, Calendar, Collection, Collections, Comparator, Date, Enumeration, HashMap, HashSet, Hashtable, Iterator, LinkedHashMap, LinkedHashSet, LinkedList, List, Locale, Map, NoSuchElementException, Objects, Optional, Properties, ResourceBundle, Set, Stack, StringTokenizer, TreeMap, Vector

java.util.concurrent
ConcurrentHashMap, ConcurrentMap

java.util.concurrent.atomic
AtomicBoolean, AtomicInteger, AtomicLong, AtomicReference

java.util.concurrent.locks
Lock, ReentrantLock

java.util.function
Consumer, Function

java.util.logging
Logger

java.util.regex
Matcher, Pattern

java.util.stream
Collectors, Stream

javax.faces.component
StateHelper, UIComponent

javax.faces.context
FacesContext, ResponseWriter

javax.xml.bind
JAXBElement

javax.xml.namespace
QName

A.2 100 MOST COMMON TYPES

TABLE A.1   Typen

TYPE NAME	OCCURENCES	PERCENTAGE DISTRIBUTION
java.lang.StringBuilder ⊙	605.692	25.28%
java.lang.String ⊙	190.854	7.97%
java.lang.Object ⊙	138.093	5.76%
java.util.Iterator ❶	102.072	4.26%
java.util.List ❶	99.833	4.17%

(Continued)

TABLE A.1 (*Continued*)   Typen

TYPE NAME	OCCURENCES	PERCENTAGE DISTRIBUTION
java.lang.StringBuffer ❶	94.562	3.95%
java.util.Map ❶	69.415	2.90%
java.lang.Class ⊙	52.435	2.19%
java.util.ArrayList ⊙	46.855	1.96%
java.lang.Integer ⊙	45.650	1.91%
java.util.Set ❶	35.131	1.47%
java.util.HashMap ⊙	28.958	1.21%
java.util.logging.Logger ⊙	26.173	1.09%
java.lang.IllegalArgumentException ⊙	25.762	1.08%
javax.xml.namespace.QName ⊙	22.050	0.92%
java.io.File ⊙	19.951	0.83%
java.lang.Boolean ⊙	19.919	0.83%
java.lang.System ⊙	18.881	0.79%
java.util.Collection ❶	15.678	0.65%
java.util.Arrays ⊙	15.533	0.65%
java.lang.AssertionError ⊙	14.927	0.62%
java.lang.IllegalStateException ⊙	14.189	0.59%
java.util.Map$Entry ❶	13.554	0.57%
java.util.Collections ⊙	13.061	0.55%
java.lang.Long ⊙	12.493	0.52%
java.util.Hashtable ⊙	11.934	0.50%
java.lang.Enum ⊙	11.191	0.47%
java.lang.Math ⊙	10.670	0.45%
java.lang.UnsupportedOperationException ⊙	10.434	0.44%
java.lang.reflect.Method ⊙	10.357	0.43%
java.io.PrintStream ⊙	10.278	0.43%
java.util.Vector ⊙	10.118	0.42%
java.lang.Character ⊙	9.904	0.41%
java.lang.Thread ⊙	9.294	0.39%
java.nio.ByteBuffer ⊙	9.285	0.39%
java.util.HashSet ⊙	8.881	0.37%
java.lang.Throwable ⊙	8.415	0.35%
java.util.Properties ⊙	8.106	0.34%
java.lang.Double ⊙	7.956	0.33%
javax.faces.component.StateHelper ❶	7.912	0.33%
java.lang.IndexOutOfBoundsException ⊙	7.799	0.33%
java.lang.RuntimeException ⊙	7.734	0.32%
java.util.Objects ⊙	7.700	0.32%
java.io.Writer ⊙	7.473	0.31%
java.io.IOException ⊙	6.902	0.29%
java.io.InputStream ⊙	6.539	0.27%
java.util.stream.Stream ❶	6.429	0.27%
java.lang.CharSequence ❶	6.170	0.26%
javax.faces.context.ResponseWriter ⊙	6.063	0.25%

(Continued)

TABLE A.1 (*Continued*)   Typen

TYPE NAME	OCCURENCES	PERCENTAGE DISTRIBUTION
java.lang.Exception ⊙	6.054	0.25%
javax.faces.context.FacesContext ⊙	6.027	0.25%
java.io.PrintWriter ⊙	5.785	0.24%
java.math.BigInteger ⊙	5.520	0.23%
java.util.Enumeration ❶	5.047	0.21%
java.util.Stack ⊙	4.904	0.20%
java.util.ResourceBundle ⊙	4.777	0.20%
java.io.OutputStream ⊙	4.682	0.20%
java.util.LinkedList ⊙	4.646	0.19%
java.util.Optional ⊙	4.169	0.17%
java.io.ByteArrayOutputStream ⊙	4.115	0.17%
java.util.AbstractList ⊙	4.074	0.17%
java.lang.Float ⊙	4.062	0.17%
java.util.StringTokenizer ⊙	4.024	0.17%
java.lang.NullPointerException ⊙	3.840	0.16%
java.util.concurrent.atomic.AtomicReference ⊙	3.579	0.15%
java.net.URI ⊙	3.491	0.15%
java.util.LinkedHashMap ⊙	3.490	0.15%
java.lang.Iterable ⊙	3.483	0.15%
javax.faces.component.UIComponent ⊙	3.481	0.15%
java.lang.reflect.Field ⊙	3.452	0.14%
java.lang.Number ⊙	3.449	0.14%
java.net.URL ⊙	3.436	0.14%
java.util.regex.Pattern ⊙	3.386	0.14%
java.util.regex.Matcher ⊙	3.343	0.14%
java.util.Calendar ⊙	3.281	0.14%
java.util.concurrent.ConcurrentHashMap ⊙	3.231	0.13%
java.text.MessageFormat ⊙	3.070	0.13%
javax.servlet.http.HttpServletRequest ❶	3.051	0.13%
javax.xml.stream.XMLStreamReader ❶	3.032	0.13%
java.util.concurrent.locks.Lock ❶	3.012	0.13%
java.lang.ClassLoader ⊙	2.861	0.12%
java.util.concurrent.atomic.AtomicInteger ⊙	2.835	0.12%
java.lang.ThreadLocal ⊙	2.706	0.11%
java.security.AccessController ⊙	2.687	0.11%
java.util.concurrent.ConcurrentMap ❶	2.579	0.11%
java.util.BitSet ⊙	2.553	0.11%
java.math.BigDecimal ⊙	2.437	0.10%
java.sql.ResultSet ❶	2.408	0.10%
java.io.BufferedReader ⊙	2.359	0.10%
java.io.DataOutputStream ⊙	2.264	0.09%
java.util.concurrent.atomic.AtomicLong ⊙	2.245	0.09%
java.sql.PreparedStatement ❶	2.237	0.09%

(Continued)

TABLE A.1 (*Continued*)   Typen

TYPE NAME	OCCURENCES	PERCENTAGE DISTRIBUTION
java.util.LinkedHashSet ☺	2.222	0.09%
java.util.Date ☺	2.212	0.09%
java.lang.ref.SoftReference ☺	2.139	0.09%
java.io.ObjectOutputStream ☺	2.119	0.09%
java.lang.reflect.Array ☺	2.048	0.09%
java.io.ObjectInputStream ☺	2.043	0.09%
java.io.StringWriter ☺	1.992	0.08%
java.util.concurrent.atomic.AtomicBoolean ☺	1.991	0.08%

A.3 100 MOST COMMON METHODS

TABLE A.2   Types with method names

METHOD NAME	OCCURENCES	PERCENTAGE DISTRIBUTION
java.lang.StringBuilder#append	377.938	15.77%
java.lang.StringBuilder#toString	111.511	4.65%
java.lang.StringBuilder#<init>	111.272	4.64%
java.lang.Object#<init>	80.559	3.36%
java.lang.StringBuffer#append	61.081	2.55%
java.lang.String#equals	56.525	2.36%
java.util.Iterator#next	50.355	2.10%
java.util.Iterator#hasNext	50.093	2.09%
java.util.ArrayList#<init>	28.413	1.19%
java.lang.Integer#valueOf	27.554	1.15%
java.lang.String#length	26.959	1.13%
java.util.Map#put	26.388	1.10%
java.util.List#add	26.041	1.09%
java.lang.IllegalArgumentException#<init>	25.190	1.05%
java.lang.Object#getClass	24.894	1.04%
java.util.List#size	21.020	0.88%
java.util.Map#get	18.625	0.78%
java.util.List#iterator	18.422	0.77%
javax.xml.namespace.QName#<init>	17.541	0.73%
java.lang.String#substring	16.687	0.70%
java.lang.StringBuffer#toString	15.771	0.66%
java.lang.Object#equals	15.554	0.65%
java.lang.StringBuffer#<init>	15.488	0.65%
java.lang.Class#getName	15.238	0.64%
java.lang.AssertionError#<init>	14.877	0.62%

(Continued)

TABLE A.2 (*Continued*)   Types with method names

METHOD NAME	OCCURENCES	PERCENTAGE DISTRIBUTION
java.lang.IllegalStateException#<init>	13.984	0.58%
java.lang.String#charAt	12.815	0.53%
java.util.Set#iterator	12.788	0.53%
java.util.logging.Logger#log	12.576	0.52%
java.util.List#get	12.204	0.51%
java.util.HashMap#<init>	12.185	0.51%
java.lang.Boolean#valueOf	10.513	0.44%
java.util.HashMap#put	10.470	0.44%
java.lang.UnsupportedOperationException#<init>	10.340	0.43%
java.util.Set#add	9.598	0.40%
java.lang.System#arraycopy	9.116	0.38%
java.lang.String#startsWith	8.501	0.35%
java.lang.Object#toString	8.418	0.35%
java.io.PrintStream#println	8.240	0.34%
java.lang.String#indexOf	8.053	0.34%
java.lang.IndexOutOfBoundsException#<init>	7.792	0.33%
java.util.Collection#iterator	7.486	0.31%
java.lang.RuntimeException#<init>	7.414	0.31%
java.lang.Long#valueOf	7.268	0.30%
java.lang.Boolean#booleanValue	7.132	0.30%
java.lang.String#valueOf	7.027	0.29%
java.lang.Integer#intValue	7.006	0.29%
java.util.Hashtable#put	6.884	0.29%
java.util.Map$Entry#getValue	6.781	0.28%
java.util.Map$Entry#getKey	6.634	0.28%
java.util.ArrayList#add	6.581	0.27%
java.util.logging.Logger#isLoggable	6.530	0.27%
java.util.HashSet#<init>	6.527	0.27%
java.lang.Object#hashCode	6.479	0.27%
java.io.Writer#write	6.423	0.27%
java.lang.Class#getClassLoader	6.378	0.27%
java.util.Arrays#asList	6.083	0.25%
java.lang.String#equalsIgnoreCase	6.070	0.25%
java.util.List#toArray	5.872	0.25%
java.lang.String#format	5.769	0.24%
java.io.File#<init>	5.631	0.24%
java.lang.Enum#<init>	5.352	0.22%
java.lang.Enum#valueOf	5.322	0.22%
java.lang.String#<init>	5.298	0.22%

(Continued)

TABLE A.2 (*Continued*)   Types with method names

METHOD NAME	OCCURENCES	PERCENTAGE DISTRIBUTION
`java.lang.String#trim`	5.115	0.21%
`java.io.IOException#<init>`	5.079	0.21%
`java.util.Objects#requireNonNull`	4.767	0.20%
`java.util.List#isEmpty`	4.748	0.20%
`java.lang.Class#isAssignableFrom`	4.468	0.19%
`java.util.Map#entrySet`	4.254	0.18%
`java.lang.Throwable#addSuppressed`	4.100	0.17%
`java.lang.String#hashCode`	3.984	0.17%
`java.lang.Math#min`	3.964	0.17%
`java.util.AbstractList#<init>`	3.943	0.16%
`javax.faces.component.StateHelper#put`	3.907	0.16%
`java.util.Map#containsKey`	3.905	0.16%
`java.lang.Class#desiredAssertionStatus`	3.884	0.16%
`javax.faces.component.StateHelper#eval`	3.830	0.16%
`java.lang.NullPointerException#<init>`	3.808	0.16%
`java.util.ArrayList#size`	3.758	0.16%
`java.lang.String#endsWith`	3.718	0.16%
`java.lang.Character#valueOf`	3.714	0.16%
`java.util.Set#contains`	3.698	0.15%
`java.io.InputStream#close`	3.684	0.15%
`java.util.ResourceBundle#getString`	3.670	0.15%
`java.lang.Thread#currentThread`	3.488	0.15%
`java.lang.Double#valueOf`	3.465	0.14%
`java.lang.Iterable#iterator`	3.363	0.14%
`java.lang.Integer#parseInt`	3.350	0.14%
`java.util.HashMap#get`	3.319	0.14%
`java.lang.System#getProperty`	3.292	0.14%
`java.util.Map#values`	3.240	0.14%
`java.util.Arrays#fill`	3.202	0.13%
`java.util.ArrayList#get`	3.189	0.13%
`java.lang.Integer#<init>`	3.181	0.13%
`java.lang.Math#max`	2.960	0.12%
`java.io.OutputStream#write`	2.951	0.12%
`java.util.Map#remove`	2.909	0.12%
`java.lang.Class#forName`	2.903	0.12%
`java.lang.String#replace`	2.887	0.12%

A.4 100 MOST COMMON METHODS INCLUDING PARAMETER LIST

TABLE A.3 Types with method names

METHOD NAME AND PARAMETER LIST	OCCURENCES	PERCENTAGE DISTRIBUTION
java.lang.StringBuilder#append(String)	296.283	12.37%
java.lang.StringBuilder#toString()	111.511	4.65%
java.lang.StringBuilder#<init>()	102.410	4.27%
java.lang.Object#<init>()	80.559	3.36%
java.lang.String#equals(Object)	56.525	2.36%
java.util.Iterator#next()	50.355	2.10%
java.util.Iterator#hasNext()	50.093	2.09%
java.lang.StringBuffer#append(String)	48.916	2.04%
java.lang.StringBuilder#append(Object)	33.491	1.40%
java.lang.Integer#valueOf(int)	27.170	1.13%
java.lang.String#length()	26.959	1.13%
java.util.Map#put(Object, Object)	26.388	1.10%
java.util.List#add(Object)	25.409	1.06%
java.lang.Object#getClass()	24.894	1.04%
java.lang.IllegalArgumentException#<init>(String)	22.429	0.94%
java.lang.StringBuilder#append(int)	21.752	0.91%
java.util.ArrayList#<init>()	21.117	0.88%
java.util.List#size()	21.020	0.88%
java.util.Map#get(Object)	18.625	0.78%
java.util.List#iterator()	18.422	0.77%
javax.xml.namespace.QName#<init>(String, String)	17.076	0.71%
java.lang.StringBuilder#append(char)	16.402	0.68%
java.lang.StringBuffer#toString()	15.771	0.66%
java.lang.Object#equals(Object)	15.554	0.65%
java.lang.Class#getName()	15.238	0.64%
java.lang.StringBuffer#<init>()	13.318	0.56%
java.lang.String#charAt(int)	12.815	0.53%
java.util.Set#iterator()	12.788	0.53%
java.util.List#get(int)	12.204	0.51%
java.lang.IllegalStateException#<init>(String)	10.673	0.45%
java.lang.AssertionError#<init>()	10.622	0.44%
java.util.HashMap#put(Object, Object)	10.470	0.44%
java.util.HashMap#<init>()	10.273	0.43%
java.util.Set#add(Object)	9.598	0.40%
java.lang.String#substring(int, int)	9.538	0.40%
java.lang.Boolean#valueOf(boolean)	9.449	0.39%
java.lang.System#arraycopy(Object, int, Object, int, int)	9.116	0.38%

(Continued)

TABLE A.3 (*Continued*)   Types with method names

METHOD NAME AND PARAMETER LIST	OCCURENCES	PERCENTAGE DISTRIBUTION
`java.lang.Object#toString()`	8.418	0.35%
`java.lang.String#startsWith(String)`	8.344	0.35%
`java.io.PrintStream#println(String)`	7.568	0.32%
`java.util.Collection#iterator()`	7.486	0.31%
`java.lang.String#substring(int)`	7.149	0.30%
`java.lang.Boolean#booleanValue()`	7.132	0.30%
`java.lang.Long#valueOf(long)`	7.066	0.29%
`java.lang.Integer#intValue()`	7.006	0.29%
`java.lang.IndexOutOfBoundsException#<init>()`	6.941	0.29%
`java.util.Hashtable#put(Object, Object)`	6.884	0.29%
`java.util.Map$Entry#getValue()`	6.781	0.28%
`java.util.Map$Entry#getKey()`	6.634	0.28%
`java.util.logging.Logger#isLoggable(java.util.logging.Level)`	6.530	0.27%
`java.lang.Object#hashCode()`	6.479	0.27%
`java.lang.Class#getClassLoader()`	6.378	0.27%
`java.util.ArrayList#add(Object)`	6.359	0.27%
`java.util.Arrays#asList(Object…)`	6.083	0.25%
`java.lang.String#equalsIgnoreCase(String)`	6.070	0.25%
`java.lang.UnsupportedOperationException#<init>()`	5.769	0.24%
`java.util.List#toArray(Object…)`	5.691	0.24%
`java.lang.Enum#<init>(String, int)`	5.352	0.22%
`java.lang.Enum#valueOf(Class, String)`	5.322	0.22%
`java.lang.String#trim()`	5.115	0.21%
`java.lang.StringBuffer#append(char)`	5.074	0.21%
`java.lang.StringBuilder#append(long)`	5.035	0.21%
`java.util.HashSet#<init>()`	5.015	0.21%
`java.util.ArrayList#<init>(int)`	4.941	0.21%
`java.util.logging.Logger#log(java.util.logging.Level, String, Throwable)`	4.766	0.20%
`java.util.List#isEmpty()`	4.748	0.20%
`java.io.Writer#write(String)`	4.690	0.20%
`java.util.logging.Logger#log(java.util.logging.Level, String)`	4.577	0.19%
`java.lang.StringBuilder#<init>(String)`	4.512	0.19%
`java.lang.UnsupportedOperationException#<init>(String)`	4.490	0.19%
`java.lang.Class#isAssignableFrom(Class)`	4.468	0.19%
`java.lang.String#format(String, Object…)`	4.411	0.18%
`java.io.IOException#<init>(String)`	4.321	0.18%
`java.lang.StringBuilder#<init>(int)`	4.314	0.18%
`java.util.Map#entrySet()`	4.254	0.18%
`java.lang.AssertionError#<init>(Object)`	4.129	0.17%
`java.lang.Throwable#addSuppressed(Throwable)`	4.100	0.17%

(Continued)

TABLE A.3 (Continued)   Types with method names

METHOD NAME AND PARAMETER LIST	OCCURENCES	PERCENTAGE DISTRIBUTION
`java.lang.String#indexOf(int)`	4.088	0.17%
`java.lang.String#hashCode()`	3.984	0.17%
`java.util.AbstractList#<init>()`	3.943	0.16%
`java.util.Map#containsKey(Object)`	3.905	0.16%
`javax.faces.component.StateHelper#put` `  (java.io.Serializable, Object)`	3.890	0.16%
`java.lang.Class#desiredAssertionStatus()`	3.884	0.16%
`java.lang.RuntimeException#<init>(String)`	3.801	0.16%
`java.util.ArrayList#size()`	3.758	0.16%
`java.lang.String#endsWith(String)`	3.718	0.16%
`java.lang.Character#valueOf(char)`	3.714	0.16%
`java.util.Set#contains(Object)`	3.698	0.15%
`java.io.InputStream#close()`	3.684	0.15%
`java.util.ResourceBundle#getString(String)`	3.670	0.15%
`java.lang.Thread#currentThread()`	3.488	0.15%
`java.lang.Iterable#iterator()`	3.363	0.14%
`java.util.HashMap#get(Object)`	3.319	0.14%
`java.lang.String#valueOf(Object)`	3.288	0.14%
`java.lang.StringBuffer#append(int)`	3.248	0.14%
`java.util.Map#values()`	3.240	0.14%
`java.lang.Double#valueOf(double)`	3.229	0.13%
`java.util.ArrayList#get(int)`	3.189	0.13%
`java.lang.Integer#<init>(int)`	3.120	0.13%
`java.util.Objects#requireNonNull(Object, String)`	3.102	0.13%

Printed in the United States
by Baker & Taylor Publisher Services

Printed in the United States
by Baker & Taylor Publisher Services